JYL STEINBACK

AMERICA'S HEALTHIEST MOM

THE BUSY MOM'S
MAKE IT
QUICK
COOKBOOK

300 TASTY RECIPES USING CONVENIENCE FOODS

Meredith₀ Books
Des Moines, Iowa

This cookbook is the ultimate timesaver for healthful fast foods from appetizers and snacks to entrées and desserts. Each chapter provides valuable information for cutting time in the kitchen and every page has a helpful tip. Many of the recipe ingredients are mixes or convenience foods—shortcuts that get you out of the kitchen as quickly as possible. And, as with all my books, the recipes are low in fat (or fat-free!) while also being full of flavor and family-friendly. Enjoy!

Jyl Steinback, "America's Healthiest Mom"
15202 North 50th Place, Scottsdale, AZ 85254
602-996-6300 fax: 602-996-9897
e-mail: Jyl@AmericasHealthiestMom.com
website: AmericasHealthiestMom.com

The Busy Mom's Make It Quick Cookbook
by Jyl Steinback
Editor: Stephanie Karpinske, R.D.
Senior Associate Design Director: Ken Carlson
Contributing Editors and Indexer: Spectrum Commuication Services, Inc.
Contributing Designer: Mary Pat Crowley
Copy Chief: Terri Fredrickson
Publishing Operations Manager: Karen Schirm
Edit and Design Production Coordinator: Mary Lee Gavin
Book Production Managers: Pam Kvitne, Marjorie J. Schenkelberg, Rick von Holdt, Mark Weaver
Contributing Copy Editor: Kim Catanzarite
Contributing Proofreaders: Maria Duryée, Gretchen Kauffman, Susan J. Kling
Photographers: Pete Krumhardt, Blaine Moats, Jay Wilde
Food Stylists: Paige Boyle, Jill Lust, Dianna Nolin, Charles Worthington
Prop Stylist: Sue Mitchell
Editorial Assistant: Cheryl Eckert

Meredith® Books
Editor in Chief: Linda Raglan Cunningham
Design Director: Matt Strelecki
Managing Editor: Gregory H. Kayko
Executive Editor: Jennifer Dorland Darling

Publisher: James D. Blume
Executive Director, Marketing: Jeffrey Myers
Executive Director, New Business Development: Todd M. Davis
Executive Director, Sales: Ken Zagor
Director, Operations: George A. Susral
Director, Production: Douglas M. Johnston
Business Director: Jim Leonard

Vice President and General Manager: Douglas J. Guendel

Meredith Publishing Group
President, Publishing Group: Stephen M. Lacy
Vice President-Publishing Director: Bob Mate

Meredith Corporation
Chairman and Chief Executive Officer: William T. Kerr

In Memoriam: E.T. Meredith III (1933-2003)

All of us at Meredith® Books are dedicated to providing you with the information and ideas you need to create delicious foods. We welcome your comments and suggestions. Write to us at: Meredith Books, Cookbook Editorial Department, 1716 Locust St., Des Moines, IA 50309-3023.

If you would like to purchase any of our cooking, crafts, gardening, home improvement, or home decorating and design books, check wherever quality books are sold. Or visit us at: meredithbooks.com

Table of Contents

Fruit and Marshmallow Salad

Chapter Index

1 Appetizers and Munchies

Chunky Tomato Bruschetta

If you're having a party or just entertaining friends, you don't need to spend a fortune on groceries. The simple recipes in this chapter are fast to make and the ingredients don't cost a lot.

After 18 years of planning, shopping, and preparing meals for my family and friends, I think I've finally mastered the art of saving! I've teetered from the nonchalant, fill-it-up-fast shopper to an expert supermarket-savvy sleuth, focusing on saving cents without sacrificing flavor and nutrition.

Top tips for slashing food costs:

- Start with a plan! Write out a weekly (or bimonthly) menu. Include foods you'll need for special events, such as a weekend cookout with friends or child's party. Dedicating a little more time to meal planning and grocery shopping can cut your spending by up to 50% if you stick to your list.
- Scan the weekly food section of your newspaper and plan meals around grocery store promotions or sales.
- Plan meals that use some of the same ingredients, such as chicken, hamburger, steak, or fish, for example: roasted chicken and mashed potatoes on Monday, chicken stir-fry with veggies and rice on Wednesday, and barbecue chicken pizza on Friday.
- Make a grocery list and STICK TO IT! Reward yourself with one impulse purchase (for instance, a pack of gum or a magazine) if you make it to the checkout line without veering off track.
- Save weekly grocery receipts and scan them for shopping ideas. Post a blank page for "must-have" items. This not only eliminates unnecessary trips to the store but also cuts impulse spending.
- Stockpile staples you regularly use. I love to bake bread so I stock up on bread flour whenever it's on sale. I can store it in the freezer for months!

- Shop once a week. Visit the same one or two stores; familiarity speeds up shopping trips and cuts impulse buying.
- Shop during off-peak hours. My favorite shopping time is early morning (about 6 a.m.). I can cruise through the aisles without distractions or temptations.
- Don't shop hungry, tired, angry, etc. Shopping when you're hungry can increase your grocery bill by up to 15% due to impulse buying. Fill yourself up before you fill up your grocery cart.
- Shop alone.
- Purchase with cash, not credit cards. This is a simple step to substantial savings.
- Take a course in supermarket psychology 101. Learn the ins and outs of supermarket schemes that tempt and tantalize your tastes.
- Compare unit prices and prices per pound to get the best buy for your money. While the large box of cereal may seem like the better buy, you may actually save more by purchasing two small boxes.
- Take advantage of bulk buying at discount stores. But buyers beware!
- Don't purchase more than you can use.
- Package, freeze, and label foods for proper storage and use.
- Prepare only what your family will eat or ... plan for leftovers.
- Plan meals around theme cooking–plan nights for Italian, pizza, chinese, vegetarian, supper salads, soup or stew, potato meals, or breakfast for dinner. Theme cooking is an excellent way to blend ingredients, flavors, and textures while using up leftover meats, veggies, and cheese.
- Keep an eye out at the checkout line–everyone (even electronic scanners) can make mistakes that can be very costly.

Appetizers and Munchies

Bacon and Cheese Potato Skins

Easy | **Do Ahead** | **Serves: 4**

4 large baking potatoes
   (each about 4 oz.)

1 tbsp. + 1 tsp. Butter Buds,
   divided

2 cups nonfat shredded
   cheddar cheese

1 1.3-oz. pkg. bacon crumbles

nonfat sour cream (optional)

Pierce potatoes with a fork in several places. Microwave on High for 9 minutes per potato until tender. Preheat oven to 450°. Line baking sheet with foil and spray with cooking spray. Cut cooked potatoes in half lengthwise. Scoop out most of the pulp, leaving about ¼ inch in skins. Sprinkle potato skins on both sides with Butter Buds (about 1 teaspoon per half) and arrange on baking sheet. Sprinkle each half with about ¼ cup cheese and 1½ teaspoons bacon crumbles. Bake until cheese is melted. Serve with nonfat sour cream, if desired.

Nutrition per serving: 349 calories, 2.2 g fat, 56 g carbohydrates, 23 g protein, 0 mg cholesterol, 6 g dietary fiber, 888 mg sodium
Exchanges: 3½ starch, 2 very lean meat
Carb Choices: 4

Shopping List

Produce
4 large baking potatoes

Dairy
8 oz. nonfat shredded cheddar
   cheese

Packaged
1.3-oz. pkg. bacon crumbles

Seasonings/Spices
Butter Buds

Optional
nonfat sour cream

It's hard to believe, but the potato is a relative of tobacco and the tomato.

Barbecued Meatballs

Easy | **Do Ahead** | **Freeze** | **Serves: 6**

1½ lb. extra-lean ground beef

½ cup nonfat half and half

1 cup quick-cooking oatmeal

¼ cup egg substitute

1½ tsp. onion powder

¾ tsp. garlic powder

1 tsp. chili powder

¼ tsp. pepper

2 cups barbecue sauce
 (regular, hickory flavor, or spicy)

Combine ground beef, half and half, oatmeal, egg substitute, onion powder, garlic powder, chili powder, and pepper in medium bowl; mix well. Line baking sheet with foil and spray with cooking spray. Shape meat mixture into 1-inch balls and arrange in single layer on baking sheet. Cover and refrigerate meatballs at least 1 hour but no longer than 8 hours. When ready to serve, preheat oven to 350°. Pour barbecue sauce over meatballs and bake for 35–45 minutes.

Nutrition per serving: 333 calories, 6.5 g fat, 42 g carbohydrates, 25 g protein, 61 mg cholesterol, 1 g dietary fiber, 1,364 mg sodium
Exchanges: 1 starch, 3 lean meat, 2 other carb
Carb Choices: 3

Appetizers and Munchies

Shopping List

Meat/Fish/Poultry
1 lb. extra-lean ground beef

Dairy
4 oz. nonfat half and half
1 oz. egg substitute

Packaged
quick-cooking oatmeal

Seasonings/Spices
onion powder
garlic powder
chili powder
pepper

Condiments
16 oz. barbecue sauce (regular, hickory flavor, or spicy)

USDA Beef Quality grades are determined by estimating the age of the animal, the amount of fat marbling, and by the texture, color, and appearance of the ribeye. USDA quality grading is optional.

Chicken and Cheese Potato Skins

Easy | Do Ahead | Serves: 4

2 large baking potatoes (each about 4 oz.)

2 tsp. Butter Buds

½ tsp. garlic powder

½ cup grilled chicken breast strips, *chopped*

¼ cup bacon crumbles

½ cup nonfat shredded cheddar cheese

¼ cup nonfat shredded mozzarella cheese

Shopping List

Produce
2 large baking potatoes

Meat/Fish/Poultry
6-oz. pkg. grilled chicken breast strips

Dairy
nonfat shredded cheddar cheese
nonfat shredded mozzarella cheese

Packaged
1.3-oz. pkg. bacon crumbles

Seasonings/Spices
Butter Buds
garlic powder

Pierce potatoes in several places with a fork. Microwave on High 9 minutes per potato until tender. Cut potatoes in half lengthwise; cut in half again. Carefully scoop out pulp, leaving ¼ inch in skins. Preheat oven to 450°. Line baking sheet with foil and spray with cooking spray. Arrange potato skins in a single layer on baking sheet (skin side down). Combine Butter Buds and garlic powder and mix well; sprinkle mixture over skins. Bake 7–8 minutes until skins are crisp. Remove from oven and sprinkle with chopped chicken, bacon crumbles, and cheeses. Bake 7–8 minutes until cheeses are completely melted. (Potato skins can also be broiled on High for 30–45 seconds; but watch carefully!)

Nutrition per serving: 195 calories, 2 g fat, 27 g carbohydrates, 15 g protein, 11 mg cholesterol, 3 g dietary fiber, 587 mg sodium
Exchanges: 1 starch, 2 very lean meat
Carb Choices: 2

During the Alaskan Klondike gold rush

(1897–1898), potatoes were practically worth their weight in gold. They were so valued for their vitamin C content that miners traded gold for potatoes. Today they are worth their weight in nutritional value!

Fajita Pizza Bites

Easy | **Serves: 6**

3   98% fat-free flour tortillas

1   16-oz. pkg. frozen pepper
    stir-fry

2   6-oz. pkgs. Southwestern
    chicken breast strips,
    cut into thirds

1   cup salsa, *divided*

1½ cups nonfat shredded
    mozzarella cheese

Preheat oven to 450°. Line baking sheet(s) with foil and spray with cooking spray. Arrange tortillas in a single layer on baking sheet(s). Spray large nonstick skillet with cooking spray. Add pepper stir-fry; cook, stirring frequently, until vegetables are crisp-tender and lightly browned. Stir in chicken and ½ cup salsa; heat 2–3 minutes. Sprinkle ½ cup cheese over each tortilla; top with chicken-vegetable mixture. Bake 10–12 minutes until cheese is melted and tortillas are lightly browned. Cut into thirds and serve with remaining salsa.

Nutrition per serving: 212 calories, 1.2 g fat, 19 g carbohydrates, 27 g protein, 33 mg cholesterol, 2 g dietary fiber, 918 mg sodium
Exchanges: 1 starch, 1 vegetable, 3 very lean meat
Carb Choices: 0

Appetizers and Munchies

Shopping List

Meat/Fish/Poultry
2 6-oz. pkgs. Southwestern
  chicken breast strips

Dairy
6 oz. nonfat shredded
  mozzarella cheese

Frozen
16-oz. pkg. frozen pepper stir-fry

Packaged
17.5-oz. pkg. 98% fat-free flour
  tortillas

Condiments
8-oz. jar salsa

One 6-ounce package of chicken breast strips contains the equivalent of 2 servings.

9

Baked 3-Cheese Tortilla Wraps

½ cup nonfat cottage cheese, *drained*

⅓ cup nonfat Parmesan cheese

½ cup nonfat pasta sauce

4 98% fat-free flour tortillas

½ cup nonfat shredded mozzarella cheese

additional pasta sauce, *heated* (optional)

Preheat oven to 350°. Line baking sheet with foil and spray with cooking spray. Combine cottage and Parmesan cheeses in small bowl and mix well. Spread 2 tablespoons pasta sauce on each tortilla; top with 2 tablespoons cottage cheese mixture and sprinkle with 2 tablespoons mozzarella cheese. Fold tortilla over and press edges to seal. Arrange in single layer on baking sheet; bake 4–5 minutes; turn tortillas over and bake 3–5 minutes until cheese is completely melted and tortilla is lightly browned. Let stand 3–5 minutes before slicing each tortilla into 4 pieces and serving with additional pasta sauce, if desired.

Nutrition per serving: 178 calories, 0.5 g fat, 29 g carbohydrates, 12 g protein, 1 mg cholesterol, 2 g dietary fiber, 611 mg sodium
Exchanges: 1 vegetable, 1½ starch, 1 very lean meat
Carb Choices: 2

Shopping List

Dairy
4 oz. nonfat cottage cheese
nonfat Parmesan cheese
nonfat shredded mozzarella cheese

Packaged
17.5-oz. pkg. 98% fat-free flour tortillas

Condiments
8 oz. nonfat pasta sauce

In addition to hors d'oeuvres, plan for some make-ahead snacks, such as cheese balls, crackers, and raw vegetables and dips.

Salmon Cheese Quesadillas

Easy | **Serves: 6**

6 98% fat-free flour tortillas

1½ cups nonfat shredded cheddar cheese

2 7.1-oz. pouches premium skinless and boneless pink salmon

½ cup diced green chiles

½ cup chopped pimientos

I Can't Believe It's Not Butter spray

1½ cups salsa

Preheat oven to 350°. Line baking sheet(s) with foil and spray with cooking spray. Arrange tortillas on baking sheet(s). Combine cheese, salmon, green chiles, and pimientos in medium bowl; toss lightly. Divide mixture among tortillas; fold tortillas in half and spray lightly with "butter" spray. Bake 10–15 minutes until cheese is melted and tortillas are lightly browned. Cut into wedges and serve with salsa.

Nutrition per serving: 271 calories, 4.1 g fat, 31 g carbohydrates, 26 g protein, 37 mg cholesterol, 3 g dietary fiber, 1,441 mg sodium
Exchanges: 1 starch, 3 very lean meat, 1 vegetable
Carb Choices: 2

Appetizers and Munchies

Shopping List

Dairy
6 oz. nonfat shredded cheddar cheese
I Can't Believe It's Not Butter spray

Canned
4-oz. can diced green chiles
chopped pimientos

Packaged
17.5-oz. pkg. 98% fat-free flour tortillas
2 7.1-oz. pouches premium skinless and boneless pink salmon

Condiments
12-oz. jar salsa

Try some exotic ingredients and inventive combinations in your appetizer recipes–this gives people a chance to nibble a little of this or that.

Honey Barbecue Chicken Tenders

Easy | Do Ahead | Freeze | Serves: 6

2   cups barbecue sauce

3   tbsp. spicy brown mustard

3   tbsp. honey

⅛   tsp. hot pepper sauce

1½ lb. boneless, skinless
    chicken tenderloins

Shopping List

Meat/Fish/Poultry

1½ lb. boneless, skinless
chicken tenderloins

Condiments

16 oz. barbecue sauce
spicy brown mustard
honey
hot pepper sauce

Combine barbecue sauce, mustard, honey, and pepper sauce in medium bowl; mix until completely blended. Remove ½ cup sauce and set aside. Pat chicken tenderloins with paper towels until dry. Place chicken in shallow baking dish. Pour barbecue sauce mixture over top and toss until well coated. Cover and refrigerate at least 2 hours or overnight. Preheat oven to 400°. Line baking sheet with foil and spray with cooking spray. Remove chicken tenderloins from sauce and arrange in single layer on baking sheet. (Discard marinating sauce.) Bake chicken tenders 15 minutes; brush with reserved sauce, turn chicken over, and bake 10–12 minutes until cooked through. Heat any remaining sauce in saucepan or microwave and serve with chicken tenders.

Nutrition per serving: 266 calories, 1.9 g fat, 39 g carbohydrates, 26 g protein, 57 mg cholesterol, 0 g dietary fiber, 1,623 mg sodium
Exchanges: 3 very lean meat, 2 other carb
Carb Choices: 3

Enjoy the finger-lickin' good taste of barbecue chicken wings without the skin and bones–keep all the flavor but cut the calories and fat!

Lobster Rolls

Easy | **Do Ahead** | **Serves: 8**

1 8-oz. pkg. nonfat cream
cheese, *softened*

¾ cup cocktail sauce, *divided*

8 oz. chunk-style imitation
lobster, *chopped*

¼ cup nonfat shredded
mozzarella cheese

¼ cup chopped green onions

4 98% fat-free flour tortillas

Combine cream cheese and ¼ cup cocktail sauce in medium
bowl; mix until blended. Stir in lobster, cheese, and green
onions. Divide mixture, spread on tortillas, and roll up tightly.
Wrap tortilla rolls in plastic wrap and refrigerate overnight.
When ready to serve, remove wrap, slice, and serve with
remaining cocktail sauce.

Nutrition per serving: 136 calories, 0.2 g fat, 23 g carbohydrates, 10 g protein,
2 mg cholesterol, 1 g dietary fiber, 866 mg sodium
Exchanges: 1 very lean meat, 1 other carb
Carb Choices: 2

Appetizers
and
Munchies

Shopping List

Produce
green onions

Meat/Fish/Poultry
8 oz. chunk-style imitation
lobster

Dairy
8-oz. pkg. nonfat cream cheese
nonfat shredded mozzarella
cheese

Packaged
17.5-oz. pkg. 98% fat-free
flour tortillas

Condiments
6 oz. cocktail sauce

Variation: Substitute crab flakes or chopped
cooked shrimp for lobster.

Chunky Tomato Bruschetta

Easy | Do Ahead | Serves: 8

1   1 lb. loaf Italian bread, *cut into 8 slices*

½   cup nonfat Italian salad dressing

1   14½-oz. can petite-cut diced tomatoes with garlic and onion, *drained*

¾   cup diced Vidalia onion

1   tbsp. roasted minced garlic

1   cup nonfat shredded mozzarella cheese

Preheat oven to 400°. Line baking sheet(s) with foil and spray with cooking spray. Arrange bread slices in single layer on baking sheet(s). Brush both sides of bread with salad dressing. Bake 2 minutes per side until lightly browned. Combine tomatoes, onion, and garlic in medium bowl and mix well; spoon mixture evenly on bread slices. Top each bread slice with 2 tablespoons cheese. Return to oven and bake until cheese is melted.

Nutrition per serving: 210 calories, 0 g fat, 37 g carbohydrates, 11 g protein, 0 mg cholesterol, 2 g dietary fiber, 530 mg sodium
Exchanges: 2 starch, 1 vegetable, 1 very lean meat,
Carb Choices: 2

Shopping List

Produce
Vidalia onion

Dairy
4 oz. nonfat shredded mozzarella cheese

Canned
14½-oz. can petite-cut diced tomatoes with garlic and onion

Packaged
Italian bread

Seasonings/Spices
minced garlic

Condiments
nonfat Italian salad dressing

Georgians value the Vidalia onion–they named it their state vegetable!

Crostini

Easy | **Do Ahead** | **Serves: 6**

6 slices Italian bread,
    cut ½ inch thick

1 14½-oz. can petite-cut
    diced tomatoes with roasted
    garlic and sweet onion,
    drained well

½ cup bottled roasted
    red peppers (not packed in
    oil), *drained and chopped*

1 tsp. Italian seasoning

1 tsp. balsamic vinegar

¾ cup nonfat shedded
    mozzarella cheese

Preheat oven to 400°. Line baking sheet with foil and spray with cooking spray. Arrange bread slices in a single layer on baking sheet; bake 3–5 minutes until lightly toasted. Combine drained tomatoes, red peppers, Italian seasoning, and balsamic vinegar in medium bowl; toss to mix. Spoon mixture on bread and top with cheese. Bake 5–6 minutes until cheese is completely melted.

Nutrition per serving: 124 calories, 0 g fat, 20 g carbohydrates, 8 g protein, 0 mg cholesterol, 1 g dietary fiber, 381 mg sodium
Exchanges: 1 starch, 1 vegetable
Carb Choices: 1

Appetizers and Munchies

Shopping List

Dairy	Condiments
nonfat shredded mozzarella cheese	7-oz. bottle roasted red peppers (not packed in oil)
Canned	balsamic vinegar
14½-oz. can petite-cut diced tomatoes with roasted garlic and sweet onion	**Seasonings/Spices**
	Italian seasoning
Packaged	
Italian bread	

Crostini are thin slices of bread that are baked; the American equivalent is melba toast.

Pretzel Twists with Hot Honey Mustard Sauce

Easy | **Serves: 6**

1 cup nonfat mayonnaise

½ cup honey-Dijon mustard

1 tbsp. prepared horseradish

1 8-oz. pkg. pretzel twists
    (or any other shape)

   fresh cut-up vegetables
    (optional)

Combine mayonnaise, mustard, and horseradish in medium bowl; mix well. Cover and refrigerate at least 1 hour. Serve cold with pretzels and, if desired, fresh cut-up vegetables.

Nutrition per serving: 218 calories, 1.3 g fat, 44 g carbohydrates, 4 g protein, 0 mg cholesterol, 0 g dietary fiber, 1,196 mg sodium
Exchanges: 2 starch, 1 other carb
Carb Choices: 3

Shopping List

Packaged
8-oz. bag pretzels

Condiments
8 oz. nonfat mayonnaise
4 oz. honey-Dijon mustard
prepared horseradish

Optional
fresh cut-up vegetables

Simply substituting nonfat mayonnaise for the regular variety will save 88 calories and 12 grams of fat per tablespoon.

Simple Stuffed Celery Sticks

Easy | **Do Ahead** | **Serves: 4**

1 8-oz. pkg. nonfat cream
   cheese, *softened*

1½ tsp. chili powder

1 tsp. Worcestershire sauce

1 7-oz. container celery sticks,
   drained and patted dry

3 tbsp. cornflake crumbs

Combine cream cheese, chili powder, and Worcestershire sauce in medium bowl; mix until creamy, smooth, and blended. Stuff celery sticks with cheese mixture and dip cheese filling in cornflake crumbs to coat.

Nutrition per serving: 69 calories, 0.2 g fat, 9 g carbohydrates, 8 g protein, 0 mg cholesterol, 1 g dietary fiber, 460 mg sodium
Exchanges: 1 vegetable, ½ other carb
Carb Choices: 0

Appetizers and Munchies

Shopping List

Produce
7-oz. container celery sticks

Dairy
8 oz. nonfat cream cheese

Packaged
cornflake crumbs

Condiments
Worcestershire sauce

Seasonings/Spices
chili powder

Using nonfat cream cheese in place of whole dairy cream cheese will save you 70 calories and 10 grams of fat per tablespoon.

Seafood Nachos

Easy | Serves: 4

8 oz. baked tortilla chips

1 cup nonfat refried beans

1½ cups chunky-style salsa, *divided*

1½ cups nonfat shredded cheddar cheese

¾ lb. cooked medium shrimp, *peeled and deveined*

Preheat oven to 450°. Line baking sheet with foil and spray with cooking spray. Spread chips in a single layer (slightly overlapping if necessary) on baking sheet. Combine refried beans and ½ cup salsa in small bowl; mix until blended. Spoon mixture over chips, spreading evenly; sprinkle with cheese. Bake 5 minutes; arrange shrimp on top and bake 4–5 minutes until cheese is completely melted and chips are lightly browned. Serve with remaining salsa.

Nutrition per serving: 465 calories, 3.1 g fat, 68 g carbohydrates, 41 g protein, 166 mg cholesterol, 2 g dietary fiber, 1,754 mg sodium
Exchanges: 4 starch, 1 vegetable
Carb Choices: 5

Shopping List

Meat/Fish/Poultry
¾ lb. cooked medium shrimp (peeled and deveined)

Dairy
6 oz. nonfat shredded cheddar cheese

Canned
15-oz. can nonfat refried beans

Packaged
8 oz. baked tortilla chips

Condiments
12 oz. chunky-style salsa

Use a variety of colors when preparing foods–this makes for an interesting and appetizing looking table!

Shrimp Quesadillas

Easy | Do Ahead | Serves: 4

4   98% fat-free flour tortillas

1   cup nonfat shredded
    cheddar cheese

1   14½-oz. can petite-cut
    diced tomatoes with green
    chiles, *drained*

4   oz. frozen cooked salad
    shrimp, *rinsed and thawed*

    salsa (optional)

Preheat oven to 300°. Spray large nonstick skillet with cooking spray and heat over medium-high heat. Place 1 tortilla at a time in skillet; fill with ¼ cup cheese, ¼ cup tomatoes, and ¼ of the shrimp. Fold tortilla over and cook 1–2 minutes; carefully turn tortilla over and cook 1 minute until cheese is melted and tortilla is crisp. Wrap in foil and keep warm in oven while preparing remaining tortillas. Serve with salsa, if desired.

Nutrition per serving: 209 calories, 0.8 g fat, 30 g carbohydrates, 19 g protein, 55 mg cholesterol, 2 g dietary fiber, 1,095 mg sodium
Exchanges: 1 starch, 3 vegetable, 2 very lean meat
Carb Choices: 2

Appetizers and Munchies

Shopping List

Dairy
1 oz. nonfat shredded cheddar cheese

Frozen
4 oz. frozen cooked salad shrimp

Canned
14½-oz. can petite-cut diced tomatoes with green chiles

Packaged
17.5-oz. pkg. 98% fat-free flour tortillas

Optional
salsa

Using canned diced tomatoes is a super timesaver; selecting varieties with additional seasonings and spices can add a splash to any recipe.

Turkey Tortilla Rollups

Easy | Do Ahead | Serves: 4

6 oz. nonfat cream cheese, *softened*

2½ tbsp. nonfat sour cream

¼ cup diced bell pepper

1 tbsp. chopped green onion

1 tbsp. chopped olives, *drained*

2 98% fat-free flour tortillas

2 6-oz. pkgs. oven roasted turkey breast, *sliced thin*

Combine cream cheese and sour cream in bowl; mix until creamy and smooth. Add bell pepper, green onion, and olives; mix well. Divide cheese mixture and spread over tortillas. Divide turkey and place on tortillas. Roll each tortilla jelly-roll fashion; wrap and refrigerate overnight. When ready to serve, cut tortilla rolls into 1-inch pieces and secure with toothpicks.

Nutrition per serving: 216 calories, 1 g fat, 16 g carbohydrates, 34 g protein, 71 mg cholesterol, 1 g dietary fiber, 491 mg sodium
Exchanges: 1 vegetable, 4 very lean meat, ½ other carb
Carb Choices: 1

Shopping List

Produce
bell pepper
green onions

Meat/Fish/Poultry
2 6-oz. pkgs. oven roasted
   turkey breast (sliced thin)

Dairy
6 oz. nonfat cream cheese
nonfat sour cream

Canned
4-oz. can chopped olives

Packaged
17.5-oz. pkg 98% fat-free flour
   tortillas

When choosing hot appetizers for party events, choose ones that will heat at the same temperature to save space and time.

Italian Garlic Pita Chips

Easy | Do Ahead | Serves: 12

6 pita pockets, *split open and cut in half*

I Can't Believe It's Not Butter spray

2 tbsp. + 2 tsp. bottled roasted minced garlic

1–2 tsp. Italian seasoning

½ cup nonfat Parmesan cheese

Preheat oven to 450°. Line baking sheet with foil and spray with cooking spray. Arrange cut pitas (rough side up) in a single layer on baking sheet. Spray pitas with "butter" spray; top with minced garlic, sprinkle with Italian seasoning, and top with Parmesan cheese. Bake pita chips 10–12 minutes until lightly browned and crisp.

Nutrition per serving: 64 calories, 0.3 g fat, 12 g carbohydrates, 3 g protein, 0 mg cholesterol, <1 g dietary fiber, 138 mg sodium
Exchanges: 1 starch
Carb Choices: 1

Appetizers and Munchies

Shopping List

Dairy
I Can't Believe It's Not Butter spray
nonfat Parmesan cheese

Packaged
6 pita pocket breads

Seasonings/Spices
bottled roasted minced garlic
Italian seasoning

Adjust the level of garlic in this recipe to suit your tastes. Or, for more herb flavor, increase the amount of Italian seasoning.

Bacon and Sun-Dried Tomato Horseradish Dip

Easy | **Do Ahead** | **Serves: 12**

2 cups nonfat sour cream

¼ cup prepared horseradish

½ cup nonfat mayonnaise

2 tbsp. lemon juice

⅓ cup bacon crumbles

¼ cup chopped sun-dried
   tomatoes *(not packed in oil)*

   parsley (optional)

   bagel chips, pita chips, or
   crackers (optional)

Combine sour cream, horseradish, mayonnaise, and lemon juice in medium bowl; mix until creamy and smooth. Fold in bacon crumbles and sun-dried tomatoes and mix well. Cover and refrigerate at least 1 hour or overnight. Garnish with parsley and serve with bagel chips, pita chips, or crackers, if desired.

Nutrition per serving: 52 calories, 0.6 g fat, 6 g carbohydrates, 4 g protein, 0 mg cholesterol, 0 g dietary fiber, 260 mg sodium
Exchanges: ½ other carb
Carb Choices: 0

Shopping List

Dairy
16 oz. nonfat sour cream

Packaged
1.3-oz. pkg. bacon crumbles
5-oz. pkg. sun-dried tomatoes

Condiments
prepared horseradish
nonfat mayonnaise
bottled lemon juice

Optional
parsley
bagel chips, pita chips,
   or crackers

You can substitute 1 tablespoon freshly grated horseradish for every 2 tablespoons prepared horseradish called for in this recipe.

Baked Northern Bean Spread

Easy | Do Ahead | Serves: 12

2 15-oz. cans Great Northern
   beans, *rinsed and drained*

1½ tbsp. onion powder

1 tbsp. bottled minced garlic

1 tsp. dried rosemary

1 tbsp. + 1 tsp. white
   wine vinegar

2–3 drops Tabasco sauce

   baked tortilla chips or raw
   vegetable sticks (optional)

Preheat oven to 350°. Spray 8-inch baking dish with cooking spray. Combine all ingredients in food processor or blender and process or blend until smooth and creamy. Spread mixture in baking dish; bake, uncovered, 20–25 minutes until bubbly hot. Serve with baked tortilla chips or raw veggie sticks, if desired.

Nutrition per serving: 84 calories, 0.2 g fat, 16 g carbohydrates, 5 g protein, 0 mg cholesterol, 0 g dietary fiber, 4 mg sodium
Exchanges: 1 starch
Carb Choices: 1

Appetizers
and
Munchies

Shopping List

Dairy
2 15-oz. cans Great Northern
   beans

Condiments
white wine vinegar
Tabasco sauce

Seasonings/Spices
onion powder
minced garlic
dried rosemary

Optional
baked tortilla chips or
raw vegetable sticks

Beans contain no cholesterol, and more than that, they can help lower your cholesterol level because they are a rich source of fiber.

Baked Spinach Dip

Easy | Do Ahead | Serves: 12

½ cup nonfat sour cream

½ cup nonfat mayonnaise

1 tsp. garlic powder

1 10-oz. pkg. frozen chopped spinach, *thawed, drained, and squeezed dry*

¼ cup chopped water chestnuts

1 cup nonfat shredded mozzarella cheese

¾ cup nonfat Parmesan cheese

assorted crackers, bagel chips, or fresh vegetables (optional)

Preheat oven to 350°. Spray 9-inch pie plate with cooking spray. Combine all the ingredients in medium bowl and mix well. Spoon mixture into pie plate and bake 25–30 minutes until bubbly hot and lightly browned on top. Serve with assorted crackers, bagel chips, or fresh vegetables, if desired.

Nutrition per serving: 52 calories, 0 g fat, 6 g carbohydrates, 7 g protein, 0 mg cholesterol, 1 g dietary fiber, 210 mg sodium
Exchanges: 1 vegetable, 1 very lean meat
Carb Choices: 0

Shopping List

Dairy
4 oz. nonfat sour cream
4 oz. nonfat shredded
    mozzarella cheese
nonfat Parmesan cheese

Condiments
nonfat mayonnaise

Seasonings/Spices
garlic powder

Frozen
10-oz. pkg. frozen
    chopped spinach

Optional
assorted crackers, bagel
    chips, or fresh
    vegetables

Canned
6-oz. can sliced water
    chestnuts

Fun fact: Spinach was the first vegetable to be sold frozen.

Ginger-Soy Shrimp Dip

Easy | Do Ahead | Serves: 4

8 oz. nonfat sour cream

¼ cup nonfat mayonnaise

2 tsp. light soy sauce

¼ tsp. ground ginger

¼ tsp. garlic powder

¼ cup diced red onions

½ cup diced celery

½ cup diced water chestnuts

1 6-oz. can baby shrimp, *rinsed, drained, and chopped*

low-fat crackers, pita chips, or raw vegetables (optional)

Combine sour cream, mayonnaise, soy sauce, ginger, and garlic powder in medium bowl; mix until blended smooth and creamy. Add onions, celery, water chestnuts, and shrimp; mix well. Cover and refrigerate until ready to serve. Serve shrimp dip with low-fat crackers, pita chips, or raw vegetables.

Nutrition per serving: 114 calories, 0.8 g fat, 10 g carbohydrates, 14 g protein, 73 mg cholesterol, <1 g dietary fiber, 327 mg sodium

Exchanges: 1 vegetable, 1 very lean meat

Carb Choices: 1

Appetizers and Munchies

Shopping List

Produce	Condiments
7-oz. container diced red onions	nonfat mayonnaise
7-oz. container celery sticks	light soy sauce
	Seasonings/Spices
	ground ginger
Dairy	garlic powder
8 oz. nonfat sour cream	
	Optional
Canned	low-fat crackers, pita
6-oz. can sliced water chestnuts	chips, or raw vegetables
6-oz. can baby shrimp	

Save 256 milligrams of sodium by substituting light soy sauce for regular.

Hot Artichoke Dip with Chiles and Bacon

Easy | Do Ahead | Serves: 6

2   15-oz. cans artichoke hearts,
    *drained and coarsely
    chopped*

1   7-oz. can diced green chiles,
    drained

¼   cup bacon crumbles

2   cups nonfat mayonnaise

2   cups nonfat Parmesan cheese

    baked chips, crackers, or
    bread cubes (optional)

Spray large saucepan with cooking spray; add all ingredients and mix well. Cook over medium heat, stirring frequently, 8–10 minutes until heated through. Serve with baked chips, crackers, or bread cubes, if desired.

Nutrition per serving: 232 calories, 1.5 g fat, 40 g carbohydrates, 17 g protein, 0 mg cholesterol, 1 g dietary fiber, 1,483 mg sodium
Exchanges: 2 vegetable, 2 very lean meat, 2 other carb
Carb Choices: 3

Shopping List

Dairy
8 oz. nonfat Parmesan cheese

Canned
2 15-oz. cans artichoke hearts
7-oz. can diced green chiles

Packaged
1.3-oz pkg. bacon crumbles

Condiments
16 oz. nonfat mayonnaise

Optional
baked chips, crackers,
or bread cubes

One-quarter cup bacon crumbles is the equivalent of 4 slices of cooked bacon.

Hot Chili Cheese Dip

Easy | **Do Ahead** | **Serves: 8**

1   8-oz. pkg. nonfat cream
    cheese, *softened*

½   cup chunky-style salsa

1½ cups nonfat shredded
    cheddar cheese, *divided*

1   16-oz. can chili beans,
    not drained

1   tbsp. diced green chiles

8   oz. baked tortilla chips

Preheat oven to 350°. Spray 9-inch pie plate with cooking spray. Combine cream cheese and salsa in medium bowl; mix well. Spread cream cheese mixture in bottom of pie plate. Sprinkle with ¾ cup cheddar cheese. Top with chili beans, green chiles, and remaining cheese. Bake 15–20 minutes until cheese is melted and mixture is bubbly hot. Serve with baked tortilla chips.

Nutrition per serving: 223 calories, 1.4 g fat, 44 g carbohydrates, 15 g protein, 0 mg cholesterol, 3 g dietary fiber, 891 mg sodium
Exchanges: 2 starch, 2 vegetable, 1 very lean meat
Carb Choices: 0

Appetizers
and
Munchies

Shopping List

Dairy
8 oz. nonfat cream cheese
6 oz. nonfat shredded
  cheddar cheese

Canned
16-oz. can chili beans
4-oz. can diced green chiles

Packaged
8 oz. baked tortilla chips

Condiments
8-oz. jar chunky-style salsa

You can determine the "heat" in your Hot Chili Cheese Dip; using jalapeños, rather than mild green chiles, and hot salsa will certainly turn up the heat!

Hot Bacon-Cheese Dip

Easy | Do Ahead | Serves: 4

1 8-oz. pkg. nonfat cream cheese, *cubed*

2 cups nonfat shredded cheddar cheese

½ cup nonfat half and half

1 tsp. Worcestershire sauce

½ tsp. onion powder

½ tsp. brown 'n spicy mustard

1 1.3-oz. pkg. bacon crumbles

baked tortilla chips, whole wheat crackers, or lahvosh cracker bread (optional)

Spray 10-inch microwave-safe dish with cooking spray. Combine cream cheese, cheddar cheese, half and half, Worcestershire sauce, onion powder, and mustard in dish; mix well. Microwave on High 1 minute; stir mixture and microwave 2–3 minutes until creamy and heated through, stirring every minute. Fold in bacon crumbles and serve with baked tortilla chips, whole wheat crackers, or lahvosh, if desired.

Nutrition per serving: 194 calories, 2 g fat, 13 g carbohydrates, 26 g protein, 0 mg cholesterol, 0 g dietary fiber, 1,247 mg sodium
Exchanges: 3 very lean meat, 1 other carb
Carb Choices: 1

Shopping List

Dairy	Seasonings/Spices
8 oz. nonfat cream cheese	onion powder
8 oz. nonfat shredded cheddar cheese	**Condiments**
4 oz. nonfat half and half	Worcestershire sauce
	brown 'n spicy mustard
Packaged	**Optional**
1.3-oz. pkg. bacon crumbles	baked tortilla chips, whole wheat crackers, or lahvosh cracker bread

Lahvosh cracker bread is available in a variety of shapes and sizes; you can also select from white or whole wheat lahvosh.

Southwest-Style Artichoke Dip

Easy | **Do Ahead** | **Serves: 6**

1 cup nonfat creamy Caesar
   salad dressing

½ cup nonfat mayonnaise

½ cup nonfat sour cream

½ cup nonfat Parmesan cheese

1 cup nonfat shredded
   mozzarella cheese

2 13¾-oz. cans quartered
   artichoke hearts, *drained
   and chopped*

1 14½-oz. can diced tomatoes
   with green chiles, *drained*

lahvosh crackers, rye crisps,
   or bread slices (optional)

Preheat oven to 350°. Spray 8×8-inch baking dish with cooking spray. Combine all the ingredients in baking dish and mix well. Bake 35–45 minutes until bubbly hot and lightly browned. Serve with lahvosh crackers, rye crisps, or toasted bread slices, if desired.

Nutrition per serving: 194 calories, 0.4 g fat, 33 g carbohydrates, 15 g protein, 0 mg cholesterol, <1 g dietary fiber, 1,106 mg sodium
Exchanges: 3 vegetable, 1 other carb
Carb Choices: 2

Appetizers and Munchies

Shopping List

Dairy
4 oz. nonfat sour cream
2 oz. nonfat Parmesan cheese
4 oz. nonfat shredded
   mozzarella cheese

Canned
2 13¾-oz. cans
   quartered artichoke hearts
14½-oz. can diced tomatoes
   with green chiles

Condiments
8 oz. nonfat creamy
   Caesar salad dressing
4 oz. nonfat mayonnaise

Optional
lahvosh crackers, rye
   crisps, or bread slices

This is the perfect addition to any party–being able to prepare it ahead saves time, energy, and stress!

Super Salsa with Chips

Easy | **Do Ahead** | **Serves: 10**

2   14½-oz. cans petite-cut diced tomatoes with jalapeños, *drained*

1   14½-oz. can stewed tomatoes with bell pepper and onion, *drained and chopped*

3   15-oz. cans black beans, *rinsed and drained*

2   11-oz. cans Mexicorn, *drained*

1   cup chopped green onions

baked tortilla chips

Combine all ingredients except tortilla chips in a large bowl; cover and refrigerate overnight. Serve salsa with baked tortilla chips.

Nutrition per serving: 93 calories, 0.3 g fat, 18 g carbohydrates, 5 g protein, 0 mg cholesterol, 3 g dietary fiber, 500 mg sodium
Exchanges: ½ starch, 2 vegetable
Carb Choices: 1

Shopping List

Produce
1 large bunch green onions

Canned
2 14½-oz. cans petite-cut diced tomatoes with jalapeños
14½-oz. can stewed tomatoes with bell pepper and onion
3 15-oz. cans black beans
2 11-oz. cans Mexicorn

Packaged
baked tortilla chips

How many appetizer items do you need per person? Although it depends on the time of day and age of your guests, you can generally figure about 5–6 pieces per person.

WOW! Tuna Dip

Easy | Do Ahead | Serves: 8

2 8-oz. pkgs. nonfat cream cheese, *softened*

⅓ cup nonfat sour cream

3 tbsp. deli-style mustard with horseradish

1 tsp. Worcestershire sauce

1 tbsp. onion powder

⅛ tsp. cayenne pepper

1 12-oz. can chunk-light tuna packed in water, *drained*

pepper to taste

fresh vegetables, low-fat crackers, lahvosh, or baked chips (optional)

Combine cream cheese, sour cream, mustard, Worcestershire sauce, onion powder, and cayenne pepper in food processor or blender; process or blend until smooth. Fold in tuna and season with pepper to taste. Cover and refrigerate several hours or overnight. Serve with fresh vegetables, low-fat crackers, lahvosh, or baked chips, if desired.

Nutrition per serving: 109 calories, 0.3 g fat, 5 g carbohydrates, 21 g protein, 8 mg cholesterol, 0 g dietary fiber, 543 mg sodium
Exchanges: 2 very lean meat, ½ other carb
Carb Choices: 0

Appetizers and Munchies

Shopping List

Dairy
2 8-oz. pkgs. nonfat cream cheese
nonfat sour cream

Canned
12-oz. can chunk-light tuna packed in water

Condiments
deli-style mustard with horseradish
Worcestershire sauce

Seasonings/Spices
onion powder
cayenne pepper
pepper

Optional
fresh vegetables, low-fat crackers, lahvosh, or baked chips

Use vegetables such as hollowed-out red cabbage or bell peppers as dip containers. They look great and save cleanup time.

Chapter Index

② Breakfast and Brunch

Mandarin Orange Pancakes

According to a study published in *The Journal of The American Dietetic Association* (1996), the nutritional quality of food Americans consume at breakfast has improved over the years, but the number of individuals eating breakfast has declined. Twenty-five percent (one out of every four) of American adults skip breakfast! If you are one of these "skippers," tune in here to find out what you've been missing.

Eight Great Reasons to Eat Breakfast

1. Breakfast gives your body the fuel it needs to start each day. Breakfast restores the body's glucose levels, the brain's energy source.

2. Breakfast provides a great opportunity to maximize your well-being.

3. Breakfast provides a substantial source of minerals and vitamins. Many foods eaten at breakfast contain significant amounts of vitamins C and D, calcium, iron, and fiber. A good breakfast can provide protein (for building and maintaining muscle), carbohydrates (for energy), fiber (for healthy digestive function), calcium (for building strong bones), iron, (for healthy red blood cells and oxygen transport around the body), plus additional vitamins and minerals. These nutrients are essential for healthy growth and development. Those who skip breakfast often don't make up for the missed nutrients later on in the day.

4. Breakfast improves mental and physical performance; a healthy breakfast is associated with better concentration, problem-solving abilities, memory, and mood.

5. Eating breakfast reduces the risk of satisfying hunger later with high-fat, less nutritious snacks. When you miss breakfast your body's metabolism slows down and remains slow for the rest of the day, making it harder for your body to use up the energy from the foods you eat later, possibly leading to weight gain over time. Skipping breakfast can leave you feeling very hungry midmorning and result in filling up on convenient snack foods, which offer poor nutriential value.

Breakfast and Brunch

6. Eating breakfast sets a proper eating pattern for the entire day.

7. Morning protein and carbohydrates provide a boost of energy that keeps your body going strong for 3–4 hours.

8. Studies show that those who regularly skip breakfast are 4.5 times more likely to be overweight.

Apple Cinnamon Pancakes

Easy | Do Ahead | Freeze | Serves: 4

2 cups fat-free buttermilk
   pancake mix

1½ cups apple juice

2 tsp. cinnamon

   syrup, jelly, or preserves
   (optional)

Prepare pancake mix according to package directions, substituting apple juice for water. Stir in cinnamon and mix well. Spray large nonstick skillet with cooking spray and heat over medium-high heat. Pour about ¼ cup batter per pancake onto skillet and cook 2–3 minutes per side until golden brown. Serve with syrup, jelly, or preserves, if desired.

Nutrition per serving: 261 calories, 0.1 g fat, 61 g carbohydrates, 5 g protein, 0 mg cholesterol, 7 g dietary fiber, 465 mg sodium
Exchanges: 3 starch, ½ fruit
Carb Choices: 4

Shopping List

Packaged
28-oz. pkg. fat-free buttermilk
   pancake mix

Canned
12-oz can or bottle apple juice

Seasonings/Spices
cinnamon

Optional
syrup, jelly, or preserves

For best results, heat skillet before adding pancake batter; you'll know it's hot enough when a drop of water "jumps" across the skillet.

Strawberry Stuffed French Toast

Easy | Do Ahead | Serves: 6

1 cup egg substitute

½ cup nonfat half and half

½ tsp. vanilla extract

2 tbsp. sugar

12 slices French bread,
    cut ½ inch thick

6 tbsp. nonfat spreadable
    cream cheese

¼ cup sugar-free strawberry
    preserves

syrup or powdered
    sugar (optional)

Combine egg substitute, half and half, vanilla, and sugar in medium bowl; whisk until ingredients are blended. Spread each of 6 slices of bread with 1 tablespoon cream cheese; spread each remaining bread slice with 2 teaspoons preserves. Sandwich bread together (1 with cheese, 1 with preserves). Spray large nonstick skillet with cooking spray and heat over medium heat. Dip "sandwiches" into egg mixture and coat on both sides. Place in hot skillet and cook 2–3 minutes per side until golden brown. Serve with syrup or powdered sugar, if desired.

Nutrition per serving: 274 calories, 2.9 g fat, 48 g carbohydrates, 13 g protein, 0 mg cholesterol, 2 g dietary fiber, 617 mg sodium
Exchanges: 2 starch, 1 very lean meat, 1 other carb, ½ fat
Carb Choices: 3

Breakfast and Brunch

Shopping List

Dairy
8 oz. egg substitute
4 oz. nonfat half and half
3 oz. nonfat spreadable
    cream cheese

Packaged
1-lb. loaf French bread

Baking goods
sugar
vanilla extract

Condiments
sugar-free strawberry
    preserves

Optional
syrup or powdered sugar

If you think skipping breakfast keeps your weight down, think again. Eating a healthy breakfast means you're much less likely to snack midmorning or overeat at lunch.

Brown Sugar Pancake Rollups

Easy | **Serves: 4**

2 cups fat-free buttermilk pancake mix

1½ cups water

½ cup brown sugar

1 tsp. cinnamon

I Can't Believe It's Not Butter spray

Prepare pancake mix with water according to package directions. Preheat oven to 300°. Spray large nonstick skillet with cooking spray and heat over medium-high heat. Pour a quarter of the batter into skillet and cook 3–4 minutes per side until golden brown. Repeat with remaining batter to make 4 large pancakes. Wrap cooked pancakes in foil and place in oven to keep warm. Combine brown sugar and cinnamon in zip-top bag; shake to mix well. Spray each pancake with "butter" spray and sprinkle with 2 tablespoons brown sugar-cinnamon mix; roll pancake up and serve.

Nutrition per serving: 319 calories, 0 g fat, 76 g carbohydrates, 5 g protein, 0 mg cholesterol, 6 g dietary fiber, 470 mg sodium
Exchanges: 4 starch, ½ other carb
Carb Choices: 5

Shopping List

Dairy
I Can't Believe It's Not Butter spray

Packaged
28-oz. pkg. fat-free buttermilk pancake mix

Baking Goods
brown sugar

Seasonings/Spices
cinnamon

In a survey conducted by General Mills, Inc., adults who ate cereal for breakfast consumed an average of 10% fewer calories than those who selected other breakfast foods. The best choices are high in fiber yet low in fat, sugar, and sodium.

Mandarin Orange Pancakes

Easy | **Do Ahead** | **Serves: 4**

2 cups fat-free buttermilk
   pancake mix

¾ cup water

¾ cup orange juice

¼ cup Mandarin oranges,
   chopped fine and drained

syrup, jelly, or fruit spread
(optional)

Combine pancake mix, water, and orange juice in medium bowl; whisk until completely blended (batter will be slightly lumpy). Fold in chopped oranges. Spray large nonstick skillet with cooking spray and heat over medium-high heat. Pour batter (about ¼ cup) into skillet and cook about 2 minutes per side until just golden brown. Serve with syrup, jelly, or fruit spread, if desired.

Nutrition per serving: 246 calories, 0 g fat, 57 g carbohydrates, 6 g protein, 0 mg cholesterol, 7 g dietary fiber, 464 mg sodium
Exchanges: 2 starch, 1½ fruit
Carb Choices: 4

Breakfast
and
Brunch

Shopping List

Refrigerated
6 oz. orange juice

Packaged
28-oz. pkg. fat-free buttermilk
pancake mix

Canned
8-oz. can Mandarin oranges

Optional
syrup, jelly, or fruit spread

For best results cook pancakes for 2–3 minutes on each side. When bubbles appear on the surface and edges seem dry, it's time to flip the pancakes.

Protein-Rich Pancakes

Easy | **Serves: 4**

6 large egg whites

¾ cup nonfat cottage cheese

½ cup flour

1 tbsp. sugar

sugar-free syrup or preserves (optional)

Combine egg whites, cottage cheese, flour, and sugar in food processor or blender; process or blend until smooth. Spray large nonstick skillet with cooking spray and heat over medium heat. Pour batter (about ¼ cup per pancake) into skillet (2–3 pancakes per batch) and cook 5–6 minutes until bottoms are lightly browned. Turn pancakes over and cook until browned on both sides. Serve with syrup or preserves, if desired.

Nutrition per serving: 101 calories, 0.1 g fat, 16 g carbohydrates, 8 g protein, 1 mg cholesterol, <1 g dietary fiber, 117 mg sodium
Exchanges: 1 starch, 1 very lean meat
Carb Choices: 1

Shopping List

Dairy
whole eggs
6 oz. nonfat cottage cheese

Baking Goods
flour
sugar

Optional
sugar-free syrup or preserves

Sugar-free products must contain less than 0.5 grams of sugar per serving. Read labels carefully–check for realistic portion sizes.

Pumpkin Pie Pancakes

Easy | Do Ahead | Freeze | Serves: 4

2 cups fat-free buttermilk pancake mix

¾ cup canned pumpkin pie mix *(not canned pumpkin puree)*

1 cup water

syrup (optional)

Combine pancake mix, pumpkin pie mix, and water; mix until blended. Spray large nonstick skillet with cooking spray and heat over medium-high heat. Pour batter (about ¼ cup per pancake) into skillet and cook 3–4 minutes per side until lightly browned and cooked through. Serve with syrup, if desired.

Nutrition per serving: 230 calories, 0.1 g fat, 53 g carbohydrates, 6 g protein, 0 mg cholesterol, 7 g dietary fiber, 464 mg sodium
Exchanges: 2 starch, 1½ fruit
Carb Choices: 4

Breakfast and Brunch

Shopping List

Packaged
28-oz. pkg. fat-free buttermilk pancake mix

Canned
16-oz. can pumpkin pie mix (not canned pumpkin puree)

Optional
syrup

Beware of labels boasting "healthy" claims.
For instance, "healthy" or "saturated fat-free" granola is often loaded with seeds, nuts, and oil, and all the calories and fat that go with them.

Applesauce Blintzes

Easy | Do Ahead | Freeze | Serves: 4

1 3-oz. pkg. nonfat cream
    cheese, *softened*

1 cup nonfat cottage cheese

¼ cup egg substitute

2 tbsp. sugar

½ tsp. almond extract

8 ready-to-use crepes

   I Can't Believe It's
     Not Butter spray

2 cups chunky homestyle
     applesauce with cinnamon

Preheat oven to 400°. Line baking sheet with foil and spray with cooking spray. Combine cream cheese, cottage cheese, egg substitute, sugar, and almond extract in food processor or blender and process or blend until smooth. Spoon 2–3 tablespoons mixture down center of each crepe. Fold sides around filling and place on baking sheet. Spray each blintz lightly with "butter" spray. Bake 10 minutes until lightly browned. Serve with applesauce.

Nutrition per serving: 295 calories, 0.2 g fat, 66 g carbohydrates, 10 g protein, 1 mg cholesterol, 6 g dietary fiber, 228 mg sodium
Exchanges: 3 starch, 1 fruit
Carb Choices: 4

Shopping List

Dairy
3-oz. pkg. nonfat cream cheese
8 oz. nonfat cottage cheese
egg substitute
I Can't Believe It's Not Butter
  spray

Packaged
4.5-oz. pkg. ready-to-use crepes

Baking Goods
sugar
almond extract

Canned
16-oz. jar chunky homestyle
  applesauce with cinnamon

Did you know the term "breakfast" dates all the way back to the 15th century when builders set out on empty stomachs to pull huge blocks of granite across the Egyptian desert?

Apple Cinnamon Quesadillas

Easy | Serves: 4

1½ cups chunky-style
    applesauce, *divided*

¼   cup nonfat vanilla yogurt

4   98% fat-free flour tortillas

2   tbsp. + 2 tsp. cinnamon-
    sugar

1   cup nonfat shredded
    mozzarella cheese

Preheat oven to 400°. Line baking sheet(s) with foil and spray with cooking spray. Combine ½ cup applesauce and vanilla yogurt in small bowl; mix well. Cover and refrigerate until ready to serve. Arrange 1 or 2 tortillas on baking sheet(s); spread each with ¼ cup applesauce. Sprinkle with 2 teaspoons cinnamon-sugar mixture and ¼ cup cheese; fold tortilla in half and bake 6–8 minutes until cheese is melted and tortilla is lightly browned. Repeat with remaining tortillas; cut tortillas in quarters and serve with apple-yogurt sauce.

Nutrition per serving: 269 calories, 0.7 g fat, 51 g carbohydrates, 14 g protein, 3 mg cholesterol, 3 g dietary fiber, 555 mg sodium
Exchanges: 2 starch, 1 very lean meat, 1½ fruit
Carb Choices: 3

Breakfast and Brunch

Shopping List

Dairy
4-oz. pkg. nonfat shredded
   mozzarella cheese
nonfat vanilla yogurt

Canned
12-oz. jar chunky-style
   applesauce

Packaged
17.5-oz. pkg. 98% fat-free flour
   tortillas

Baking Goods
cinnamon-sugar

Don't throw away overripe fruit. Instead, puree it in the blender or food processor and use in smoothies, dessert toppings, or as sauce for pancakes and waffles. You can also freeze pureed fruit in a plastic freezer bag and use as needed.

Pumpkin Spiced Oatmeal with Raisins

Easy | **Serves: 2**

1 cup quick-cooking oatmeal

¾–1 cup skim milk *(depending on desired consistency)*

½ cup canned pumpkin pie mix *(not canned pumpkin puree)*

2 tbsp. raisins

Combine oatmeal and ¾ cup skim milk in microwave-safe bowl. Cook on High 1–2 minutes, stirring once while cooking. Stir in pumpkin pie mix and add milk as needed to reach desired consistency. Microwave 30–45 seconds until heated through. Fold in raisins and serve.

Nutrition per serving: 247 calories, 2.9 g fat, 45 g carbohydrates, 12 g protein, 2 mg cholesterol, 4 g dietary fiber, 69 mg sodium
Exchanges: 2 starch, 1 fruit, ½ fat
Carb Choices: 3

Shopping List

Dairy
8 oz. skim milk

Canned
16-oz. can pumpkin pie mix
    (not canned pumpkin puree)

Packaged
quick-cooking oatmeal
raisins

Selecting vitamin-fortified cereals and eating them with skim milk helps you meet the Recommended Daily Allowance for calcium, vitamins, riboflavin, and folate.

Chocolate Banana Instant Oatmeal

Easy | **Serves: 1**

½ cup quick-cooking oatmeal

¾–1 cup water *(depending on desired consistency)*

½ banana, *mashed*

2 tbsp. brown sugar

skim milk (optional*)*

1 tsp. miniature chocolate chips

Combine oatmeal and water in microwave-safe bowl; cook on High 1½–2 minutes. Immediately stir in mashed banana and brown sugar, mixing well. Add milk to thin if oatmeal is too thick (or increase water when preparing). Fold in chocolate chips and serve immediately.

Nutrition per serving: 336 calories, 4.3 g fat, 70 g carbohydrates, 7 g protein, 1 mg cholesterol, 3 g dietary fiber, 15 mg sodium
Exchanges: 2 starch, 1 fruit, 1 other carb
Carb Choices: 5

Breakfast and Brunch

Shopping List

Produce
1 banana

Packaged
quick-cooking oatmeal

Baking Goods
brown sugar
miniature chocolate chips

Optional
skim milk

One banana can help reduce blood pressure and relieve heartburn. The good news is many of us eat about 27 pounds of bananas a year!

Apple Cider Oatmeal with Raisins

Easy | Serves: 1

⅓ cup quick-cooking oatmeal

⅔ cup water

1 packet instant sugar-free
   spiced cider

1 tsp. brown sugar

2 tbsp. raisins

   skim milk as needed
   (optional)

Combine quick-cooking oatmeal and water in microwave-safe bowl; mix well. Microwave on High 1½–2 minutes. Stir in spiced cider packet, brown sugar, and raisins. If oatmeal is too thick, thin with skim milk.

Nutrition per serving: 175 calories, 1.7 g fat, 37 g carbohydrates, 5 g protein, 0 mg cholesterol, 2 g dietary fiber, 5 mg sodium
Exchanges: 1 starch, 1 fruit, ½ other carb
Carb Choices: 2

Shopping List

Packaged
quick-cooking oatmeal
1.4-oz. box instant sugar-free
   spiced cider
raisins

Baking Goods
brown sugar

Optional
skim milk

You can lower LDL (bad) cholesterol by adding soluble fiber to your diet. Oatmeal, whole wheat bread, and brown rice are a few favorites.

Breakfast Shake

Easy | **Serves: 2**

1 cup nonfat vanilla yogurt

½ cup canned crushed pineapple in juice, *not drained*

1 banana, *peeled and sliced*

1 cup frozen sliced strawberries, *slightly thawed*

1 tbsp. wheat germ

ice cubes (optional)

Combine all ingredients in blender; puree until smooth and creamy. If shake is too thick, add several cubes of ice and blend again until desired consistency.

Nutrition per serving: 174 calories, 0.7 g fat, 39 g carbohydrates, 6 g protein, 3 mg cholesterol, 4 g dietary fiber, 73 mg sodium
Exchanges: 2 fruit, ½ milk
Carb Choices: 3

Breakfast and Brunch

Shopping List

Produce
1 banana

Dairy
8 oz. nonfat vanilla yogurt

Frozen
10-oz. pkg. frozen sliced strawberries

Canned
8-oz. can crushed pineapple in juice

Packaged
wheat germ

Wheat germ, a good source of selenium, works with vitamin E to help preserve elasticity of tissues, utilize protein, and promote proper functioning of red and white blood cells.

Banana-Berry Breakfast Shake

Easy | **Serves: 4**

2 bananas, *peeled and sliced*

½ cup nonfat cottage cheese

1¼ cups nonfat vanilla yogurt

1½ cups frozen blueberries, *slightly thawed*

4 or 5 ice cubes

fresh peach, sliced, or strawberries (optional)

Combine all the ingredients in food processor or blender; process or blend until smooth. Garnish with fresh peach slices or strawberries, if desired.

Nutrition per serving: 116 calories, 0.4 g fat, 26 g carbohydrates, 4 g protein, 2 mg cholesterol, 2 g dietary fiber, 71 mg sodium
Exchanges: 1 fruit, ½ milk
Carb Choices: 2

Shopping List

Produce
2 bananas

Dairy
4 oz. nonfat cottage cheese
10 oz. nonfat vanilla yogurt

Frozen
10-oz. pkg. frozen blueberries

Optional
fresh peach or strawberries

Vary the flavor of Banana-Berry Breakfast Shake by substituting strawberries, raspberries, blackberries, or mixed berries for the blueberries–or blend up a combination of your favorites.

O'Brien Omelet

Easy | **Serves: 4**

3 cups frozen Potatoes O'Brien, *thawed*

1 cup egg substitute

4 egg whites

3 tbsp. nonfat cottage cheese

dash pepper

¾ cup nonfat shredded cheddar cheese

Spray large nonstick skillet with cooking spray and heat over medium heat. Add potatoes; cook, stirring frequently, until tender. Combine egg substitute, egg whites, cottage cheese, and pepper in medium bowl; beat until blended. Pour egg mixture over potatoes and cook over medium heat. As the eggs begin to set, lift edges with a spatula and let uncooked portion flow underneath. Continue cooking until eggs are completely set. Sprinkle cheddar cheese on top, cover skillet, and cook over medium-low heat until cheddar is melted.

Nutrition per serving: 143 calories, 0 g fat, 16 g carbohydrates, 17 g protein, <1 mg cholesterol, 2 g dietary fiber, 474 mg sodium

Exchanges: 1 starch, 2 very lean meat

Carb Choices: 2

Breakfast and Brunch

Shopping List

Dairy
8 oz. egg substitute
whole eggs
nonfat cottage cheese
nonfat shredded cheddar cheese

Frozen
28-oz. pkg. frozen Potatoes O'Brien

Seasonings/Spices
pepper

Eggs are marketed according to grade and size standards established by the USDA or state departments of agriculture. All eggs sold in retail markets must meet standards for Grade B or higher.

Skillet Quiche

Easy | Serves: 4

1 cup egg substitute

4 egg whites

⅓ cup bacon crumbles

1 tbsp. onion powder

1¾ cups nonfat shredded Swiss or cheddar cheese, *divided*

dash pepper

Combine egg substitute, egg whites, bacon crumbles, onion powder, 1½ cups cheese, and pepper in medium bowl; beat until frothy and well mixed. Spray large broiler-safe nonstick skillet with cooking spray and heat over medium heat. Pour egg mixture into skillet; reduce heat to medium-low and cook until eggs are set. Lift sides of eggs several times while cooking to allow the uncooked portion to flow underneath. Preheat broiler; sprinkle remaining cheese over top of eggs. Place skillet under broiler and cook 1–2 minutes until cheese is melted and eggs are completely set.

Nutrition per serving: 163 calories, 2 g fat, 6 g carbohydrates, 19 g protein, 0 mg cholesterol, 0 g dietary fiber, 945 mg sodium
Exchanges: 3 very lean meat, ½ other carb
Carb Choices: 0

Shopping List

Dairy
8 oz. egg substitute
whole eggs
8 oz. nonfat shredded Swiss or cheddar cheese

Packaged
1.3-oz. pkg. bacon crumbles

Seasonings/Spices
onion powder
pepper

Because many breakfast foods are fortified with vitamins and minerals, skipping breakfast can mean missing out on important nutrients you need each day.

Peppers, Mushrooms, and Corn Egg Scramble

Easy | Serves: 6

1 tsp. nonfat vegetable or chicken broth

3 tbsp. chopped green onions

1 tsp. minced garlic

8 oz. sliced mushrooms

¾ cup frozen diced green bell peppers, *thawed and drained*

1 cup frozen corn kernels, *thawed and drained*

1 cup Garden Vegetable Egg Beaters

4 whole egg whites

2 tbsp. skim milk

pepper to taste

Spray large nonstick skillet with cooking spray; add broth and heat over medium-high heat. Add onions, garlic, mushrooms, bell peppers, and corn. Cook, stirring frequently, 5–6 minutes until vegetables are tender. Combine Egg Beaters, egg whites, milk, and pepper in medium bowl; beat until frothy and blended. Pour egg mixture over vegetables and cook, stirring frequently, until eggs are cooked through and scrambled. Serve immediately.

Nutrition per serving: 69 calories, 0.1 g fat, 9 g carbohydrates, 8 g protein, 0 mg cholesterol, 1 g dietary fiber, 166 mg sodium
Exchanges: 1 vegetable, 1 very lean meat
Carb Choices: 1

Breakfast and Brunch

Shopping List

Produce
green onions
8 oz. sliced mushrooms

Dairy
8 oz. Garden Vegetable Egg Beaters
whole eggs
skim milk

Frozen
10-oz. pkg. frozen diced green bell peppers
10-oz. pkg. frozen corn kernels

Canned
nonfat vegetable or chicken broth

Seasonings/Spices
minced garlic
pepper

The key to large, light, fluffy scrambled eggs is to let the eggs sit in the pan for about 30 seconds without stirring.

Spinach-Cheese Omelet

Easy | Serves: 4

1 cup frozen chopped spinach, *thawed and well drained*

¼ cup nonfat cottage cheese

½ tsp. garlic powder

dash pepper

2 tsp. cilantro herb blend

½ cup nonfat shredded cheddar cheese

2 cups egg substitute

4 egg whites

Preheat oven to 350°. Spray 10-inch baking dish with cooking spray. Combine all the ingredients in large bowl; whisk ingredients until frothy and blended. Pour egg mixture into baking dish. Bake 20–30 minutes until toothpick inserted in center comes out clean.

Nutrition per serving: 117 calories, 0.1 g fat, 6 g carbohydrates, 22 g protein, <1 mg cholesterol, 1 g dietary fiber, 611 mg sodium
Exchanges: 1 vegetable, 3 very lean meat
Carb Choices: 0

Shopping List

Produce
cilantro herb blend

Dairy
nonfat cottage cheese
nonfat shredded cheddar cheese
16 oz. egg substitute
whole eggs

Frozen
10-oz. pkg. frozen chopped spinach

Seasonings/Spices
garlic powder
pepper

Egg storage tips: Eggs keep for 3–5 weeks in your refrigerator. It's best to keep them in the carton because it insulates the eggs and helps maintain moisture.

"Sausage" Breakfast Soufflé

Easy | **Do Ahead** | **Serves: 6**

¾ lb. Gimme Lean
  sausage-style

½ cup + 1 tbsp. egg substitute

4 egg whites

1½ cup skim milk

¾ tsp. dry mustard

1½ slices low-fat bread,
  cut into cubes

¾ cup nonfat shredded
  cheddar cheese

Spray large nonstick skillet with cooking spray; add "sausage" and cook, stirring frequently, until browned and crumbled. Preheat oven to 350°. Spray 9×13-inch baking dish with cooking spray. Combine all the ingredients (including cooked sausage) in a medium bowl and mix well. Pour mixture into baking dish and bake 55–60 minutes until toothpick inserted in center comes out clean. Remove from oven and let stand 5 minutes before serving.

Nutrition per serving: 139 calories, 0.1 g fat, 13 g carbohydrates, 19 g protein, 1 mg cholesterol, 2 g dietary fiber, 643 mg sodium
Exchanges: 1 starch, 2 very lean meat
Carb Choices: 1

Breakfast
and
Brunch

Shopping List

Meat/Fish/Poultry
¾ lb. Gimme Lean sausage-style

Dairy
6 oz. egg substitute
whole eggs
12 oz. skim milk
nonfat shredded cheddar cheese

Packaged
low-fat bread

Seasonings/Spices
dry mustard

It's when you eat, not what you eat that makes it breakfast! Some of the most unconventional foods, such as leftover pizza, bean tortillas, or peanut butter and jelly sandwiches, can provide great nutrition for your body.

Scrambled Eggs with Potatoes O'Brien

Easy | **Serves: 4**

1 cup egg substitute

4 egg whites

3 tbsp. skim milk

2 tbsp. nonfat vegetable or chicken broth

1½ cups frozen Potatoes O'Brien

¾ cup petite-cut diced tomatoes, *well drained*

Combine egg substitute, egg whites, and skim milk in medium bowl; mix until blended and frothy. Spray large nonstick skillet with cooking spray; add broth and heat over medium-high heat. Add potatoes and tomatoes; cook, stirring frequently, until potatoes are lightly browned and heated through. Pour egg mixture over top; cook, without stirring, 2–3 minutes. Gently lift eggs so the uncooked portion can run underneath. Continue cooking until eggs are set and cooked through.

Nutrition per serving: 90 calories, 0.1 g fat, 10 g carbohydrates, 11 g protein, <1 mg cholesterol, 1 g dietary fiber, 348 mg sodium
Exchanges: ½ starch, 1 vegetable, 1 very lean meat
Carb Choices: 1

Shopping List

Dairy
8 oz. egg substitute
whole eggs
skim milk

Frozen
28-oz. pkg. frozen Potatoes O'Brien

Canned
nonfat vegetable or chicken broth
14½-oz. can petite-cut diced tomatoes

Skipping breakfast plays havoc with your metabolism; fight back by fueling up!

PB&E Breakfast Tostada

Average | Serves: 4

4 low-fat white corn tortillas

2 cups packaged shredded potatoes

1 cup egg substitute

8 egg whites

2 tbsp. diced green chiles

1 16-oz. can nonfat refried beans

salsa (optional)

Shopping List

Produce
18-oz. pkg. shredded potatoes

Dairy
8 oz. egg substitute
whole eggs

Canned
4-oz. can diced green chiles
16-oz. can nonfat refried beans

Packaged
low-fat white corn tortillas

Optional
salsa

Preheat oven to 450°. Line baking sheet with foil; arrange corn tortillas in a single layer, spray lightly with cooking spray, and bake 30–45 seconds until lightly crisp. Remove from oven and set aside. Spread potatoes in a single layer on the baking sheet; bake 12–15 minutes until lightly browned and crisp. Combine egg substitute, egg whites, and diced green chiles in medium bowl; beat well. Spray nonstick skillet with cooking spray and heat over medium heat. Pour egg mixture into skillet and cook, stirring constantly, over medium heat until scrambled and cooked through. Spoon refried beans into microwave-safe dish; heat on High 1–2 minutes. Spread warm beans on tortillas; top with cooked potatoes and scrambled eggs. Serve with salsa, if desired.

Breakfast and Brunch

Nutrition per serving: 294 calories, 0.4 g fat, 47 g carbohydrates, 23 g protein, 0 mg cholesterol, 6 g dietary fiber, 820 mg sodium
Exchanges: 3 starch, 2 very lean meat
Carb Choices: 3

The key factors in egg quality include proper handling and refrigeration. Because eggs lose quality very quickly at room temperature, it is best to refrigerate them immediately at temperatures of 35°F–45°F.

Microwave Spinach Frittata

Easy | Do Ahead | Serves: 2

8 egg whites

2 tbsp. nonfat cottage cheese

½ tsp. onion powder

2 cups fresh baby spinach
   leaves

Combine egg whites, cottage cheese, and onion powder in bowl; beat until egg whites are frothy. Fold in spinach. Spray microwave-safe baking dish with cooking spray; pour egg mixture into dish. Microwave on High 3 minutes; turn dish in microwave and cook 1–2 minutes until eggs are completely set. Eggs can be prepared, covered, and refrigerated at night and quickly made in the morning.

Nutrition per serving: 85 calories, 0.2 g fat, 4 g carbohydrates, 16 g protein, <1 mg cholesterol, 1 g dietary fiber, 276 mg sodium
Exchanges: 1 vegetable, 2 very lean meat
Carb Choices: 0

Shopping List

Produce
9-oz. pkg. baby spinach leaves

Dairy
whole eggs
nonfat cottage cheese

Seasonings/Spices
onion powder

Store leftover egg whites in the refrigerator, tightly covered, for up to four days. Store yolks for only two days; discard any leftovers after that time.

Breakfast Quesadillas

Easy | **Serves: 4**

2 cups Southwestern Egg Beaters

2 tbsp. diced green chiles

4 10-inch 98% fat-free flour tortillas

2 cups nonfat shredded cheddar cheese

1 cup chunky-style salsa

Combine Egg Beaters and green chiles in bowl; beat until blended. Spray large nonstick skillet with cooking spray and heat over medium-high heat. Add egg mixture; let eggs cook, lifting several times to let liquid portion run underneath. Cook over medium heat until eggs are set and cooked through. Cut eggs into 4 equal pieces. Place one piece on each tortilla; top with ½ cup cheese. Fold tortilla in half. Respray nonstick skillet with cooking spray and heat over medium-high heat. Add tortillas to skillet and cook until lightly browned and cheese is melted. Serve with salsa.

Nutrition per serving: 287 calories, 0.5 g fat, 33 g carbohydrates, 33 g protein, 0 mg cholesterol, 2 g dietary fiber, 1,624 mg sodium
Exchanges: 1½ starch, 1 vegetable, 4 very lean meat
Carb Choices: 2

Breakfast and Brunch

Shopping List

Dairy

16 oz. Southwestern Egg Beaters

8 oz. nonfat shredded cheddar cheese

Canned

4-oz. can diced green chiles

Packaged

17.5-oz. pkg. 98% fat-free flour tortillas

Condiments

8 oz. chunky-style salsa

Avoid the problem of heated food sticking to spatulas; spray the spatula with cooking spray before using.

Baked Eggs with Chiles and Cheese

Easy | Do Ahead | Serves: 6

1 7-oz. can whole green chiles, *split in half*

2½ cups nonfat shredded cheddar cheese, *divided*

2 cups Southwestern Egg Beaters

1 11-oz. can Mexicorn, *drained*

¾ cup skim milk

1 tbsp. flour

1 tsp. baking powder

½ tsp. garlic powder

Preheat oven to 350°. Spray 9×11-inch baking dish with cooking spray. Arrange green chiles in baking dish; top with 1¼ cup cheese. Combine Egg Beaters, Mexicorn, milk, flour, baking powder, and garlic powder in medium bowl; mix well. Pour egg mixture over chiles and top with remaining cheese. Bake 25–30 minutes until lightly browned and puffy. Let stand 5 minutes before serving.

Nutrition per serving: 179 calories, 0.3 g fat, 19 g carbohydrates, 24 g protein, <1 mg cholesterol, 2 g dietary fiber, 1,346 mg sodium
Exchanges: ½ starch, 2 vegetable, 3 very lean meat
Carb Choices: 1

Shopping List

Dairy
10 oz. nonfat shredded cheddar cheese
16 oz. Southwestern Egg Beaters
6 oz. skim milk

Canned
7-oz. can whole green chiles
11-oz. can Mexicorn

Baking goods
flour
baking powder

Seasonings/Spices
garlic powder

Meal idea: Serve Baked Eggs with Chiles and Cheese with chunky-style salsa or a dollop of nonfat sour cream.

Breakfast Fajita Wrap

Easy | **Serves: 4**

1 cup Southwestern
Egg Beaters

4 large egg whites

⅓ cup nonfat cottage cheese

1 16-oz. pkg. frozen
pepper stir-fry

1 tbsp. packaged fajita
seasoning mix

4 98% fat-free flour tortillas

salsa (optional)

Shopping List

Dairy
8 oz. Southwestern Egg Beaters
whole eggs
nonfat cottage cheese

Frozen
16-oz. pkg. frozen pepper
stir-fry

Packaged
17.5-oz. pkg. 98% fat-free
flour tortillas

Seasonings/Spices
1.27-oz. pkg. fajita
seasoning mix

Optional
salsa

Combine Egg Beaters, egg whites, and cottage cheese in food processor or blender; process or blend until blended and frothy. Spray large nonstick skillet with cooking spray and heat over medium heat. Add pepper stir-fry and season with fajita seasoning. Cook, stirring frequently, until vegetables are tender and heated through. Remove from skillet and set aside; keep warm. Respray skillet with cooking spray; pour egg mixture into skillet and let set; while cooking, gently lift cooked portion so uncooked portion can run underneath. Continue cooking until eggs are completely set. Wrap tortillas in paper towels; microwave on High 30–45 seconds per tortilla. Place one-quarter of egg mixture in center of each tortilla; top with vegetables, roll up, and serve with salsa, if desired.

Breakfast
and
Brunch

Nutrition per serving: 212 calories, 0.5 g fat, 33 g carbohydrates, 15 g protein, <1 mg cholesterol, 3 g dietary fiber, 772 mg sodium
Exchanges: 2 starch, 1 vegetable, 1 very lean meat
Carb Choices: 2

When bringing eggs or egg whites to room temperature, don't allow them to stand out for more than 30 minutes.

Baked Cheese Omelet Roll

Easy | **Do Ahead** | **Serves: 6**

1 cup egg substitute

4 egg whites

1 cup skim milk

½ cup flour

½ tsp. Mrs. Dash seasoning

1 cup nonfat shredded
  cheddar cheese

Preheat oven to 450°. Spray 9×13-inch baking dish with cooking spray. Combine egg substitute, egg whites, milk, flour, and Mrs. Dash seasoning in blender; blend until smooth. Egg mixture can be refrigerated at this point and baked later. Pour egg mixture into baking dish; bake 20–25 minutes until eggs are completely set. Remove from oven; sprinkle with cheese and return to oven for 1–2 minutes until cheese is melted. Carefully loosen eggs from pan and roll jelly-roll fashion. Cut into 6 equal pieces and serve immediately.

Nutrition per serving: 204 calories, 0.1 g fat, 16 g carbohydrates, 30 g protein, 1 mg cholesterol, <1 g dietary fiber, 925 mg sodium
Exchanges: 4 very lean meat, 1 other carb
Carb Choices: 1

Shopping List

Dairy
8 oz. egg substitute
whole eggs
8 oz. skim milk
4 oz. nonfat shredded cheddar
  cheese

Baking Goods
flour

Seasonings/Spices
Mrs. Dash seasoning

The color of egg shells and yolks varies, but color has nothing to do with egg quality, flavor, nutritive value, or cooking characteristics.

Crustless Vegetable Quiche

Easy | Do Ahead | Serves: 4

¾ cup Garden Vegetable
    Egg Beaters

1 cup nonfat cottage cheese

1½ tsp. onion powder

½ cup nonfat Parmesan cheese

1 10-oz. pkg. frozen chopped
    spinach, *thawed*

pepper to taste

Preheat oven to 350°. Spray 9-inch pie pan with cooking spray. Combine Egg Beaters, cottage cheese, onion powder, and Parmesan cheese in blender; process until blended. Pour egg mixture into pie plate; fold in spinach and season with pepper. Bake 25–30 minutes until toothpick inserted in center comes out clean. Let stand 3–5 minutes before slicing and serving.

Nutrition per serving: 85 calories, 0.1 g fat, 10 g carbohydrates, 13 g protein, 1 mg cholesterol, 2 g dietary fiber, 333 mg sodium
Exchanges: 2 vegetable, 1 very lean meat
Carb Choices: 1

Breakfast
and
Brunch

Shopping List

Dairy
8-oz. Garden Vegetable
    Egg Beaters
8 oz. nonfat cottage cheese
nonfat Parmesan cheese

Frozen
10-oz. pkg. frozen chopped
    spinach

Seasonings/Spices
onion powder
pepper

Most quiche dishes are baked in a crust, but you'll never miss it when the recipe is as good as this one. Full of flavor without added calories or fat, Crustless Vegetable Quiche is the perfect meal for breakfast, lunch, or dinner.

Chapter Index

3 Breads and Muffins

Strawberry Banana Muffins

Nothing brings a smile to the morning like the aroma of freshly baked muffins and breads. And the recipes in this chapter are so easy to make! Some are even made and baked in the same pan.

Quick breads don't contain yeast, so there's no need to wait for the dough to rise. You simply mix, spread batter, and bake! Most quick bread and muffin recipes are interchangeable, but cooking times may vary slightly according to the size of the muffin tin or bread pan. Follow these simple steps and you'll be baking up several batches in no time!

1. Preheat the oven according to the recipe. Once you get used to working with your oven, you may want to make adjustments to temperatures or time. It is always best to follow the test for doneness rather than simply relying on the stated cooking time—a recommendation based on testing.

2. Spray muffin tin or loaf pan with cooking spray. You can also use paper muffin cups to line a muffin tin. Use two paper muffin cups per muffin if you plan to freeze the muffins.

3. While standard recipes suggest mixing the dry ingredients first and gradually adding wet ingredients, I have found that the muffins and quick breads have a much lighter texture and flavor with the reverse method. I recommend putting the liquid ingredients plus sugars in first and blending well until sugar is dissolved. Then gradually add dry ingredients, mixing just until moistened. The batter will be slightly lumpy. Do NOT overmix. Overmixed batter results in tough, rubbery muffins and quick breads.

4. Spoon batter into muffin tin or loaf pan. Most recipes recommend filling the muffin cups two-thirds full, but doing so usually results in 12 small muffins. Fill each muffin cup just short of the top and you'll get about nine average-size muffins. If you want bakery-huge muffins, fill the tin completely to the top. Fill any empty muffin cups with water or stuff them with foil before cooking to prevent burning.

5. Bake according to recipe directions, but don't rely on suggested cooking times because ovens vary. (See step 1.)

6. Test muffins or loaves for doneness using a toothpick inserted in the center of the baked good. If it comes out clean, it's done—if it comes out with gooey batter, it needs a little more baking time.

7. Once the muffins or loaves are done, immediately remove from pan and cool on racks.

8. While it's all right to eat muffins straight from the oven, some quick breads taste better the following day (this is based on personal preference).

Breads
and
Muffins

Magical Muffin Mix

8 cups flour

¼ cup baking powder

2 cups sugar

1 cup brown sugar

Combine all ingredients in large bowl and mix until completely blended. Store in covered container or zip-top bag. Follow directions for muffin or bread recipes that call for Magical Muffin Mix.

Shopping List

Baking Goods

flour

baking powder

sugar

brown sugar

The possibilities are endless–once you get used to working with Magical Muffin Mix, let your imagination run wild. You can vary flavor and texture according to liquids and extracts added to basic mix.

Basic Magic Muffins

½ cup egg substitute

½ cup nonfat yogurt or
   skim milk

¼ tsp. vanilla extract

2 cups Magical Muffin Mix
   (See recipe on page 62.)

Preheat oven to 350°. Spray muffin tin with cooking spray. Combine egg substitute, yogurt, and vanilla in large bowl; mix until creamy and smooth. Gradually add Magical Muffin Mix, blending until dry ingredients are moistened. If mixture is too dry, add additional yogurt 1 tablespoon at a time until batter is desired consistency. If mixture is too moist, sprinkle with additional Muffin Mix 1 tablespoon at a time until batter is desired consistency. Fill muffin cups ¾ full with batter. Bake 20–23 minutes until toothpick inserted in center comes out clean.

Nutrition per serving: 97 calories, 0.1 g fat, 22 g carbohydrates, 3 g protein, <1 mg cholesterol, <1 g dietary fiber, 96 mg sodium
Exchanges: 1 other carb
Carb Choices: 1

Breads and Muffins

Shopping List

Dairy
4 oz. egg substitute
4 oz. nonfat yogurt or skim milk

Baking Goods
Magical Muffin Mix (see recipe)
vanilla extract

You can store Magical Muffin Mix in the refrigerator or freezer; bring it to room temperature before adding other ingredients.

Blueberry Streusel Muffins

Easy | Do Ahead | Serves: 12

½ cup egg substitute

¼ cup French vanilla nonfat creamer

¼ cup nonfat vanilla yogurt

¼ tsp. vanilla extract

2 cups Magical Muffin Mix (See recipe on page 62.)

1 cup fresh or frozen blueberries

½ cup flour

¼ cup sugar

¼ cup powdered sugar

2 tbsp. Butter Buds

Preheat oven to 350°. Spray muffin tin with cooking spray. Combine egg substitute, creamer, yogurt, and vanilla in large bowl; mix until creamy and smooth. Gradually add Magical Muffin Mix, blending until dry ingredients are moistened. Fold in blueberries. Fill muffin cups ¾ full with batter. For streusel topping, combine flour, sugar, and powdered sugar in small bowl; sprinkle Butter Buds over top. Blending with fingertips, add just enough water until crumbly and moist. Sprinkle streusel topping over muffin batter. Bake 25–30 minutes until toothpick inserted in center comes out clean. Cool slightly before removing from tin.

Nutrition per serving: 148 calories, 0.2 g fat, 34 g carbohydrates, 3 g protein, <1 mg cholesterol, 1 g dietary fiber, 94 mg sodium
Exchanges: 2 other carb
Carb Choices: 2

Shopping List

Dairy	Seasonings/Spices
8 oz. egg substitute	Butter Buds
French vanilla nonfat creamer	
nonfat vanilla yogurt	**Frozen**
	10-oz. pkg. frozen blueberries
Baking Goods	(or ½ pint fresh blueberries)
vanilla extract	
Magical Muffin Mix (see recipe)	
flour	
sugar	
powdered sugar	

You can make simple substitutions when you don't have certain ingredients on hand: 2 egg whites = ¼ cup egg substitute; ¼ cup nonfat sour cream can replace yogurt; and skim milk flavored with vanilla extract can replace French vanilla nonfat creamer.

p. 87   Sesame Breadsticks

Strawberry Banana Muffins p. 80

Banana Nut Bread   p. 82

Chili Cheese Cornbread **p. 85**

p. 81 Pineapple Pumpkin Bread

Cinnamon Raisin Whole Wheat Bread   p. 83

Mocha Chip Muffins

Easy | Do Ahead | Serves: 24

½ cup café mocha nonfat creamer

½ cup nonfat vanilla yogurt

1 tsp. vanilla extract

1 cup egg substitute

4 cups Magical Muffin Mix (See recipe on page 62.)

2 tbsp. miniature chocolate chips

Preheat oven to 350°. Spray muffin tin with cooking spray. Combine creamer, yogurt, vanilla extract, and egg substitute in large bowl; mix until blended smooth. Gradually add Magical Muffin Mix, blending until dry ingredients are moistened. Fold in chocolate chips. Fill muffin cups ¾ full with batter. Bake 20–25 minutes until toothpick inserted in center comes out clean. Cool slightly; remove from pan. Repeat with remaining batter.

Nutrition per serving: 102 calories, 0.3 g fat, 23 g carbohydrates, 3 g protein, <1 mg cholesterol, <1 g dietary fiber, 93 mg sodium
Exchanges: 1½ other carb
Carb Choices: 2

Breads and Muffins

Shopping List

Dairy
4 oz. café mocha nonfat creamer
4 oz. nonfat vanilla yogurt
8 oz. egg substitute

Baking Goods
vanilla extract
miniature chocolate chips
Magical Muffin Mix (see recipe)

Make your own mocha creamer: Add a teaspoon of nonfat chocolate syrup to fat-free half and half and mix well. Prepare recipe as directed.

Apple-Apple Muffins

Easy | **Do Ahead** | **Freeze** | **Serves: 12**

1 19-oz. pkg. fat-free apple
cinnamon muffin mix

1 tsp. cinnamon

¾ cup apple juice

½ cup water

Preheat oven to 400°. Spray muffin tin with cooking spray. Combine apple muffin mix, cinnamon, apple juice, water, and packet of apples (enclosed with mix) in medium bowl; mix just until ingredients are moistened and blended. Fill muffin cups ¾ full with batter and bake 15–20 minutes until toothpick inserted in center comes out clean.

Nutrition per serving: 185 calories, 0 g fat, 44 g carbohydrates, 3 g protein, 0 mg cholesterol, 3 g dietary fiber, 436 mg sodium
Exchanges: 3 other carb
Carb Choices: 3

Shopping List

Canned/Bottled
6 oz. apple juice

Baking Goods
19-oz. pkg. fat-free apple
cinnamon muffin mix

Seasonings/Spices
cinnamon

One more reason to make your own:

A bakery apple-cinnamon muffin can contain as much as 573 calories, 16 grams of fat, and 49 milligrams of cholesterol.

Tropical Banana Muffins

Easy | **Do Ahead** | **Freeze** | **Serves: 12**

1   14-oz. pkg. fat-free banana
    muffin mix

½   cup water

½   cup pineapple juice

¾   cup dried tropical fruit medley

Preheat oven to 400°. Spray muffin tin with cooking spray. Prepare muffin mix, using ½ cup water and ½ cup pineapple juice in place of water required by package directions. Fold in dried fruit and mix until blended. Fill muffin cups ¾ full with batter and bake 18–20 minutes until toothpick inserted in center comes out clean.

Nutrition per serving: 161 calories, 0 g fat, 39 g carbohydrates, 2 g protein, 0 mg cholesterol, 2 g dietary fiber, 322 mg sodium
Exchanges: 2½ other carb
Carb Choices: 3

Breads and Muffins

Shopping List

Canned/Bottled
4 oz. pineapple juice

Packaged
14-oz. pkg. fat-free banana
    muffin mix

Baking Goods
6-oz. pkg. dried tropical fruit
    medley

Avoid bananas that have brown spots or feel very soft. Always select fruit that is firm and free of bruises.

Very Berry Muffins with Crumb Topping

Easy | **Do Ahead** | **Freeze** | **Serves: 12**

1 17.5-oz. pkg. fat-free blueberry muffin mix

¼ cup sliced strawberries

¼ cup raspberries, *cut in half*

¼ cup flour

2 tbsp. sugar

2 tbsp. powdered sugar

1½ tsp. Butter Buds

1½ tbsp. water

Preheat oven to 400°. Spray muffin tin with cooking spray. Prepare muffin mix according to package directions; fold in strawberries and raspberries and mix gently. Fill muffin cups ¾ full with batter. Combine flour, sugar, powdered sugar, and Butter Buds in small bowl; mix well. Drizzle water over top and blend with fingertips until mixture is moist and crumbly. Sprinkle over muffin batter and bake 20–23 minutes until lightly browned and toothpick inserted in center comes out clean.

Nutrition per serving: 186 calories, 0 g fat, 44 g carbohydrates, 3 g protein, 0 mg cholesterol, 3 g dietary fiber, 401 mg sodium
Exchanges: 3 other carb
Carb Choices: 3

Shopping List

Produce
strawberries
raspberries

Baking Goods
17.5-oz. pkg. fat-free blueberry muffin mix
flour
sugar
powdered sugar

Seasonings/Spices
Butter Buds

Use this crumb topping on your favorite muffins, quick breads, or coffee cakes.

Orange Cranberry Swirl Muffins

Easy | **Do Ahead** | **Freeze** | **Serves: 12**

1   17.5-oz. pkg. orange-
cranberry fat-free muffin mix

¾   cup orange juice

¾   cup whole cranberry sauce

Preheat oven to 350°. Spray muffin tin with cooking spray. Combine all ingredients in large bowl; mix until blended and moistened. Fill muffin cups ¾ full with batter and bake 20–25 minutes until toothpick inserted in center comes out clean.

Nutrition per serving: 195 calories, 0 g fat, 47 g carbohydrates, 3 g protein, 0 mg cholesterol, 3 g dietary fiber, 406 mg sodium
Exchanges: 3 other carb
Carb Choices: 3

Breads and Muffins

Shopping List

Refrigerated
6 oz. orange juice

Canned
16-oz. can whole cranberry sauce

Packaged
17.5-oz. pkg. orange-cranberry fat-free muffin mix

You do the math: One 4-oz. Cranberry Orange Walnut Muffin from the Atlanta Bread Company weighs in at 440 calories and 23 grams of fat.

Pine-apple Zucchini Muffins

Easy | Do Ahead | Freeze | Serves: 12

1   17.5-oz. pkg. fat-free
    apple cinnamon muffin mix
1   cup canned crushed pineapple
    in juice, *do not drain*
½   cup applesauce
½   cup shredded zucchini
¾   tsp. cinnamon

Preheat oven to 350°. Spray muffin tin with cooking spray. Combine all ingredients in large bowl; blend until dry ingredients are moistened. Fill muffin cups ¾ full with batter and bake 20–25 minutes until toothpick inserted in center comes out clean.

Nutrition per serving: 185 calories, 0 g fat, 45 g carbohydrates, 3 g protein, 0 mg cholesterol, 3 g dietary fiber, 402 mg sodium
Exchanges: 3 other carb
Carb Choices: 3

Shopping List

Produce
1 medium zucchini

Canned
8-oz. can crushed
    pineapple in juice
4 oz. applesauce

Packaged
17.5-oz. pkg. fat-free apple
    cinnamon muffin mix

Seasonings/Spices
cinnamon

Variations: Substitute shredded carrots for zucchini. Add raisins, chopped dates, or other dried fruit, if desired.

Chocolate Banana Chip Muffins

Easy | Do Ahead | Serves: 12

1   14-oz. pkg. fat-free banana
    muffin mix

¼   cup miniature
    chocolate chips

½   cup flour

2   tbsp. unsweetened
    cocoa powder

¼   cup sugar

¼   cup brown sugar

1   tbsp. Butter Buds

3   tbsp. water

Preheat oven to 400°. Spray muffin tin with cooking spray. Prepare muffin mix according to package directions; fold in chocolate chips. Fill muffin cups ¾ full with batter. Combine flour, cocoa powder, sugar, and brown sugar in small bowl; mix well. Sprinkle Butter Buds over top and mix in; gradually drizzle water over mixture and blend with fingertips just until moist and crumbly. Sprinkle topping over muffin batter. Bake 20 minutes until top is lightly browned and toothpick inserted in center comes out clean.

Nutrition per serving: 197 calories, 0.9 g fat, 46 g carbohydrates, 3 g protein, 0 mg cholesterol, 2 g dietary fiber, 323 mg sodium

Exchanges: 3 other carb

Carb Choices: 3

Breads and Muffins

Shopping List

Baking Goods

14-oz. pkg. fat-free banana
   muffin mix
miniature chocolate chips
flour
unsweetened cocoa powder
sugar
brown sugar

Seasonings/Spices

Butter Buds

The best conditions for storing ripe bananas is 65°F with 80% humidity and good air circulation. They will keep for a week or so.

Strawberry Banana Muffins

Easy | Do Ahead | Serves: 12

1 19-oz. pkg. fat-free banana muffin mix

½ cup strawberry preserves

Preheat oven to 400°. Spray muffin tin with cooking spray. Prepare muffin mix according to package directions. Fill muffin cups ½ full with batter; top each with ½ teaspoon preserves and cover with remaining batter. Bake 18–20 minutes until lightly browned. Cool slightly before removing from tin.

Nutrition per serving: 213 calories, 0 g fat, 52 g carbohydrates, 3 g protein, 0 mg cholesterol, 3 g dietary fiber, 437 mg sodium
Exchanges: 3 other carb
Carb Choices: 3

Shopping List

Baking Goods
19-oz. pkg. fat-free banana
  muffin mix

Condiments
4 oz. strawberry preserves

To ripen green-tip bananas quickly,
keep them at 70°F, with very high humidity and no air circulation for two to three days.

Pineapple Pumpkin Bread

Easy | **Do Ahead** | **Freeze** | **Serves: 12**

½ cup egg substitute

½ cup canned pumpkin puree
  (*not pumpkin pie mix*)

¾ cup canned crushed
  pineapple in juice, *drained*

½ tsp. vanilla

1½ tsp. pumpkin pie spice

2 cups Magical Muffin Mix
  (See recipe on page 62.)

Preheat oven to 350°. Spray 9×5-inch loaf pan with cooking spray. Combine egg substitute, pumpkin puree, pineapple, vanilla, and pumpkin pie spice in large bowl; blend until creamy and smooth. Add Magical Muffin Mix; blending until dry ingredients are moistened. Spoon batter into loaf pan and bake 25–35 minutes until toothpick inserted in center comes out clean. Cool slightly in pan, remove from pan, and let cool before slicing.

Nutrition per serving: 107 calories, 0.2 g fat, 25 g carbohydrates, 3 g protein, 0 mg cholesterol, 1 g dietary fiber, 91 mg sodium
Exchanges: 1½ other carb
Carb Choices: 2

Breads
and
Muffins

Shopping List

Dairy
4 oz. egg substitute

Canned
16-oz. can pumpkin
8-oz. can crushed pineapple
  in juice

Baking Goods
Magical Muffin Mix (see recipe)

Seasonings/Spices
vanilla
pumpkin pie spice

You can substitute ½ cup canned pumpkin pie mix for the canned pumpkin and pumpkin pie spice.

Banana Nut Bread

Easy | **Do Ahead** | **Freeze** | **Serves: 16**

1 cup mashed bananas

1 cup egg substitute

¾ cup nonfat vanilla yogurt

½ tsp. banana extract

4 cups Magical Muffin Mix
(See recipe on page 62.)

2 tbsp. chopped nuts

Preheat oven to 350°. Spray two 9×5-inch loaf pans with cooking spray. Combine mashed bananas, egg substitute, vanilla yogurt, and banana extract in large bowl; mix until blended, smooth, and creamy. Gradually add Magical Muffin Mix, blending until dry ingredients are moistened. Fold in nuts. Divide batter among loaf pans. Bake 45–60 minutes until toothpick inserted in center comes out clean. Cool slightly in pans, remove from pans, and let cool before slicing.

Nutrition per serving: 176 calories, 0.8 g fat, 40 g carbohydrates, 5 g protein, <1 mg cholesterol, 1 g dietary fiber, 142 mg sodium
Exchanges: 2½ other carb
Carb Choices: 3

Shopping List

Produce
3 large bananas

Dairy
8 oz. egg substitute
6 oz. nonfat vanilla yogurt

Baking Goods
banana extract
Magical Muffin Mix (see recipe)

Packaged
chopped nuts

If bananas ripen before they are picked, they lose their taste and texture.

Cinnamon Raisin Whole Wheat Bread

Easy | **Do Ahead** | **Freeze** | **Serves: 8**

1   1-lb. 2-oz. pkg. fat-free
    hearty cracked wheat
    bread mix

1½ tbsp. cinnamon, *divided*

1½ cups club soda, seltzer,
    or beer, *room temperature*

½   cup raisins

2   tbsp. sugar

Preheat oven to 350°. Spray 8×4-inch loaf pan with cooking spray. Combine bread mix, 1½ teaspoons cinnamon, and liquid in a medium bowl; mix until completely blended. Fold in raisins. Combine remaining cinnamon and sugar in small cup; mix well. Press dough into loaf pan; sprinkle top with cinnamon-sugar mixture and bake 45–50 minutes until crust is golden brown. Remove bread from pan and let cool before slicing.

Nutrition per serving: 266 calories, 1.6 g fat, 56 g carbohydrates, 7 g protein, <1 mg cholesterol, 3 g dietary fiber, 525 mg sodium
Exchanges: 2 starch, 1½ fruit
Carb Choices: 4

Breads and Muffins

Shopping List

Canned/Bottled
12 oz. club soda, seltzer, or beer
    (regular or light)

Packaged
raisins

Baking Goods
1-lb. 2-oz. pkg. fat-free hearty
    cracked wheat bread mix
sugar

Seasonings/Spices
cinnamon

For a lighter loaf of whole wheat bread, add a tablespoon of lemon juice to the dough while you mix it.

Bacon and Sun-Dried Tomato Cornbread

Easy | **Do Ahead** | **Serves: 12**

1 14.5-oz. pkg. fat-free honey cornbread mix

½ cup Tomato 'n Bacon Parmesano salad topping

Preheat oven to 400°. Spray 8×8-inch baking dish with cooking spray. Prepare cornbread mix according to package directions; fold in Parmesano salad topping and mix lightly. Spoon batter into baking dish. Bake 18–22 minutes until toothpick inserted in center comes out clean.

Nutrition per serving: 141 calories, 0.6 g fat, 29 g carbohydrates, 3 g protein, 0 mg cholesterol, 2 g dietary fiber, 436 mg sodium
Exchanges: 2 other carb
Carb Choices: 2

Shopping List

Produce
5-oz. pkg. Tomato 'n Bacon Parmesano salad topping

Baking Goods
14.5-oz. pkg. fat-free honey cornbread mix

You can prepare cornbread mix in a baking dish or muffin tin. Depending on the size of the muffin tin, you will probably need to reduce baking time.

Chili Cheese Cornbread

Easy | **Do Ahead** | **Serves: 12**

1 14.5-oz. pkg. fat-free honey
   cornbread mix

¾ cup Mexicorn, *drained*

2 tbsp. diced green chiles

½ cup nonfat shredded
   cheddar cheese

Preheat oven to 400°. Spray 8×8-inch baking dish with cooking spray. Prepare cornbread mix according to package directions; fold in Mexicorn and green chiles. Spread batter into baking dish. Bake 10–15 minutes until toothpick inserted in center comes out clean. Sprinkle cheese over top of cornbread and bake 5–8 minutes until cheese is melted and bread is lightly browned.

Nutrition per serving: 139 calories, 0 g fat, 30 g carbohydrates, 4 g protein, 0 mg cholesterol, 1 g dietary fiber, 526 mg sodium
Exchanges: 2 starch
Carb Choices: 2

Breads
and
Muffins

Shopping List

Dairy
nonfat shredded cheddar cheese

Canned
11-oz. can Mexicorn
4-oz. can diced green chiles

Baking Goods
14.5-oz. pkg. fat-free honey
   cornbread mix

If you don't have Mexicorn, you can use canned or frozen corn kernels with 2–3 tablespoons of chopped bell peppers.

Parmesan Garlic Bread

Easy | **Do Ahead** | **Serves: 8**

1   1-lb. 2-oz. pkg. fat-free garlic and herbs bread mix

1½   cups club soda, seltzer, or beer, *at room temperature*

1   tbsp. + 1 tsp. Butter Buds

½   tsp. garlic powder

½   cup nonfat Parmesan cheese

     butter-flavored cooking spray

Prepare and bake bread mix according to package directions, using liquid of choice. Remove from oven and let cool; slice bread into 8 pieces. Preheat broiler on High heat. Line baking sheet with foil and spray with cooking spray. Arrange bread slices in a single layer on baking sheet. Combine Butter Buds and garlic powder; mix well. Sprinkle about ½ teaspoon garlic mixture and 1 tablespoon cheese over each bread slice. Spray lightly with butter-flavored cooking spray. Broil 30–45 seconds (watch carefully) until bread is lightly browned and crisp on top.

Nutrition per serving: 221 calories, 0 g fat, 49 g carbohydrates, 8 g protein, 0 mg cholesterol, 2 g dietary fiber, 703 mg sodium
Exchanges: 3 starch
Carb Choices: 3

Shopping List

Dairy
nonfat Parmesan cheese

Canned/Bottled
12-oz. can or bottle seltzer, club soda, or beer

Baking Goods
1-lb. 2-oz. pkg. fat-free garlic and herbs bread mix

Seasonings/Spices
Butter Buds
garlic powder
butter-flavored cooking spray

One slice of purchased frozen Garlic Parmesan Bread can add up to more than 150 calories and 7 grams of fat.

Sesame Breadsticks

Easy | **Do Ahead** | **Serves: 8**

1   1-lb. 2-oz. pkg. fat-free garlic
    and herbs bread mix

1½   cups seltzer, club soda,
      or beer, *at room temperature*

     butter-flavored cooking spray

2   tbsp. + 2 tsp. sesame seeds

Preheat oven to 350°. Line baking sheet with foil and spray with cooking spray. Prepare bread mix dough according to package directions, using liquid of choice. Divide bread into 8 equal pieces; roll each piece about 2–3 inches long and 1 inch thick. Arrange breadsticks on baking sheet; spray lightly with cooking spray and sprinkle with sesame seeds. Bake 30–35 minutes until golden brown and cooked through.

Nutrition per serving: 222 calories, 1.4 g fat, 45 g carbohydrates, 6 g protein, 0 mg cholesterol, 3 g dietary fiber, 638 mg sodium
Exchanges: 3 starch
Carb Choices: 3

Breads and Muffins

Shopping List

Canned/Bottled
12-oz. can or bottle seltzer, club soda, or beer

Baking Goods
1-lb. 2-oz. pkg. fat-free garlic and herbs bread mix

Seasonings/Spices
butter-flavored cooking spray
sesame seeds

If you don't have butter-flavored cooking spray, you can substitute I Can't Believe It's Not Butter spray or regular cooking spray and a sprinkling of Butter Buds.

Chapter Index

4 Sandwiches and Wraps

Lemon Basil Chicken Salad Sandwiches

Rolled, wrapped, stuffed, spread … filled, folded, or open-face, these fuss-free foods satisfy any time of day. From breakfast to dinner or in-between snacks, sandwiches and wraps are the perfect packages, the all-in-one meal.

These portable, handheld meals are the original fast food, versatile and filled with a world of ingredients. Unlock your imagination to create sandwiches and wraps far beyond the standard peanut butter and jelly, grilled cheese, and burger. Pick your package (sliced bread, tortilla, pita, or others); stuff, spread, or pile on unlimited possibilities; and spruce it up with a variety of condiments from typical mayo and mustard to wasabi and chutney.

The history of the sandwich stretches back to the first century when Rabbi Hillel sandwiched Passover filling between two matzos. Years later, John Montague the Fourth Earl of Sandwich, ordered his valet to deliver meat tucked inside two bread slices so he could gamble straight through meal times. From simple sandwiches with bread, meat, and cheese to universal favorites, the ultimate fast food crosses all cultural lines. The category encompasses everything from Chinese egg rolls or lettuce wraps to Mexican tacos and burritos from Greek gyros and French crepes to Cuban tortas and Middle Eastern pockets, filling the bill for quick, healthful, simple meals any time of day.

Step One: Pick Your Packaging
- Tortilla (low-fat flour, corn, spinach, sun-dried tomato, whole wheat, pesto-flavored, and more)
- Naan, a flat-round Indian bread
- Lahvosh, Armenian flatbread
- Pita pockets, plain or whole wheat
- Focaccia
- Whole lettuce or cabbage leave
- Sliced bread or whole rolls

Step Two: Stuff, Spread, or Stack
Anything goes! Meat, fish, and poultry; sliced or spreadable cheese; chopped, sliced, or diced veggies; leftover stir-fries, pilafs, taco meat; appetizer spreads; chopped fruit

Step Three: Spice It Up
- Mustard varieties (honey mustard, spicy, whole grain, and more)
- Mayonnaise (substitute a nonfat variety to save 100 calories and 12 grams of fat per tablespoon)
- Barbecue sauce
- Wasabi
- Flavored cream cheese spread
- Chutney
- Horseradish

For perfectly packaged sandwiches and wraps …
- Freeze bread before spreading with peanut butter, hummus, cream cheese, or others to prevent bread from breaking when you spread topping on.
- Prevent sandwich freezer burn: Wrap sandwiches in aluminum foil and store in plastic freezer bags.
- Stop sogginess: Spread sauces between layers of meat, cheese, and other ingredients rather than directly on bread.
- Keep the crunch in veggies: Add veggies to sandwich (or wrap) just before eating.

Sandwiches and Wraps

Caesar Chicken Wraps with Feta Cheese

Easy | **Serves: 4**

½ cup nonfat Caesar salad
   dressing

2 tbsp. sliced black olives

½ cup nonfat crumbled
   feta cheese

2 6-oz. pkgs. honey roasted
   chicken breast strips

4 98% fat-free flour tortillas

Combine salad dressing, olives, feta cheese, and chicken strips in medium bowl; cover and microwave on High 30–45 seconds until warm. Wrap tortillas in paper towels; microwave on High 30–45 seconds until softened. Divide chicken mixture among tortillas, roll up, and serve immediately.

Nutrition per serving: 311 calories, 2.3 g fat, 40 g carbohydrates, 31 g protein, 50 mg cholesterol, 2 g dietary fiber, 1,124 mg sodium
Exchanges: 2 starch, 3 very lean meat, ½ other carb
Carb Choices: 3

Shopping List

Meat/Poultry/Fish
2 6-oz. pkgs. honey roasted
   chicken breast strips

Dairy
6 oz. nonfat crumbled feta cheese

Canned
4-oz. can sliced black olives

Packaged
17.5-oz. pkg. 98% fat-free flour
   tortillas

Condiments
nonfat Caesar salad dressing

The greatest convenience or fast food, sandwiches have been around for more than 240 years!

Chili Chicken Wraps

Easy | **Do Ahead** | **Serves: 4**

1   8-oz. pkg. nonfat cream cheese, *softened*

¼   cup chili spice blend

4   98% fat-free flour tortillas

2   cups shredded lettuce

2   6-oz. pkgs. cooked chicken breast strips

¼   cup chopped fresh cilantro

    salsa (optional)

Shopping List

Produce
chili spice blend
8-oz. pkg. shredded lettuce
fresh cilantro

Meat/Fish/Poultry
2 6-oz. pkgs. cooked chicken
   breast strips

Dairy
8-oz. pkg. nonfat cream cheese

Packaged
17.5-oz. pkg. 98% fat-free
   flour tortillas

Optional
salsa

Combine cream cheese and chili spice blend in bowl; mix until creamy and smooth. Spread cheese-chili mixture on tortillas; sprinkle ½ cup shredded lettuce, one-quarter of the chicken strips, and 1 tablespoon chopped cilantro down center of each tortilla. Roll tortillas and serve; secure with toothpick, if necessary. Serve with salsa, if desired.

Nutrition per serving: 307 calories, 2 g fat, 33 g carbohydrates, 33 g protein, 50 mg cholesterol, 2 g dietary fiber, 1,895 mg sodium
Exchanges: 1 starch, 1 vegetable, 4 very lean meat, 1 other carb
Carb Choices: 2

Sandwiches
and
Wraps

Spread mustard directly on the meat rather than the bread to enhance the flavor of your sandwich and prevent soggy bread.

Honey-Roasted Chicken and Salsa Wraps

Easy | **Serves: 4**

2 14½-oz. cans diced tomatoes with green chiles, *drained*

¼ cup herb and garlic marinade with lemon juice

1 tbsp. red wine vinegar

1 tbsp. cilantro herb blend

½ tsp. Mrs. Dash seasoning

2 6-oz. pkgs. honey roasted chicken breast strips, *cubed*

4 98% fat-free flour tortillas

Combine all ingredients except tortillas in medium bowl; toss to mix. Cover and refrigerate at least 1 hour. Wrap tortillas in paper towels; microwave on High 30–45 seconds per tortilla. Divide chicken filling among tortillas; roll up and serve.

Nutrition per serving: 294 calories, 2.1 g fat, 40 g carbohydrates, 27 g protein, 50 mg cholesterol, 3 g dietary fiber, 1,846 mg sodium
Exchanges: 1 starch, 2 vegetable, 3 very lean meat, 1 other carb
Carb Choices: 3

Shopping List

Produce	Packaged
cilantro herb blend	17.5-oz. pkg. 98% fat-free flour tortillas
Meat/Fish Poultry	
2 6-oz. pkgs. honey-roasted chicken breast strips	**Condiments**
	16-oz. bottle herb and garlic marinade with lemon juice
Canned	red wine vinegar
2 14½-oz. cans diced tomatoes with green chiles	**Seasonings/Spices**
	Mrs. Dash seasoning

Tortillas can be warmed as directed in the microwave or wrapped in foil and heated in a 350°F oven for 3–5 minutes.

Spicy Chicken and Cheese Wraps

Easy | Do Ahead | Serves: 4

- 2 6-oz. pkgs. Southwestern chicken breast strips
- 1 11-oz. can whole kernel corn, *drained*
- 1 cup chunky-style salsa with beans
- 2 tbsp. diced green chiles
- ½ cup nonfat refried beans, *heated*
- 1 cup nonfat shredded cheddar cheese
- 4 98% fat-free flour tortillas
  nonfat sour cream, salsa (optional)

Combine chicken, corn, salsa, and green chiles in medium saucepan; bring to a boil over medium-high heat. Reduce heat to low and cook 3–5 minutes. Place refried beans in small microwave-safe bowl; microwave on High 45–60 seconds until warm. Spread 2 tablespoons beans on each tortilla. Top with ¼ cup cheese. Divide chicken mixture and spread down center of tortillas. Roll up and serve with nonfat sour cream and salsa, if desired.

Nutrition per serving: 393 calories, 3.5 g fat, 53 g carbohydrates, 39 g protein, 50 mg cholesterol, 5 g dietary fiber, 1,527 mg sodium
Exchanges: 3 starch, 2 vegetable, 3½ very lean meat
Carb Choices: 4

Sandwiches and Wraps

Shopping List

Meat/Fish/Poultry	Packaged
2 6-oz. pkgs. Southwestern chicken breast strips	17.5-oz. pkg. 98% fat-free flour tortillas

Dairy	Condiments
4 oz. nonfat shredded cheddar cheese	8-oz. jar chunky-style salsa with beans

Canned	Optional
11-oz. can whole kernel corn	nonfat sour cream salsa
4-oz. can diced green chiles	
15-oz. can nonfat refried beans	

Chicken of the Sea's new pink-salmon-in-a-pouch offers skinless, boneless salmon that is even fresher tasting than canned.

Chicken Teriyaki and Pineapple Sandwiches

Easy | Do Ahead | Serves: 4

1 lb. boneless, skinless chicken breasts

½ cup + 2 tbsp. teriyaki marinade with pineapple juice, *divided*

1 8-oz. can sliced pineapple in juice, *well drained*

4 low-fat hamburger buns

Place chicken breasts in shallow dish; pour ½ cup marinade over top, cover, and refrigerate 30 minutes. Preheat broiler on High heat. Line broiler pan with foil and spray with cooking spray. Arrange chicken breasts on pan; broil 10–12 minutes per side until cooked through, turning once. Remove chicken from oven, wrap in foil, and keep warm. Arrange pineapple slices on pan; brush with remaining marinade. Broil 1–2 minutes until heated through. Place chicken breast on bottom half of bun; top with pineapple slice and top half of bun.

Nutrition per serving: 292 calories, 3.1 g fat, 36 g carbohydrates, 27 g protein, 0 mg cholesterol, 1 g dietary fiber, 1,290 mg sodium
Exchanges: 2 starch, ½ fruit, 3 very lean meat
Carb Choices: 2

Shopping List

Meat/Fish/Poultry
1 lb. boneless, skinless chicken breasts

Canned
8-oz. can pineapple rings in juice

Packaged
low-fat hamburger buns

Condiments
teriyaki marinade with pineapple juice

The basics of any sandwich begin with its wrapping–you can use anything from bread and bagels to tortillas, pita pockets, cracker crisps, and crisp lettuce leaves.

Lemon Basil Chicken Salad Sandwiches

Easy | **Do Ahead** | **Serves: 4**

¼ cup nonfat mayonnaise

¼ cup nonfat sour cream

1½ tsp. onion powder

2½ tbsp. basil herb blend

½ tsp. grated lemon peel

⅛ tsp. sugar

pepper to taste

2 6-oz. pkgs. grilled chicken breast strips, *cubed*

1½ cups diced celery

1½ cups shredded carrots

8 slices low-fat whole wheat bread, 4 pita pocket breads, *cut in half*, or 4 low-fat tortillas

Combine mayonnaise, sour cream, onion powder, basil herb blend, lemon peel, sugar, and pepper in medium bowl; mix until creamy and smooth. Add chicken, celery, and carrots to mayonnaise mixture; toss until well coated. This can be refrigerated several hours or overnight until ready to serve in bread of choice.

Nutrition per serving: 263 calories, 2.2 g fat, 34 g carbohydrates, 26 g protein, 50 mg cholesterol, 3 g dietary fiber, 884 mg sodium
Exchanges: 2 starch, 3 very lean meat
Carb Choices: 2

Sandwiches and Wraps

You can substitute 2½ tablespoons freshly chopped basil or 2 teaspoons dried basil for the basil herb blend.

Shopping List

Produce	Packaged
8-oz. pkg. shredded carrots	low-fat whole wheat bread,
small bunch celery (or	pita pocket breads, or
ready-pac celery sticks)	low-fat tortillas
basil herb blend	
lemon	**Baking Goods**
	sugar
Dairy	
nonfat sour cream	**Condiments**
	nonfat mayonnaise
Meat/Fish/Poultry	
2 6-oz. pkgs. grilled	**Seasonings/Spices**
chicken breast strips	onion powder
	pepper

Orange Chicken Pitas

Easy | **Do Ahead** | **Serves: 4**

2 6-oz. pkgs. honey roasted
   chicken breast strips, *cubed*

1 6-oz. pkg. orange-flavored
   dried cranberries

3 tbsp. chopped walnuts

¾ cup sliced green onions

¾ cup nonfat mayonnaise

¼ cup + 2 tbsp. nonfat
   sour cream

1½ tbsp. lemon juice

¾ tsp. Italian seasoning

4 large lettuce leaves

4 whole wheat pita pocket
   breads, *cut in half*

chopped fresh parsley
   (optional)

Combine chicken, dried cranberries, walnuts, and green onions in large bowl; mix well. For dressing, combine mayonnaise, sour cream, lemon juice, and Italian seasoning in medium bowl; mix until blended smooth. Spoon dressing over chicken mixture and toss until well coated. Cover and refrigerate 1–2 hours. Place 1 large lettuce leaf in each pita pocket. Fill with chicken mixture and garnish with chopped fresh parsley, if desired.

Nutrition per serving: 459 calories, 5.4 g fat, 71 g carbohydrates, 29 g protein, 50 mg cholesterol, 3 g dietary fiber, 1,049 mg sodium
Exchanges: 2 starch, 2 fruit, 3 very lean meat, ½ fat, ½ other carb
Carb Choices: 5

To easily chop nuts, place them in a zip-top bag and roll with a rolling pin.

Shopping List

Produce	chopped walnuts
⅓ lb. green onions	whole wheat pita pocket
whole lettuce leaves	breads

Dairy	Condiments
8 oz. nonfat sour cream	nonfat mayonnaise
	bottled lemon juice

Meat/Fish/Poultry	
2 6-oz. pkg. honey roasted	Seasonings/Spices
chicken breast strips	Italian seasoning

Packaged	Optional
6-oz. pkgs. orange-flavored	parsley
dried cranberries	

BLT Sandwiches

Easy | **Serves: 4**

½ cup nonfat Thousand Island
  salad dressing

8 98% fat-free flour tortillas

4 whole lettuce leaves

4 large tomato slices

12 oz. deli-style low-fat
  turkey breast

8 slices extra-lean turkey
  bacon, *cooked*

4 oz. nonfat Swiss cheese
  slices

Spread 2 tablespoons salad dressing on each tortilla. Top each of 4 tortillas with lettuce leaf, sliced tomato, 3 ounces turkey breast, 2 slices cooked bacon, and 1 slice Swiss cheese. Top with remaining tortillas and cut into quarters.

Nutrition per serving: 430 calories, 1.3 g fat, 58 g carbohydrates, 39 g protein, 81 mg cholesterol, 4 g dietary fiber, 1,476 mg sodium
Exchanges: 3 starch, 4 very lean meat, 1 other carb
Carb Choices: 3

Sandwiches and Wraps

Shopping List

Produce
lettuce leaves
large tomato

Meat/Fish/Poultry
12 oz. deli-style low-fat turkey
  breast
12-oz. pkg. extra-lean turkey bacon

Dairy
4 oz. nonfat Swiss cheese slices

Packaged
17.5-oz. pkg. 98% fat-free flour
  tortillas

Condiments
nonfat Thousand Island salad
  dressing

Sandwich fillings can easily meet the nutritional needs of vegetarians and meat-eaters alike; the combinations and possibilities are endless.

Tuna Tortilla Wraps

Easy | Serves: 4

2 7.1-oz. pouches chunk
   light tuna

1 6½-oz. can diced chiles,
   do not drain

¾ cup diced onions

½ cup nonfat mayonnaise

¾ tsp. cilantro herb blend

4 98% fat-free flour tortillas

Shopping List

Produce
7-oz. pkg. diced onions
cilantro herb blend

Canned
6½-oz. can diced chiles

Packaged
2 7.1-oz. pouches chunk
  light tuna
17.5-oz. pkg. 98% fat-free
  flour tortillas

Condiments
nonfat mayonnaise

Combine tuna, chiles, and onions in medium bowl; toss to mix. Combine mayonnaise and cilantro herb blend in small cup; mix until blended. Add to tuna mixture and toss until moist. Divide mixture among tortillas; roll up and serve.

Nutrition per serving: 294 calories, 1.2 g fat, 33 g carbohydrates, 34 g protein, 18 mg cholesterol, 3 g dietary fiber, 1,450 mg sodium
Exchanges: 1 starch, 1 vegetable, 4 very lean meat, ½ other carb
Carb Choices: 2

You can substitute ¾ teaspoon freshly chopped cilantro or ½ teaspoon dried cilantro for the cilantro herb blend.

Salmon Stuffed Pitas

Easy | **Do Ahead** | **Serves: 6**

2 7.1-oz. pouches premium
   skinless and boneless
   pink salmon

½ cup nonfat mayonnaise

1 cup chopped cucumber

1 cup diced celery

½ cup diced onion

½ tsp. celery seeds

6 Whole Wheat 'n Honey Pita
   Pocket breads, *cut in half*

Combine salmon, mayonnaise, cucumber, celery, onion, and celery seeds in bowl; mix well. Cover and refrigerate until ready to serve. Fill each pita pocket half with ½–¾ cup salmon mixture and serve.

Nutrition per serving: 222 calories, 4.6 g fat, 26 g carbohydrates, 18 g protein, 37 mg cholesterol, 1 g dietary fiber, 745 mg sodium
Exchanges: 1 starch, 2 vegetable, 2 lean meat
Carb Choices: 2

Sandwiches
and
Wraps

Shopping List

Produce
medium cucumber
celery
small onion

Packaged
2 7.1-oz. pouches premium
   skinless and boneless
   pink salmon
12-oz. pkg. Whole Wheat 'n
   Honey Pita Pocket breads

Condiments
nonfat mayonnaise

Seasonings/Spices
celery seeds

You can substitute a 14-ounce can of pink salmon for two 7.1-ounce pouches.

Shrimp and Artichoke Pita Pockets

Easy | **Do Ahead** | **Serves: 6**

⅔ cup nonfat sour cream

1 tsp. dried dill weed

1 tsp. sugar

1 tbsp. lemon juice

1 lb. cooked small shrimp, *peeled and deveined*

1 14½-oz. can artichoke hearts, *drained and chopped*

1 cup canned petite-cut diced tomatoes, *well drained and patted dry*

3 Whole Wheat 'n Honey Pita Pocket breads, *cut in half*

Combine sour cream, dill weed, sugar, and lemon juice in medium bowl; add shrimp, chopped artichokes, and tomatoes. Toss ingredients until coated and well mixed. Cover and refrigerate 30–45 minutes. Stuff shrimp mixture in pita halves and serve.

Nutrition per serving: 196 calories, 1.9 g fat, 23 g carbohydrates, 22 g protein, 117 mg cholesterol, 1 g dietary fiber, 369 mg sodium
Exchanges: 1 starch, 2 vegetable, 2 very lean meat
Carb Choices: 2

Shopping List

Meat	Packaged
1 lb. cooked small shrimp, *peeled and deveined*	12-oz. pkg. Whole Wheat 'n Honey Pita Pocket breads

Dairy	Baking Goods
8 oz. nonfat sour cream	sugar

Canned	Condiments
14½-oz. can artichoke hearts	bottled lemon juice
14½-oz. can petite-cut diced tomatoes	**Seasonings/Spices** dried dill weed

During the Middle Ages, thick blocks of bread were used instead of plates; meat and other foods were piled on top of the bread, and it was usually eaten at the end of the meal.

Tarragon Crab Melts

Easy | **Serves: 4**

2 8-oz. cans crabmeat,
    drained, flaked, and
    cartilage removed

¼ cup diced water chestnuts

½ cup nonfat mayonnaise

1¼ tbsp. lemon juice

¼ tsp. dried tarragon

    pepper to taste

4 English muffins, *cut in half*

1½ cups nonfat shredded
    cheddar cheese

Combine crabmeat, water chestnuts, mayonnaise, lemon juice, tarragon, and pepper in medium bowl; mix well. Toast English muffin halves in toaster, toaster oven, or broiler. Preheat broiler on High heat. Line baking sheet with foil and spray with cooking spray. Divide crabmeat mixture among English muffins; sprinkle each with cheddar cheese. Broil 1–3 minutes until cheese is melted and lightly browned.

Nutrition per serving: 339 calories, 3.7 g fat, 35 g carbohydrates, 37 g protein, 113 mg cholesterol, 1 g dietary fiber, 1,556 mg sodium
Exchanges: 2 starch, 4 very lean meat, ½ other carb
Carb Choices: 2

Sandwiches and Wraps

Shopping List

Dairy
6 oz. nonfat shredded
   cheddar cheese

Canned
2 8-oz. cans crabmeat
6-oz. can sliced water chestnuts

Packaged
English muffins

Condiments
nonfat mayonnaise
bottled lemon juice

Seasonings/Spices
dried tarragon
pepper

You can substitute ⅛ teaspoon chervil, fennel seeds, or anise seeds for tarragon, if desired.

Tuna Sourdough Sub Sandwiches

Easy | Do Ahead | Serves: 4

1 12-oz. can chunk light tuna
   in water, *drained*

½ cup diced celery

1 small apple, *diced*

¼ cup raisins

¼ cup nonfat mayonnaise

½ tsp. onion powder

¼ tsp. dry mustard

4 sourdough sandwich rolls,
   cut in half

lettuce leaves, tomato slices,
onion slices, mild and creamy
Dijon mustard (optional)

Combine tuna, celery, apple, and raisins in medium bowl; mix well. Combine mayonnaise, onion powder, and dry mustard in small bowl; mix well. Add to tuna mixture and toss until coated. Divide tuna mixture and spoon onto 4 sourdough bread halves. Garnish with lettuce, tomatoes, and onions as desired. Top with remaining bread halves. Spread mustard on top half for spicier flavor, if desired.

Nutrition per serving: 281 calories, 2.7 g fat, 34 g carbohydrates, 29 g protein, 15 mg cholesterol, 2 g dietary fiber, 664 mg sodium
Exchanges: 2 starch, ½ fruit, 3 very lean meat,
Carb Choices: 2

The submarine sandwich, aka "Italian Hero," "Hoagie," "Grinder," "Poor Boy," or "Dagwood," originated in Naples, Italy, as small meat and cheese sandwiches on little rolls with pointed ends. The Naples original developed into the super-size American version with a variety of meats, cheeses, and condiments on a hard bread roll.

Shopping List

Produce	Condiments
celery	nonfat mayonnaise
small apple	
	Seasonings/Spices
Packaged	onion powder
sourdough sandwich rolls	dry mustard
raisins	**Optional**
	lettuce
Canned	tomato
12-oz. can chunk light tuna in water	onion
	mild and creamy Dijon mustard

Pineapple Tuna Melts

Easy | **Do Ahead** | **Serves: 4**

1 12-oz. can chunk light tuna in water, *drained*

2 tbsp. nonfat mayonnaise

1 tbsp. mild and creamy Dijon mustard

¼ cup chopped jicama

2 English muffins or bagels, *cut in half*

1 16-oz. can sliced pineapple, *drained*

4 oz. nonfat sliced cheese (American, cheddar, or Swiss)

Shopping List

Produce
jicama

Dairy
4 oz. sliced nonfat cheese

Canned
12-oz. can chunk light tuna
16-oz. can sliced pineapple

Packaged
English muffins or bagels

Condiments
mild and creamy Dijon mustard
nonfat mayonnaise

Preheat broiler on High heat. Line baking sheet with foil and spray with cooking spray. Combine tuna, mayonnaise, mustard, and jicama in medium bowl; mix well. Divide tuna mixture among English muffin or bagel halves; top each with 1 slice of pineapple and cheese. Arrange open-faced sandwiches on baking sheet; broil 1-2 minutes just until cheese is melted.

Nutrition per serving: 295 calories, 1.5 g fat, 37 g carbohydrates, 33 g protein, 15 mg cholesterol, 1 g dietary fiber, 874 mg sodium
Exchanges: 1 starch, 1½ fruit, 4 very lean meat
Carb Choices: 2

Sandwiches and Wraps

For variety, substitute two 7-ounce packages premium chicken breast for tuna, and substitute celery for jicama.

Open-Faced Lobster Sandwiches

Easy | Do Ahead | Serves: 4

1 8-oz. pkg. chunk-style imitation lobster, *flaked*

¼ cup Salad Confetti (or diced vegetables)

½ cup nonfat shredded cheddar cheese

¼ cup nonfat sour cream

¾ tsp. Worcestershire sauce

4 sourdough sandwich rolls, *cut in half*

3 oz. nonfat cream cheese, *softened*

4 whole lettuce leaves

4 slices tomatoes

Combine imitation lobster, salad confetti, cheddar cheese, sour cream, and Worcestershire sauce; mix well. Cut bread rolls in half and toast lightly. Spread 4 halves with cream cheese. Arrange lettuce leaf and tomato slice on top of cream cheese for each. Top with imitation lobster mixture and replace bread tops.

Nutrition per serving: 225 calories, 2.2 g fat, 32 g carbohydrates, 17 g protein, 6 mg cholesterol, 2 g dietary fiber, 852 mg sodium
Exchanges: 2 starch, 2 very lean meat
Carb Choices: 2

Shopping List

Produce
7-oz. container Salad Confetti
medium tomato
lettuce leaves

Meat/Fish/Poultry
8-oz. pkg. chunk-style imitation lobster

Dairy
nonfat shredded cheddar cheese
nonfat sour cream
3 oz. nonfat cream cheese

Packaged
sourdough sandwich rolls

Condiments
Worcestershire sauce

Substitute diced carrots, celery, jicama, cabbage, and bell peppers for packaged Salad Confetti.

Lemon Basil Chicken Salad Sandwiches p. 95

Orange Chicken Pitas **p. 96**

p. 94 Chicken Teriyaki and Pineapple Sandwiches

Tuna Sourdough Sub Sandwiches p. 102

p. **91** Chili Chicken Wraps

Pineapple Tuna Melts p. 103

Open-Faced Veggie-Wich

Easy | Do Ahead | Serves: 4

4   English muffins, *cut in half*

1   tbsp. + 1 tsp. Dijon or Bold & Spicy Brown Mustard

1   16-oz. pkg. frozen broccoli, cauliflower, and carrots, *thawed and drained*

1   cup nonfat shredded cheddar cheese

¼   cup nonfat Parmesan cheese

Preheat broiler on high heat. Line baking sheet with foil and spray with cooking spray. Arrange English muffin halves on baking sheet; spread each half with ½ teaspoon mustard. Arrange vegetables on top; sprinkle each half with 2 tablespoons cheddar and 1 tablespoon Parmesan cheese. Place on baking sheet and broil until vegetables are cooked, cheese is melted, and English muffin is lightly browned.

Nutrition per serving: 228 calories, 1.5 g fat, 36 g carbohydrates, 17 g protein, 0 mg cholesterol, 5 g dietary fiber, 786 mg sodium
Exchanges: 2 starch, 1 vegetable, 1½ very lean meat
Carb Choices: 2

Shopping List

Frozen
16-oz. pkg. frozen broccoli, cauliflower, and carrots

Dairy
4 oz. nonfat shredded cheddar cheese
nonfat Parmesan cheese

Packaged
English muffins

Condiments
Dijon or Bold & Spicy Brown Mustard

Sandwiches and Wraps

Round out your sandwich meal with fruit; try ½ cup strawberries, 1 medium apple, or ½ cup seedless grapes.

Black Bean and Vegetable Pocket

Easy | **Serves: 4**

1 16-oz. pkg. frozen broccoli florets, *cooked and drained*

1 11-oz. can Mexicorn or whole kernel corn

1 15-oz. can black beans, *rinsed and drained*

1 16-oz. can diced tomatoes with green chiles, *drained*

2 tbsp. cilantro herb blend

dash Tabasco sauce

4 pita pocket breads, *cut in half*

salsa or nonfat sour cream (optional)

Combine broccoli, Mexicorn, beans, and tomatoes in medium bowl; add cilantro herb blend and Tabasco and mix well. Fill pita pockets with broccoli, corn, bean mixture. Garnish with salsa or nonfat sour cream, if desired. Serve immediately.

Nutrition per serving: 309 calories, 1.5 g fat, 63 g carbohydrates, 16 g protein, 0 mg cholesterol, 10 g dietary fiber, 1,376 mg sodium
Exchanges: 3 starch, 3 vegetable
Carb Choices: 4

One of the greatest versatile aspects of sandwiches is that they can be served hot or cold.

Shopping List

Produce	Packaged
cilantro herb blend	pita pocket breads

Frozen	Condiments
16-oz. pkg. frozen broccoli florets	Tabasco sauce

Canned	Optional
11-oz. can Mexicorn or whole kernel corn	salsa
15-oz. can black beans	nonfat sour cream
16-oz. can diced tomatoes with green chiles	

Roasted Vegetable Wraps

Easy | **Do Ahead** | **Serves: 6**

½ lb. eggplant

½ lb. yellow squash

½ lb. zucchini

1 large portabello mushroom

1 14-oz. bottle Sweet Roasted Onion & Garlic Cooking Sauce

6 98% fat-free flour tortillas

Preheat oven to 450°. Line baking sheet with foil and spray with cooking spray. Slice eggplant, squash, zucchini, and mushroom into 3-inch strips, about ¼ inch thick. Arrange vegetables on baking sheet; top with Roasted Onion & Garlic Sauce and toss lightly. Bake 10–15 minutes until vegetables are tender. Wrap tortillas in paper towels and microwave on High 30–45 seconds per tortilla. Divide vegetable mixture among tortillas; roll up and serve. Vegetables can be prepared ahead and reheated in microwave before wrapping in tortillas.

Nutrition per serving: 183 calories, 0.7 g fat, 50 g carbohydrates, 5 g protein, 0 mg cholesterol, 4 g dietary fiber, 329 mg sodium
Exchanges: 1 starch, 2 vegetable, 1 other carb
Carb Choices: 3

Sandwiches and Wraps

Shopping List

Produce
eggplant
yellow squash
zucchini
large portabello mushroom

Packaged
17.5-oz. pkg. 98% fat-free flour tortillas

Condiments
14-oz. bottle Sweet Roasted Onion & Garlic Cooking Sauce

Roasted vegetables can also be served in a pita pocket or as topping for a baked or sweet potato.

Chapter Index

5 Soups and Chowders

4-Minute Chili

Soup is the ultimate fast food. It's a quick-fix main-dish meal that's made in one pot, making cleanup a breeze. Serving soup for dinner is a great way to save time in the kitchen. Find more timesaving tips below.

- Plan meals at least a week in advance to make the most of leftovers.
- Plan ahead for busy nights. If you know tomorrow night will be crazy, prepare double the night before and reheat as needed.
- Clean your kitchen work space as you go. When you're done cooking, you'll have little left to clean.
- After returning from the grocery store, package snack foods in individual snack bags so they're ready to pack in lunches. Individually wrap hamburger patties, chicken breasts, and the like so you can thaw as needed.
- Keep your shopping list on the front of your refrigerator, and as soon as you run out of something, write it down! You can also review old grocery receipts for shopping and cooking ideas.
- Prepare drink mixes in large pitchers so you don't have to make them as often.
- Keep your pantry stocked with canned broths, vegetables, fruits, fish, and chicken for quick-to-prepare healthful meals in minutes.
- Preserve nutrients by cooking quickly. Minimizing the time, temperature, and amount of water needed to prepare food will maximize nutritional benefits.
- Add ½ teaspoon uncooked rice to your salt shaker to prevent clogging and waste.
- Save cooking liquid from vegetables to use for nutritious soup stock.

- Keep your cupboard stocked with nonfat cooking sprays! They save cleanup time as well as calories and fat!
- Use seasoning blends such as Italian, Cajun, Mexican, fajita seasoning, pumpkin pie spice, poultry seasoning, and apple pie spice. A little goes a long way, and you don't have to mix them yourself.
- Buy garlic in minced or powdered form to prevent waste—½ teaspoon minced garlic or ¼ teaspoon garlic powder is equivalent to one garlic clove.
- Keep supplies of ground nuts, grated ginger, and shredded citrus peels in the freezer and use as needed.
- Skip serving dishes; serve meals right onto the plate. Doing so saves cleanup time and also controls portion sizes.
- Line casseroles and roasting pans with foil and spray with cooking spray before adding ingredients. After the meal, simply discard foil and rinse out the pan.
- Make use of your timesaving kitchen appliances such as slow cookers, microwaves, and bread machines.
- Take advantage of prepared and packaged food items. They may cost more, but the time you save is well worth it.

Soups and Chowders

Beef-Vegetable Soup

3 14-oz. cans nonfat beef broth

¾ tsp. Italian seasoning

1 16-oz. pkg. rosemary and
   garlic diced potatoes

1 16-oz. pkg. frozen mixed
   vegetables *(corn, carrots,
   green beans, and peas)*

Combine all ingredients in a large saucepan; bring to a boil over high heat. Reduce heat to low, cover, and simmer 15–20 minutes until heated through.

Nutrition per serving: 135 calories, 0.3 g fat, 26 g carbohydrates, 6 protein, 0 mg cholesterol, 3 dietary fiber, 1,078 mg sodium
Exchanges: 1 starch, 2 vegetable
Carb Choices: 2

Shopping List

Produce
16-oz. pkg. rosemary and
   garlic diced potatoes

Frozen
16-oz. pkg. frozen mixed
   vegetables (corn, carrots,
   green beans, and peas)

Canned
3 14-oz. cans nonfat beef broth

Seasonings/Spices
Italian seasoning

Quick fix: If you accidentally "overspice" soup, add a few potato slices, simmer for 30–45 minutes, and discard potatoes before serving.

Meatball Soup

Easy | Do Ahead | Freeze | Serves: 8

6 cups nonfat beef broth

1 28-oz. can crushed tomatoes

1 7-oz. can diced green chiles

3 tbsp. onion powder, *divided*

1 tbsp. + 1½ tsp. Italian seasoning, *divided*

½ cup uncooked long grain rice *(not instant)*

dash cayenne pepper

1 lb. extra-lean ground beef

1 tsp. garlic powder

⅓ cup seasoned bread crumbs

⅓ cup nonfat Parmesan cheese

⅓ cup nonfat half and half

¼ cup egg substitute

Combine beef broth, crushed tomatoes, green chiles, 2 tablespoons onion powder, and 1 tablespoon Italian seasoning in large soup pot; bring to a boil over high heat. Add rice and cayenne pepper; reduce heat to low, cover, and simmer 15–18 minutes. While rice is cooking, combine ground beef, garlic powder, 1 tablespoon onion powder, 1½ teaspoons Italian seasoning, bread crumbs, Parmesan cheese, half and half, and egg substitute; mix until ingredients are blended. Preheat broiler on high heat. Line broiler pan with foil and spray with cooking spray. Rinse your hands with water, but do not dry them. Roll beef mixture into 1-inch balls and arrange in a single layer on broiler pan. Broil meatballs 5 minutes; turn meatballs over and broil 5 minutes longer until cooked through. Add cooked meatballs to soup; heat and serve.

Soups and Chowders

Nutrition per serving: 203 calories, 3.1 g fat, 25 g carbohydrates, 18 g protein, 30 mg cholesterol, 1 g dietary fiber, 1,215 mg sodium
Exchanges: 1 starch, 2 vegetable. 1½ lean meat
Carb Choices: 2

Shopping List

Meat/Fish/Poultry
1 lb. extra-lean ground beef

Dairy
nonfat Parmesan cheese
8 oz. nonfat half and half
egg substitute

Canned
3 14-oz. cans beef broth
28-oz. can crushed tomatoes
7-oz. can diced green chiles

Packaged
long grain rice
seasoned bread crumbs

Seasonings/Spices
Italian seasoning
onion powder
cayenne pepper
garlic powder

Meal idea: Serve this soup with Parmesan Garlic Bread (p. 86) or Sesame Breadsticks (p. 87) for a meal your family will love!

Beef and Red Bean Chili

Easy | Do Ahead | Freeze | Serves: 6

1 lb. extra-lean ground beef

1 tsp. garlic powder

1 tbsp. onion powder

1 15-oz. can vegetable garden
4-bean chili

1 15-oz. can red kidney beans,
rinsed and drained

3 8-oz. cans tomato sauce with
roasted garlic

1 6-oz. can Italian tomato paste
with roasted garlic

Shopping List

Meat/Fish/Poultry
1 lb. extra-lean ground beef

Canned
15-oz. can vegetable garden
4-bean chili
15-oz. can red kidney beans
3 8-oz. cans tomato sauce
with roasted garlic
6-oz. can Italian tomato paste
with roasted garlic

Seasonings/Spices
garlic powder
onion powder

Spray large nonstick skillet with cooking spray and heat over medium-high heat. Add beef, garlic powder, and onion powder. Cook, stirring frequently, until beef is crumbled and browned. Add chili, beans, tomato sauce, and tomato paste. Bring to a boil over medium-high heat. Reduce heat to low and cook 15–20 minutes until heated through.

Nutrition per serving: 285 calories, 3.8 g fat, 37 g carbohydrates, 24 g protein, 41 mg cholesterol, 8 g dietary fiber, 1,426 mg sodium
Exchanges: 2 starch, 1 vegetable, 2 lean meat
Carb Choices: 2

To save hours of prep time purchase precooked kidney beans–commonly used in chili, salads, and rice dishes–in cans.

Taco Soup

Easy | Do Ahead | Freeze | Serves: 4

1 lb. extra-lean ground beef

2 tbsp. + ¼ cup dried
   minced onion

1 1-oz. packet taco seasoning
   mix

1 cup water

2 14½-oz. cans petite-cut
   diced tomatoes with
   jalapeños, *do not drain*

2 15-oz. cans chili beans,
   do not drain

1 15-oz. can black beans,
   drained

1 15-oz. can cream-style corn,
   do not drain

Spray large soup pot or Dutch oven with cooking spray and heat over medium-high heat. Add ground beef and 2 tablespoons dried minced onion; cook, stirring frequently, until beef is browned and crumbled. Add remaining ingredients and mix well; bring to a boil over high heat. Reduce heat to low and simmer 15–20 minutes until heated through.

Nutrition per serving: 605 calories, 7 g fat, 97 g carbohydrates, 40 g protein, 61 mg cholesterol, 17 g dietary fiber, 2,460 mg sodium
Exchanges: 5 starch, 4 vegetable, 2 lean meat
Carb Choices: 6

Soups and Chowders

Shopping List

Meat/Fish/Poultry
1 lb. extra-lean ground beef

Canned
2 14½-oz. cans petite-cut
   diced tomatoes with jalapeños
2 15-oz. cans chili beans
15-oz. can black beans
15-oz. can cream-style corn

Seasonings/Spices
1-oz. packet taco seasoning mix
dried minced onion

Learn to read food labels; it will help you cut calories, fat, cholesterol, and sodium while increasing your intake of dietary fiber.

Chicken-Barley Soup

2 14-oz. cans nonfat chicken broth

½ cup water

1 tbsp. onion powder

½ cup quick-cooking barley

1½ tsp. chili powder

1 16-oz. pkg. frozen mixed vegetables (corn, carrots, green beans, and peas)

2 6-oz. pkgs. Southwestern chicken breast strips, *cubed*

1 14½-oz. can petite-cut diced tomatoes with green chiles, *drained*

¼ cup chopped cilantro (optional)

Combine chicken broth, water, and onion powder in large saucepan; bring to a boil over high heat. Add barley and chili powder; cook over low heat 5–6 minutes. Add vegetables and cook over low heat until barley is tender. Add chicken and tomatoes; increase heat to medium and cook, stirring frequently, until soup is heated through. Garnish with chopped cilantro, if desired.

Nutrition per serving: 293 calories, 2.5 g fat, 37 g carbohydrates, 31 g protein, 50 mg cholesterol, 6 g dietary fiber, 1,654 mg sodium
Exchanges: 1½ starch, 2 vegetable, 4 very lean meat
Carb Choices: 2

It's easy to make your own chicken broth! Just place chicken pieces in a soup pot and fill with water. Add peeled and sliced onion, celery tops, carrot pieces, and parsley; bring to a boil over high heat. Reduce heat to low and simmer at least one hour. Strain the liquid and store in refrigerator or freezer.

Shopping List

Meat/Fish/Poultry
2 6-oz. pkgs. Southwestern chicken breast strips

14½-oz. can petite-cut diced tomatoes with green chiles

Frozen
16-oz. pkg. frozen mixed vegetables (corn, carrots, green beans, and peas)

Packaged
quick-cooking barley

Seasonings/Spices
onion powder
chili powder

Canned
2 14-oz. cans nonfat chicken broth

Optional
fresh cilantro

Chicken Noodle Soup

Easy | **Do Ahead** | **Freeze** | **Serves: 6**

5¼ cups nonfat chicken broth

1 16-oz. pkg. frozen
   baby carrots

1 10-oz. pkg. frozen seasoning
   vegetables

1 8-oz. pkg. no-yolk egg noodles

2 6-oz. pkgs. grilled chicken
   breast strips, *cubed*

Pour broth into large saucepan; bring to a boil over high heat. Add carrots, seasoning vegetables, and no-yolk egg noodles; reduce heat to medium and cook 10–12 minutes until vegetables and noodles are tender. Stir in chicken and heat through.

Nutrition per serving: 268 calories, 1.4 g fat, 39 g carbohydrates, 23 g protein, 33 mg cholesterol, 6 g dietary fiber, 1,096 mg sodium
Exchanges: 2 starch, 1 vegetable, 2 very lean meat
Carb Choices: 2

Soups
and
Chowders

Shopping List

Meat/Fish/Poultry
2 6-oz. pkgs. grilled chicken
  breast strips

Frozen
16-oz. pkg. baby carrots
10-oz. pkg. frozen seasoning
  vegetables

Canned
3 14-oz. cans nonfat
  chicken broth

Packaged
8-oz. pkg. no-yolk egg noodles

Beware of packaged noodle soups; most contain prefried noodles and are loaded with sodium. A 3-ounce package of chicken flavor ramen noodle soup contains 380 calories, 14 grams of fat, and 1,820 milligrams of sodium.

Special Chicken Noodle Soup

Easy | Do Ahead | Freeze | Serves: 6

3 14-oz. cans nonfat chicken broth

1 tsp. garlic powder

½ cup uncooked ditalini, orzo, or tubetti pasta

3 6-oz. pkgs. chicken breast strips, *cut in half*

1 5-oz. pkg. baby spinach

¼ cup nonfat Parmesan cheese

Pour chicken broth into large saucepan; add garlic powder and bring to a boil over high heat. Add pasta and cook according to package directions (simmer about 8–9 minutes until tender). Add chicken and spinach to soup; cook until spinach is wilted and soup is heated through. Garnish with Parmesan cheese.

Nutrition per serving: 174 calories, 1.9 g fat, 13 g carbohydrates, 26 g protein, 50 mg cholesterol, 1 g dietary fiber, 1,102 mg sodium
Exchanges: ½ starch, 1 vegetable, 3 very lean meat
Carb Choices: 1

Shopping List

Produce
5-oz. pkg. baby spinach

Meat/Fish/Poultry
3 6-oz. pkgs. chicken breast strips

Dairy
nonfat Parmesan cheese

Canned
3 14-oz. cans nonfat chicken broth

Packaged
8-oz. ditalini, orzo, or tubetti pasta

Seasonings/Spices
garlic powder

Select low-sodium canned foods when possible. The National Academy of Sciences recommends consuming no more than 500 milligrams of sodium each day, yet the average American consumes at least 10 times this amount (5,000–7,000 milligrams).

Chicken Cannellini Soup

Easy | **Do Ahead** | **Freeze** | **Serves: 4**

1 15-oz. can cannellini
   beans, *drained and mashed*

2½ cups nonfat chicken broth

2 tbsp. Italian tomato paste with
   roasted garlic

2 tbsp. red wine vinegar

1½ cups frozen seasoning
   vegetables

¾ tsp. garlic powder

¼ tsp. red pepper flakes

2 6-oz. pkgs. grilled chicken
   breast strips, *cubed*

Combine beans, chicken broth, tomato paste, and vinegar in large saucepan. Bring to a boil over medium-high heat. Add seasoning vegetables, garlic powder, and red pepper flakes; bring to a boil. Reduce heat to low and simmer 15–20 minutes. Stir in chicken and cook until heated through.

Nutrition per serving: 262 calories, 1.9 g fat, 31 g carbohydrates, 30 g protein, 50 mg cholesterol, 1 g dietary fiber, 1,081 mg sodium
Exchanges: 1 starch, 3 vegetable, 4 very lean meat
Carb Choices: 2

Soups and Chowders

Shopping List

Meat/Fish/Poultry
2 6-oz. pkgs. grilled
  chicken breast strips

Frozen
10-oz. pkg. frozen
  seasoning vegetables

Canned
15-oz. can cannellini beans
2 14-oz. cans nonfat
  chicken broth
6-oz. can Italian tomato
  paste with roasted garlic

Condiments
red wine vinegar

Seasonings/Spices
garlic powder
red pepper flakes

Be creative! Add leftover meats and vegetables to soups– the possibilities are endless!

Chipotle Chicken Soup

Easy | **Do Ahead** | **Serves: 4**

1½ cups frozen seasoning vegetables

1½ tsp. chipotle chile pepper seasoning

1 tbsp. minced garlic

1 tsp. ground cumin

2 14-oz. cans nonfat chicken broth

1 14½-oz. can petite-cut diced tomatoes with green chiles, *undrained*

1 11-oz. can Mexicorn, *drained*

2 6-oz. pkgs. Southwestern chicken breast strips

baked tortilla chips, *crumbled* (optional)

Spray large saucepan with cooking spray and heat over medium-high heat. Add seasoning vegetables and cook, stirring frequently, until softened. Stir in chile pepper seasoning, garlic, and cumin. Add broth, tomatoes, corn, and chicken; bring to a boil over high heat. Reduce heat to low and simmer 15–20 minutes. Garnish with crumbled baked tortilla chips, if desired.

Nutrition per serving: 212 calories, 2.6 g fat, 22 g carbohydrates, 28 g protein, 50 mg cholesterol, 3 g dietary fiber, 1,926 mg sodium
Exchanges: ½ starch, 2 vegetable, 3 very lean meat
Carb Choices: 1

Bake up a batch of fat-free cornbread (from package mix) for a quick and easy side dish.

Shopping List

Meat/Fish/Poultry	Seasonings/Spices
2 6-oz. pkgs. Southwestern chicken breast strips	chipotle chile pepper seasoning
	minced garlic
	ground cumin
Frozen	
10-oz. pkg. frozen seasoning vegetables	**Optional**
	baked tortilla chips
Canned	
2 15-oz. cans nonfat chicken broth	
14½-oz. can petite-cut diced tomatoes with green chiles	
11-oz. can Mexicorn	

Chicken Taco Soup

Easy | Do Ahead | Serves: 4

1 14-oz. can nonfat
   chicken broth

1 16-oz. can nonfat
   refried beans

2½ cups chunky-style salsa

1 15-oz. can black beans,
   drained

2 6-oz. pkgs. Southwestern
   chicken breast strips,
   cut in thirds

Combine broth and refried beans in large saucepan; cook over medium heat, stirring constantly, until mixture is blended and thickened. Stir in remaining ingredients; bring to a boil over high heat. Reduce heat to low and simmer, uncovered, 10–15 minutes until heated through.

Nutrition per serving: 374 calories, 2.3 g fat, 41 g carbohydrates, 38 g protein, 50 mg cholesterol, 7 g dietary fiber, 2,517 mg sodium
Exchanges: 2 starch, 3 vegetable, 4 very lean meat
Carb Choices: 3

Soups and Chowders

Shopping List

Meat/Fish/Poultry
2 6-oz. pkgs. Southwestern
   chicken breast strips

Canned
15-oz can nonfat chicken broth
16-oz. can nonfat refried beans
15-oz. can black beans

Condiments
24 oz. bottle chunky style salsa

Canned beans, packed with protein and fiber, are on the list of pantry essentials for quick, healthful cooking.

4-Minute Chili

Easy | Do Ahead | Serves: 6

2 16-oz. cans chili beans

2 14½-oz. cans diced tomatoes
with jalapeños, *lightly drained*

3 6-oz. pkgs. Southwestern
chicken breast strips

shredded nonfat cheddar
cheese, nonfat sour cream,
chopped green onions, diced
red or white onions (optional)

Combine beans, tomatoes, and chicken in large saucepan or microwave-safe dish; bring to a boil over high heat or microwave on High for 4 minutes until bubbly hot. Garnish with optional ingredients, if desired.

Nutrition per serving: 255 calories, 1.9 g fat, 28 g carbohydrates, 30 g protein, 50 mg cholesterol, 1 g dietary fiber, 1,341 mg sodium
Exchanges: 1½ starch, 1 vegetable, 3 very lean meat
Carb Choices: 2

Shopping List

Meat
3 6-oz. pkgs. Southwestern
chicken breast strips

Canned
2 16-oz. cans chili beans
2 14½-oz. cans diced tomatoes
with jalapeños

Optional
shredded nonfat cheddar cheese
nonfat sour cream
green onions
red or white onion packaged
diced onions

Open cans from the bottom to avoid having to scoop out food that usually gets stuck.

Chicken Chili Corn Chowder

Easy | **Do Ahead** | **Serves: 6**

2　15-oz. cans vegetable garden chili

1　15¼-oz. can whole kernel corn

1　14½-oz. can stewed tomatoes with bell pepper and onion

1　tsp. chili powder

1　tbsp. cilantro herb blend

3　6-oz. pkgs. Southwestern chicken breast strips

1½　cups nonfat shredded cheddar cheese

1　7-oz. container diced red or yellow onions (optional)

Combine vegetable chili, corn, stewed tomatoes, chili powder, and cilantro herb blend in medium saucepan. Bring to a boil over medium-high heat. Add chicken and cook over medium heat until bubbly hot. Serve with nonfat shredded cheese and, if desired, diced onions.

Nutrition per serving: 336 calories, 2.6 g fat, 40 g carbohydrates, 38 g protein, 50 mg cholesterol, 5 g dietary fiber, 1,712 mg sodium
Exchanges: 2 starch, 2 vegetable, 4 very lean meat
Carb Choices: 3

Soups and Chowders

If you purchase canned soups, avoid creamy premixed varieties. Instead buy the kind you can add skim milk or nonfat half and half to.

Shopping List

Produce
cilantro herb blend

Meat/Fish/Poultry
3 6-oz. pkgs. Southwestern chicken breast strips

Dairy
6-oz. nonfat shredded cheddar cheese

Canned
2 15-oz. cans vegetable garden chili
15¼-oz. whole kernel corn
14½-oz. can stewed tomatoes with bell pepper and onion

Seasonings/Spices
chili powder

Optional
7-oz. container diced red or yellow onions

Timesaving Tortilla Soup

Easy | Do Ahead | Freeze | Serves: 8

1 49-oz. can nonfat chicken broth

2 14½-oz. cans petite-cut diced tomatoes with jalapeños, *do not drain*

2 11-oz. cans Mexicorn

4 6-oz. pkg. Southwestern chicken breast strips

red pepper sauce to taste

2 cups nonfat shredded cheddar cheese

8 oz. baked tortilla chips, *broken into small pieces*

Combine broth, tomatoes, and Mexicorn in large soup pot; bring to a boil over high heat. Add chicken and red pepper sauce. Cook over medium heat, stirring occasionally, 15–20 minutes until heated through. Stir in cheese and mix until melted. Garnish soup with broken tortilla pieces. If freezing soup, freeze before adding cheese and tortillas.

Nutrition per serving: 358 calories, 4.3 g fat, 44 g carbohydrates, 37 g protein, 60 mg cholesterol, 3 g dietary fiber, 2,266 mg sodium
Exchanges: 2 starch, 3 vegetable, 4 very lean meat
Carb Choices: 3

Shopping List

Meat/Fish/Poultry
4 6-oz. pkgs. Southwestern chicken breast strips

Dairy
8 oz. nonfat shredded cheddar cheese

Canned
49-oz. can nonfat chicken broth
2 14½-oz. cans petite-cut diced tomatoes with jalapeños
2 11-oz. cans Mexicorn

Packaged
8-oz. pkg. baked tortilla chips

Seasonings/Spices
red pepper sauce

Don't overcook soup you plan to freeze; it cooks further when reheated.

Vegetable Pasta Soup

Easy | **Do Ahead** | **Serves: 4**

2   14-oz. cans nonfat
     chicken broth

2   cups water

1   16-oz. pkg. frozen mixed
     vegetables (corn, carrots,
     green beans, and peas)

¾   cup uncooked elbow
     macaroni

¼   tsp. Italian seasoning

     dash pepper

1   6-oz. pkg. grilled chicken
     breast strips, *cubed*

Combine chicken broth and water in large saucepan; bring to a boil over high heat. Add vegetables; return to a boil. Add macaroni, Italian seasoning, and pepper; bring to a boil over high heat. Reduce heat to medium-high and cook 7–9 minutes until pasta and vegetables are tender. Stir in chicken and heat through.

Nutrition per serving: 167 calories, 1.4 g fat, 26 g carbohydrates, 19 g protein, 25 mg cholesterol, 6 g dietary fiber, 1,152 mg sodium
Exchanges: 1½ starch, 1½ very lean meat
Carb Choices: 2

Soups
and
Chowders

Shopping List

Meat/Fish/Poultry	Packaged
6-oz. pkg. grilled chicken breast strips	8-oz. pkg. elbow macaroni

Frozen	Seasonings/Spices
16-oz. pkg. frozen mixed vegetables (corn, carrots, green beans, and peas)	Italian seasoning pepper

Canned
2 14-oz. cans nonfat
chicken broth

Make soups ahead of time and freeze them for a quick meal or snack. Because seasonings intensify during freezing, it's better to add them as needed during reheating.

New England Clam Chowder

Easy | **Do Ahead** | **Serves: 6**

6 cups nonfat chicken broth

2 6-oz. cans minced clams, *drained*

2 cups garden herb pearl potatoes

4 cups nonfat half and half

¼ cup bacon crumbles

pepper to taste

Combine broth, clams, and potatoes in large saucepan; bring to a boil over high heat. Reduce heat to low and simmer until potatoes are tender. Gradually add half and half; cook over medium heat, stirring constantly, until soup thickens and is heated through (do not boil). Add bacon crumbles and season with pepper to taste.

Nutrition per serving: 200 calories, 1.2 g fat, 33 g carbohydrates, 7 g protein, 35 mg cholesterol, 1 g dietary fiber, 405 mg sodium
Exchanges: 1 starch, 1 very lean meat, 1 other carb
Carb Choices: 2

Shopping List

Produce
18-oz. pkg. garden herb pearl potatoes

Dairy
1 quart nonfat half and half

Canned
4 14-oz. cans nonfat chicken broth
2 6-oz. cans minced clams

Packaged
1.3-oz. pkg. bacon crumbles

Seasonings/Spices
pepper

Start your meal with soup to take the edge off your appetite. Studies have shown that people who consume 1 cup of soup before eating consume about 25% fewer calories.

Chili Corn Soup

Easy | **Do Ahead** | **Serves: 4**

2 cups nonfat beef broth

1 15-oz. can vegetable
   garden 4-bean chili

1 10-oz. pkg. frozen whole
   kernel corn, *thawed
   and drained*

1 16-oz. pkg. precooked
   roasted onion potato cubes

½ cup nonfat shredded
   cheddar cheese,
   diced onions (optional)

Combine all the ingredients in a large saucepan or Dutch oven; bring to a boil over high heat. Reduce heat to low and simmer, uncovered, 20–25 minutes until heated through. Garnish with shredded cheese or diced onions, if desired.

Nutrition per serving: 256 calories, 0.7 g fat, 54 g carbohydrates, 10 g protein, 0 mg cholesterol, 7 g dietary fiber, 990 mg sodium
Exchanges: 3 starch
Carb Choices: 4

Soups and Chowders

Shopping List

Produce
16-oz. pkg. precooked roasted
   onion potato cubes

Frozen
10-oz. pkg. frozen whole
   kernel corn

Canned
15-oz. can vegetable garden
   4-bean chili
2 10¾-oz. cans nonfat
   beef broth

Optional
nonfat shredded cheddar cheese
diced onions

You can turn this into a vegetarian meal by substituting vegetable broth for the beef broth.

Black Bean and Noodle Soup

Easy | **Do Ahead** | **Serves: 6**

3 14-oz. cans nonfat chicken or vegetable broth

1 16-oz. jar chunky-style salsa

1 15-oz. can black beans, *rinsed and drained*

1 11-oz. can Mexicorn, *drained*

6 oz. uncooked spaghetti

1 tbsp. lime juice

1¼ tsp. Mexican seasoning

dash pepper

¼ cup + 2 tbsp. nonfat shredded cheddar cheese

Pour broth into large saucepan; bring to a boil over high heat. Add salsa, beans, Mexicorn, spaghetti, lime juice, Mexican seasoning, and pepper; mix well and bring to a boil over high heat. Reduce heat to medium and cook, stirring occasionally, 15–20 minutes until spaghetti is tender and soup is heated through. Sprinkle cheese over top and mix lightly.

Nutrition per serving: 257 calories, 1.4 g fat, 47 g carbohydrates, 14 g protein, 0 mg cholesterol, 4 g dietary fiber, 1,678 mg sodium
Exchanges: 3 starch, 1 vegetable
Carb Choices: 3

Shopping List

Dairy
nonfat shredded cheddar cheese

Canned
3 14-oz. cans nonfat chicken or vegetable broth
15-oz. can black beans
11-oz. can Mexicorn

Packaged
6 oz. spaghetti

Condiments
16-oz. jar chunky-style salsa
bottled lime juice

Seasonings/Spices
Mexican seasoning
pepper

Black beans are also called turtle beans, Mexican black, or Spanish beans.

Timesaving Black Bean Soup

Easy | **Do Ahead** | **Serves: 4**

- 2 14-oz. cans nonfat chicken or vegetable broth
- 2 15-oz. cans black beans, *rinsed, drained, and divided*
- 3 tbsp. onion powder
- 2 tsp. garlic powder
- 2 tsp. Italian seasoning
- dash cayenne pepper

Shopping List

Canned
2 14-oz. cans nonfat chicken
   or vegetable broth
2 15-oz. cans black beans

Seasonings/Spices
onion powder
garlic powder
Italian seasoning
cayenne pepper

Combine broth, 1 can beans, onion powder, garlic powder, Italian seasoning, and cayenne pepper in food processor or blender; process or blend until smooth. Pour mixture into medium saucepan; bring to a boil over high heat. Reduce heat to low, add remaining beans, and cook, uncovered, 15–20 minutes until slightly thickened and heated through.

Nutrition per serving: 228 calories, 0.9 g fat, 42 g carbohydrates, 16 g protein, 0 mg cholesterol, 6 g dietary fiber, 1,489 mg sodium
Exchanges: 3 starch
Carb Choices: 3

Soups and Chowders

Black beans are most often used in Mexican, Caribbean, and Latin American soups or side dishes.

Bean and Macaroni Soup

Average | **Do Ahead** | **Freeze** | **Serves: 8**

2 16-oz. cans nonfat chili beans

2 tbsp. nonfat chicken broth

1 8-oz. pkg. sliced mushrooms

1 cup frozen diced onions

2 cups frozen sliced carrots

2 tbsp. dried celery flakes

1 tsp. minced garlic

2 14½-oz. cans stewed tomatoes with oregano and basil, *lightly drained*

2½ tsp. Italian seasoning

pepper to taste

4 cups cooked elbow macaroni water

Drain beans and reserve liquid; set aside. Spray Dutch oven or large soup pot with cooking spray; add chicken broth and heat over medium-high heat. Add mushrooms, onions, carrots, celery flakes, and minced garlic; cook, stirring frequently, 5–7 minutes until vegetables are softened. Add tomatoes, Italian seasoning, and pepper to taste. Bring to a boil over medium-high heat. Reduce heat to low, cover, and cook 25–30 minutes. Combine reserved liquid (from beans) with enough water to equal 4 cups. Add liquid, beans, and macaroni to pot; bring to a boil over medium-high heat. Cover and cook over low heat, stirring occasionally, 25–30 minutes.

Nutrition per serving: 231 calories, 1 g fat, 45 g carbohydrates, 10 g protein, 0 mg cholesterol, 3 g dietary fiber, 738 mg sodium
Exchanges: 2 starch, 3 vegetable
Carb Choices: 3

Shopping List

Produce
8-oz. pkg. sliced mushrooms

Frozen
12-oz. pkg. frozen diced onions
16-oz. pkg. frozen sliced carrots

Canned
2 16-oz. cans nonfat chili beans
nonfat chicken broth

2 14½-oz. cans stewed tomatoes with oregano and basil

Packaged
8-oz. pkg. elbow macaroni

Seasonings/Spices
celery flakes
minced garlic
pepper
Italian seasoning

Soups are very versatile; they serve as an all-in-one meal, appetizer, or side dish. Most soups freeze well, so you can make a batch ahead of time and store it in individual containers to heat in the microwave as needed.

Creamy Vegetable Rice Soup

Easy | **Do Ahead** | **Serves: 4**

1½ cups nonfat half and half

2 cups skim milk

1 cup nonfat shredded cheddar cheese

½ tsp. chili powder

2 cups cooked rice (brown or white)

1 16-oz. pkg. frozen broccoli, cauliflower, and carrots, *thawed and drained*

Combine half and half, milk, and cheese in large saucepan; cook over low heat, stirring frequently, until cheese is melted and soup is thickened. Stir in chili powder, rice, and vegetables. Cook over medium heat, stirring occasionally, 15–20 minutes until vegetables are tender and soup is heated through.

Nutrition per serving: 311 calories, 0.7 g fat, 55 g carbohydrates, 17 g protein, 2 mg cholesterol, 5 g dietary fiber, 383 mg sodium
Exchanges: 2½ starch, ½ milk, 1 vegetable. 1 very lean meat
Carb Choices: 4

Soups and Chowders

Shopping List

Dairy
12 oz. nonfat half and half
16 oz. skim milk
4 oz. nonfat shredded cheddar cheese

Frozen
16-oz. pkg. frozen broccoli, cauliflower, and carrots

Packaged
instant rice (brown or white)

Seasonings/Spices
chili powder

For thicker soup you can substitute nonfat half and half for the skim milk; cook as directed, stirring constantly, until soup is thickened.

Cream of Broccoli Soup

Easy | Do Ahead | Serves: 6

1 cup nonfat half and half

1 cup skim milk

2 10¾-oz. cans condensed 98% fat-free cream of chicken soup

1 tbsp. onion powder

4 cups frozen broccoli florets, *thawed and drained*

2 cups nonfat shredded cheddar cheese

Combine half and half, milk, chicken soup, and onion powder in large saucepan; cook over medium heat, stirring frequently, until heated. Add broccoli and cook 10 minutes. Gradually add cheese, stirring until melted, and cook until heated through (do not boil).

Nutrition per serving: 198 calories, 1.9 g fat, 27 g carbohydrates, 18 g protein, 2 mg cholesterol, 6 g dietary fiber, 831 mg sodium
Exchanges: 1 starch, 2 very lean meat, ½ other carb
Carb Choices: 2

Shopping List

Dairy
8 oz. nonfat half and half
8 oz. skim milk
8 oz. nonfat shredded cheddar cheese

Frozen
20-oz. pkg. frozen broccoli florets

Canned
2 10¾-oz. cans condensed 98% fat-free cream of chicken soup

Seasonings/Spices
onion powder

Don't boil soup after adding milk products!

Cauliflower-Potato Soup

Easy | **Do Ahead** | **Serves: 4**

2 14-oz. cans + 1 tbsp.
    nonfat chicken broth,
    divided

⅔ cup frozen seasoning
    vegetables

1 16-oz. pkg. frozen cauliflower
    florets

2 cups packaged sliced
    home fries

¼ tsp. cayenne pepper

chopped green onions
    (optional)

Shopping List

Produce
1-lb. 4-oz. pkg. sliced home
    fries

Frozen
10-oz. pkg. frozen seasoning
    vegetables
16-oz. pkg. cauliflower florets

Canned
3 14-oz. cans nonfat
    chicken broth

Seasonings/Spices
cayenne pepper

Optional
green onions

Spray large saucepan or Dutch oven with cooking spray; add 1 tablespoon broth and heat over medium-high heat. Add seasoning vegetables; cook, stirring frequently, until vegetables are softened. Stir in remaining broth, cauliflower, home fries, and cayenne pepper; bring to a boil over high heat. Reduce heat to low, cover, and simmer 20–25 minutes until vegetables are tender. Remove soup from heat and cool slightly. Working in batches, process or blend soup in food processor or blender until smooth. Return to saucepan and cook over medium heat until heated through. Garnish with chopped green onions before serving, if desired.

Nutrition per serving: 108 calories, 0.5 g fat, 20 g carbohydrates, 6 g protein, 0 mg cholesterol, 3 g dietary fiber, 768 mg sodium
Exchanges: 1 starch, 1 vegetable
Carb Choices: 1

Soups and Chowders

For a chunky soup, puree only half the vegetables from the soup with 1 cup of liquid in a food processor or blender; return the mixture to the pot and heat through.

Lentil-Tomato Soup

Easy | Do Ahead | Freeze | Serves: 4

1 6-oz. pkg. lentil soup mix

1 15½-oz. can stewed tomatoes with bell pepper and onion, *lightly drained*

1 15½-oz. can petite-cut diced tomatoes with roasted garlic and sweet onion, *lightly drained*

Prepare soup mix according to package directions. After adding seasoning packet, add stewed and diced tomatoes. Bring to a boil; reduce heat to low, cover and simmer 10–15 minutes before serving.

Nutrition per serving: 148 calories, 0.1 g fat, 27 g carbohydrates, 8 g protein, 0 mg cholesterol, 4 g dietary fiber, 1,025 mg sodium
Exchanges: 1 starch, 3 vegetable
Carb Choices: 2

Shopping List

Packaged
6-oz. pkg. lentil soup mix

Canned
15½-oz. can stewed tomatoes with bell pepper and onion
15½-oz. can petite-cut diced tomatoes with roasted garlic and sweet onion

Fill up on fiber! Soluble fiber found in oats, legumes, fruits, and vegetables helps lower blood cholesterol and manage blood sugar.

Mushroom Barley Soup

Easy | **Do Ahead** | **Freeze** | **Serves: 4**

2 14-oz. cans + 1 tbsp.
    nonfat chicken broth,
    divided

2 8-oz. pkgs. sliced mushrooms

1 cup frozen seasoning
    vegetables

1 tsp. minced garlic

1 tsp. Italian seasoning

¼ tsp. pepper

1 14½-oz. can petite-cut
    diced tomatoes, *drained*

1 tbsp. balsamic vinegar

½ cup uncooked quick-cooking
    barley

Spray large saucepan or Dutch oven with cooking spray; add 1 tablespoon broth and heat over medium-high heat. Add mushrooms, seasoning vegetables, garlic, Italian seasoning, and pepper; cook, stirring frequently, until vegetables are softened. Add remaining broth, tomatoes, balsamic vinegar, and barley; bring to a boil over high heat. Reduce heat to low and simmer 12–15 minutes until barley is tender.

Nutrition per serving: 156 calories, 1.3 g fat, 29 g carbohydrates, 9 g protein, 0 mg cholesterol, 6 g dietary fiber, 876 mg sodium
Exchanges: 1 starch, 3 vegetable
Carb Choices: 2

Soups and Chowders

Shopping List

Produce	Packaged
2 8-oz. pkgs. sliced mushrooms	quick-cooking barley
Frozen	**Condiments**
10-oz. pkg. frozen seasoning vegetables	balsamic vinegar
Canned	**Seasonings/Spices**
3 14-oz. cans nonfat chicken broth	minced garlic
14½-oz. can petite-cut diced tomatoes	Italian seasoning
	pepper

Nonfat canned broths make homemade soups easy–add canned vegetables, cooked meat or poultry, and instant rice for a quick-fix meal.

Chapter Index

6 Meat Entrées

Sloppy Joe Mix

Spices make it possible to add flavor to your food without adding fat. You can personalize recipes to fit your family's tastes by adding more or less of a spice. When you're experimenting with spices, it's helpful to know what flavors work with what foods. Use this chart as a quick reference when you're looking to boost the flavor in any dish.

Seasoning/Spices	Best used for	Substitutions
Basil	Tomato sauces, pesto, and vinaigrettes	Oregano, thyme (use half of basil amount)
Bell pepper flakes: dehydrated sweet red and green peppers	Soup, sauces, salads, and stews	1 tbsp. dried = 3 tbsp. chopped fresh
Celery flakes	Soups, sauces, salads, dips, and stuffings	½ cup fresh, chopped celery per tablespoon of celery flakes
Celery salt or seeds	Coleslaw, potato salad, and pickles	Ground celery seeds
Chili powder: a blend of chile peppers, cumin, garlic, oregano, salt, paprika, and other spices	Chili con carne, spare ribs, stews, and appetizers	Dash bottled hot pepper sauce plus ⅛ teaspoon oregano and ⅛ teaspoon cumin per teaspoon of chili powder
Coriander seeds	Pickles, Oriental dishes, curried dishes, and meat dishes	1 tbsp. cumin per 1 tbsp. ground coriander seeds (or 1½ tablespoons whole seeds)
Cumin	Chili powders, pickles, spare ribs, and other meat dishes	½ teaspoon chili powder or caraway seeds per teaspoon of cumin
Lemon-Pepper	Salads, broiled meats, poultry, and seafood	Lemon zest, black pepper, and salt
Marjoram leaves	Poultry stuffings, sausage, stews, sauces, soups, veal dishes, meat dishes, potato dishes, and most Italian sauces	Basil, thyme, and savory
Oregano leaves	Italian dishes, soups or sauces, meat stews, and bean dishes	½-¾ teaspoon thyme or basil or 1 teaspoon marjoram per teaspoon of oregano leaves
Parsley	To garnish or season stocks, soups, sauces, salads, and egg and potato dishes	½-¾ teaspoon chervil or cilantro per tablespoon fresh parsley
Rosemary leaves	Stuffings, roasted dishes such as lamb, pork, beef, poultry, and wild game	Thyme, tarragon, and savory
Saffron	In Spanish and Italian foods for mild flavor and yellow coloring	Dash turmeric
Sage	To season stuffings, pork, poultry, and veal dishes	½-¾ teaspoon poultry seasoning, savory, marjoram, or rosemary per teaspoon of sage
Tarragon leaves	Béarnaise sauce and egg, seafood, and poultry dishes	½-¾ teaspoon chervil or dash fennel or anise seeds per teaspoon of tarragon
Thyme leaves	Seafood chowders, sauces, stocks, and meat dishes	½-¾ teaspoon basil, marjoram, oregano, or savory per teaspoon thyme

Meat Entrées

Hamburger Pie with Corn Bread Topping

Easy | Do Ahead | Serves: 4

1 lb. extra-lean ground beef

1 cup frozen diced onions

1 cup frozen diced green bell
  peppers

1 cup tomato sauce

¼ cup water

¼ cup + 2 tbsp. chunky-style
  salsa

1 14½-oz. pkg. fat-free honey
  corn bread mix

Spray large nonstick skillet with cooking spray and heat over medium heat. Add beef, onions, and bell pepper; cook, stirring frequently, until beef is browned and crumbled and vegetables are tender; drain well. Return beef mixture to skillet; stir in tomato sauce, water, and salsa. Preheat oven to 400°. Spray baking dish with cooking spray; spoon beef mixture into baking dish. Prepare corn bread batter according to package directions; let batter stand 5 minutes to thicken. Drop batter by tablespoons onto beef mixture and spread carefully to cover. Bake 15–20 minutes until corn bread is lightly browned and cooked through.

Nutrition per serving: 550 calories, 4.7 g fat, 92 g carbohydrates, 29 g protein, 61 mg cholesterol, 5 g dietary fiber, 1,731 mg sodium
Exchanges: 4 starch, 4 vegetable, 2½ lean meat
Carb Choices: 6

Shopping List

Meat/Fish/Poultry
1 lb. extra-lean ground beef

Frozen
12-oz. pkg. frozen diced onions
10-oz. pkg. frozen diced green
  bell peppers

Canned
8-oz. can tomato sauce

Packaged
14½-oz. pkg. fat-free honey
  corn bread mix

Condiments
chunky-style salsa

For a change of pace, add 1 cup of canned corn kernels or 2 tablespoons chopped green chiles to the honey corn bread mix.

 p. 166 Cranberry Upside-Down Meat Loaf

Sloppy Joes p. 161

p. 169 Canadian Bacon and Pineapple Pizza

Beef Ziti Bake p. 159

p. 155 Beef and Potato Tex-Mex Hash

Chili-Beef with Rice p. 158

Beef Skillet Meal

Easy | **Serves: 4**

3 tbsp. nonfat beef broth

1 lb. extra-lean ground beef

1 cup cornflake crumbs

⅛ tsp. pepper

1 16-oz. pkg. frozen baby gold and white corn, *thawed and drained*

1 cup frozen pepper stir-fry, *thawed and drained*

2 14½-oz. cans petite-cut diced tomatoes with roasted garlic and sweet onion, *drained*

Spray large nonstick skillet with cooking spray; add beef broth and heat over medium-high heat. Combine beef, cornflake crumbs, and pepper; mix well and add to skillet. Cook, stirring frequently, until beef is browned and crumbled. Stir in corn and pepper stir-fry; cook, stirring frequently, 3–4 minutes. Add tomatoes; bring to a boil over high heat. Reduce heat to low, cover, and simmer 20–25 minutes.

Nutrition per serving: 363 calories, 4.6 g fat, 47 g carbohydrates, 29 protein, 61 mg cholesterol, 4 g dietary fiber, 607 mg sodium
Exchanges: 2 starch, 3 vegetable, 2½ lean meat
Carb Choices: 3

Meat Entrées

Shopping List

Meat/Fish/Poultry	Packaged
1 lb. extra-lean ground beef	21-oz. pkg. cornflake crumbs

Frozen	
16-oz. pkg. frozen baby gold and white corn	**Seasonings/Spices**
16-oz. pkg. frozen pepper stir-fry	pepper

Canned
nonfat beef broth
2 14½-oz. cans petite-cut diced tomatoes with roasted garlic and sweet onion

The USDA recommends reheating meat to 165°F to make sure any bacteria is destroyed.

Barbecued Beef and Beans

Easy | **Do Ahead** | **Serves: 6**

- 1 lb. extra-lean ground beef
- 1 tbsp. onion powder
- 1 28-oz. can nonfat vegetarian baked beans, *drained*
- ½ cup ketchup
- 1 tbsp. Worcestershire sauce
- 2 tbsp. vinegar
- ⅛ tsp. red pepper flakes

Preheat oven to 350°. Spray 1½-quart casserole with cooking spray. Spray large nonstick skillet with cooking spray and heat over medium-high heat. Add ground beef and onion powder; cook, stirring frequently, until beef is browned and crumbled. Remove skillet from heat; add remaining ingredients and mix well. Pour mixture into casserole and bake 30–40 minutes until bubbly hot.

Nutrition per serving: 242 calories, 3.6 g fat, 34 g carbohydrates, 21 g protein, 41 mg cholesterol, 10 g dietary fiber, 750 mg sodium
Exchanges: 2 starch, 1½ lean meat
Carb Choices: 2

Shopping List

Meat/Fish/Poultry
1 lb. extra-lean ground beef

Canned
28-oz. can nonfat vegetarian baked beans

Condiments
ketchup
Worcestershire sauce
vinegar

Seasonings/Spices
onion powder
red pepper flakes

You can substitute bottled steak sauce for Worcestershire if you don't have the latter on hand.

Beef and Potato Tex-Mex Hash

Average | **Serves: 4**

1 lb. extra-lean ground beef

1 tbsp. onion powder

1 tbsp. nonfat beef broth

3 cups frozen Potatoes O'Brien

1 cup chunky-style salsa

2 tsp. Mexican seasoning

1½ cups nonfat shredded
    cheddar cheese

Shopping List

Meat/Fish/Poultry
1 lb. extra-lean ground beef

Dairy
6 oz. nonfat shredded
   cheddar cheese

Frozen
28-oz. pkg. frozen Potatoes
   O'Brien

Canned
nonfat beef broth

Condiments
8 oz. chunky-style salsa

Seasonings/Spices
onion powder
Mexican seasoning

Spray large nonstick skillet with cooking spray and heat over medium-high heat. Add ground beef and onion powder. Cook, stirring frequently, until beef is browned and crumbled. Remove beef and set aside. Respray skillet with cooking spray; add broth and heat over medium-high heat. Add potatoes; cook, stirring frequently, 8–10 minutes until lightly browned. Add salsa, Mexican seasoning, and ground beef to skillet; cook over medium heat 10–12 minutes until heated through. Sprinkle cheese over top; cover skillet and cook over medium-low heat until cheese is melted.

Nutrition per serving: 292 calories, 4.6 g fat, 21 g carbohydrates, 34 g protein, 61 mg cholesterol, 2 g dietary fiber, 861 mg sodium
Exchanges: 1 starch, 1 vegetable, 3½ lean meat
Carb Choices: 1

Meat
Entrées

Taking the time to plan meals cuts grocery spending by up to 50%, if you stick to your list. Impulse buying digs a big hole in your pocket!

Beef Stroganoff

Easy | Do Ahead | Serves: 4

1 lb. extra-lean ground beef

1 tbsp. onion powder

1 tbsp. nonfat beef broth

2 cups sliced mushrooms

1 tbsp. cornstarch

½ cup cold water

1 cup nonfat sour cream

8 oz. yolk-free egg
    noodles, *cooked
    and drained*

Shopping List

Produce
6 oz. sliced mushrooms

Meat/Fish/Poultry
1 lb. extra-lean ground beef

Dairy
8 oz. nonfat sour cream

Canned
nonfat beef broth

Packaged
8 oz. yolk-free egg noodles
cornstarch

Seasonings/Spices
onion powder

Spray large nonstick skillet with cooking spray and heat over medium-high heat. Add ground beef and onion powder; cook, stirring frequently, until beef is browned and crumbled. Drain beef, remove from skillet and set aside. Respray skillet with cooking spray. Add broth and heat over medium-high heat. Add mushrooms; cook, stirring frequently, until mushrooms are tender. Stir in cooked beef. Combine cornstarch and water in small bowl; mix until blended. Add cornstarch mixture to skillet and cook, stirring constantly, until mixture thickens. Reduce heat to low; gradually stir in sour cream, mixing well. Serve beef and mushroom mixture over cooked egg noodles. If desired, prepare beef mixture ahead of time, reheat in microwave or skillet, and serve over hot noodles.

Nutrition per serving: 416 calories, 5.2 g fat, 50 g carbohydrates, 35 g protein, 61 mg cholesterol, 4 g dietary fiber, 74 mg sodium
Exchanges: 2 starch, 1 vegetable, 3½ lean meat, 1 other carb
Carb Choices: 3

To assure that you get extra-lean ground beef, look for packages that give the percentages of the fat and choose ground beef that contains no more than 10% fat.

Spanish Rice with Ground Beef

Easy | Do Ahead | Serves: 4

1 lb. extra-lean ground beef

1½ tbsp. onion powder

2 tbsp. nonfat beef broth

1 6.8-oz. pkg. Spanish rice

2 cups water

1 16-oz. jar chunky-style salsa

Spray large nonstick skillet with cooking spray and heat over medium heat. Add ground beef and onion powder; cook, stirring frequently, until meat is browned and crumbled. Remove from skillet and set aside. Respray skillet with cooking spray; add broth and heat over medium-high heat. Add rice mix and cook, stirring frequently, until rice is golden brown. Add water, seasonings from rice package, and salsa. Reduce heat to low, cover, and cook 15–20 minutes. Stir in ground beef and heat through.

Nutrition per serving: 343 calories, 5 g fat, 44 g carbohydrates, 27 g protein, 61 mg cholesterol, 2 g dietary fiber, 1,360 mg sodium
Exchanges: 2½ starch, 3 lean meat
Carb Choices: 3

Meat
Entrées

Shopping List

Meat/Fish/Poultry
1 lb. extra-lean ground beef

Canned
nonfat beef broth

Packaged
6.8-oz. pkg. Spanish rice

Condiments
16-oz. jar chunky-style salsa

Seasonings/Spices
onion powder

Refrigerate hot foods within two hours of cooking; discard any food left at room temperature for more than two hours. Even a small amount of contaminated food can cause illness.

Chili Beef with Rice

Easy | **Do Ahead** | **Serves: 6**

1 lb. extra-lean ground beef

1½ tsp. Mrs. Dash seasoning

3 15-oz. cans vegetable garden 4-bean chili

1 cup nonfat shredded cheddar cheese

3 cups cooked rice

Spray large nonstick skillet with cooking spray and heat over medium-high heat. Add ground beef; sprinkle with Mrs. Dash seasoning. Cook, stirring frequently, until beef is browned and crumbled. Add chili; bring to a boil over high heat; reduce heat to low. Sprinkle cheese over top; cover, and cook over low heat about 5 minutes until cheese is melted. Serve chili-beef mixture over cooked rice.

Nutrition per serving: 429 calories, 4.1 g fat, 62 g carbohydrates, 31 g protein, 41 mg cholesterol, 7 g dietary fiber, 938 mg sodium
Exchanges: 4 starch, 2 lean meat
Carb Choices: 4

Shopping List

Meat/Fish/Poultry
1 lb. extra-lean ground beef

Dairy
6 oz. nonfat shredded cheddar cheese

Canned
3 15-oz. cans vegetable garden 4-bean chili

Packaged
rice

Seasonings/Spices
Mrs. Dash

Mrs. Dash seasoning is an excellent salt-free spice that comes in a variety of flavors and flavor blends.

Beef Ziti Bake

Easy | Do Ahead | Freeze | Serves: 6

1 lb. extra-lean ground beef

1 tbsp. onion powder

1 tbsp. dried sweet pepper flakes

1 14½-oz. can stewed tomatoes
   with bell pepper and onion,
   do not drain

1 8-oz. can tomato sauce

1 tsp. Italian seasoning

½ tsp. garlic powder

8 oz. ziti pasta, *cooked*
   and drained

2 cups nonfat shredded
   mozzarella cheese, *divided*

½ cup nonfat Parmesan cheese

Preheat oven to 350°. Spray 9×13-inch baking dish with cooking spray. Spray nonstick skillet with cooking spray and heat over medium-high heat. Add ground beef, onion powder, and pepper flakes. Cook, stirring frequently, until beef is browned and crumbled. Add stewed tomatoes, tomato sauce, Italian seasoning, and garlic powder; mix well. Add cooked ziti and 1 cup mozzarella cheese. Spoon mixture into baking dish; top with remaining mozzarella and Parmesan cheese. Bake 30–35 minutes until lightly browned and bubbly hot. Remove from oven and let stand 5–10 minutes before serving.

Nutrition per serving: 345 calories, 3.7 g fat, 37 g carbohydrates, 35 g protein, 41 mg cholesterol, 1 g dietary fiber, 670 mg sodium
Exchanges: 2 starch, 1 vegetable, 3 lean meat
Carb Choices: 2

Meat
Entrées

Shopping List

Dairy
8 oz. nonfat shredded
   mozzarella cheese
nonfat Parmesan cheese

Meat/Fish/Poultry
1 lb. extra-lean
   ground beef

Canned
14½-oz. can stewed
   tomatoes with bell
   pepper and onion
8-oz. can tomato sauce

Packaged
8-oz. pkg. ziti pasta

Seasonings/Spices
onion powder
dried sweet
   pepper flakes
Italian seasoning
garlic powder

For food safety, keep your refrigerator at a temperature of 41°F or less. Surveys show many households keep refrigerator temperatures above 50°F. While lower temperatures don't kill bacteria, they do keep it from multiplying.

Beef Tamale Skillet Meal

Easy | **Serves: 4**

1 lb. extra-lean ground beef

2 cups chunky-style salsa

1 11-oz. can Mexicorn, *drained*

6 white corn tortillas, cut into
   ½-inch strips

2 tbsp. water

1½ cups nonfat shredded
   cheddar cheese

Spray large nonstick skillet with cooking spray and heat over medium-high heat. Add ground beef and cook, stirring frequently, until beef is browned and crumbled. Add salsa, Mexicorn, tortilla strips, and water; toss to mix. Reduce heat to medium, cover, and cook 10–15 minutes. Sprinkle cheese over top, cover, and cook on medium-low heat until cheese is melted.

Nutrition per serving: 396 calories, 6.7 g fat, 42 g carbohydrates, 39 g protein, 61 mg cholesterol, 5 g dietary fiber, 1,377 mg sodium
Exchanges: 2 starch, 2 vegetable, 3½ lean meat
Carb Choices: 3

Shopping List

Meat/Fish/Poultry
1 lb. extra-lean ground beef

Dairy
6 oz. nonfat shredded cheddar cheese

Canned
11-oz. can Mexicorn

Packaged
8.5-oz. pkg. white corn tortillas

Condiments
16-oz. jar chunky-style salsa

Freeze ground meat in humidity-free wrapping to prevent meat from drying out and ice from forming. Always write the freezing date on the package; frozen raw ground meat keeps safely for two to three months.

Sloppy Joe Mix

Easy | **Do Ahead** | **Yields: 18 servings (3 tbsp. per 1 lb. meat)**

1 tbsp. onion powder

1 tbsp. dried sweet pepper flakes

1½ tsp. Mrs. Dash seasoning

1 tbsp. cornstarch

¾ tsp. garlic powder

¾ tsp. dry mustard

¾ tsp. celery seeds

¾ tsp. chili powder

Sloppy Joes

1 lb. extra-lean ground beef

3 tbsp. Sloppy Joe Mix (above)

1 cup seasoned diced tomato sauce for chili

½ cup water

For spice mix, combine all dry ingredients in zip-top bag; seal and shake to mix. Store at room temperature up to 3 months. To make Sloppy Joes, spray a large nonstick skillet with cooking spray; heat over medium-high heat. Add ground beef; cook, stirring frequently, until browned and crumbled. Add 3 tablespoons mix, 1 cup seasoned diced tomato sauce for chili, and ½ cup water. Bring to a boil over high heat; reduce heat to low and simmer 10–15 minutes. Serve over baked potatoes, low-fat buns, or stuffed in pita pockets.

Nutrition per serving: 118 calories, 3.2 g fat, 5 g carbohydrates, 15 g protein, 41 mg cholesterol, 1 g dietary fiber, 172 mg sodium
Exchanges: 1 vegetable, 2 lean meat
Carb Choices: 0

Meat Entrées

Shopping List

Meat/Fish/Poultry	Seasonings/Spices
1 lb. extra-lean ground beef	onion powder
	dried sweet pepper flakes
	Mrs. Dash
Canned	garlic powder
15-oz. can seasoned diced tomato sauce for chili	dry mustard
	celery seeds
	chili powder
Baking Goods	
cornstarch	

Want to change "meat and potatoes" night? Make it a vegetarian dinner by substituting cooked bulgur for the ground beef in your favorite recipes.

Beef 'n Oat Burgers

Easy | **Do Ahead** | **Freeze** | **Serves: 6**

1½ lbs. extra-lean ground beef

¼ cup quick-cooking oatmeal

¼ cup + 2 tbsp. chili sauce

1½ tsp. onion powder

2 tsp. Worcestershire sauce

Combine all ingredients in medium bowl and mix well. Shape into 6 patties. Preheat grill or broiler on high heat. If using broiler, line broiler pan with foil and spray with cooking spray. Cook burgers 7 minutes per side until browned and cooked through.

Nutrition per serving: 174 calories, 4.7 g fat, 7 g carbohydrates, 22 g protein, 61 mg cholesterol, <1 g dietary fiber, 219 mg sodium
Exchanges: 3 lean meat, ½ other carb
Carb Choices: 0

Shopping List

Meat/Fish/Poultry
1½ lbs. extra-lean ground beef

Packaged
quick-cooking oatmeal

Condiments
chili sauce
Worcestershire sauce

Seasonings/Spices
onion powder

Good news concerning the health claims you find on food labels: Manufacturers can include nutrient content and health claims only under certain circumstances, such as when the food contains appropriate levels of the stated nutrients. That means consumers can believe them.

Chili Dogs with Cheese

Easy | **Serves: 4**

4 97% fat-free beef franks

1 15-oz. can vegetable garden
   4-bean chili

¼ cup nonfat shredded
   cheddar cheese

Preheat broiler on high heat. Line baking sheet with foil and spray with cooking spray. Cut beef franks down center (not all the way through), open, and arrange on baking sheet. Broil 5–6 minutes. Turn franks over and broil until browned on both sides. While franks are cooking, pour chili into microwave-safe bowl; cook on High 2–3 minutes. Stir in cheese and heat 1–2 minutes until cheese is melted; stir to mix. Serve chili-cheese mixture over broiled franks.

Nutrition per serving: 147 calories, 1.9 g fat, 18 g carbohydrates, 12 g protein, 15 mg cholesterol, 3 g dietary fiber, 864 mg sodium
Exchanges: 1 starch, 2 very lean meat
Carb Choices: 1

Meat
Entrées

Shopping List

Meat/Fish/Poultry
12-oz pkg. 97% fat-free
   beef franks

Dairy
nonfat shredded
   cheddar cheese

Canned
15-oz. can vegetable garden
   4-bean chili

Not all vegetarian chilies are low calorie or low fat; some varieties pack 345 calories and 18 grams into each cup.

Honey Dijon Meat Loaf

Easy | **Do Ahead** | **Freeze** | **Serves: 6**

1½ lbs. extra-lean ground beef

⅓ cup seasoned breadcrumbs

1½ tbsp. onion powder

¼ tsp. pepper

½ cup egg substitute

1 tsp. basil herb blend

¼ cup honey

¼ cup Dijon mustard

Shopping List

Produce
basil herb blend

Dairy
4 oz. egg substitute

Meat/Fish/Poultry
1½ lbs. extra-lean ground beef

Packaged
seasoned breadcrumbs

Condiments
honey
Dijon mustard

Seasonings/Spices
onion powder
pepper

Preheat oven to 350°. Line baking sheet with foil and spray with cooking spray. Combine beef, breadcrumbs, onion powder, and pepper in medium bowl. Add egg substitute and basil herb blend; mix thoroughly and shape into loaf. Place loaf on baking sheet. Combine honey and mustard in small cup; mix until blended. Spread half the honey-mustard mixture on meat loaf; bake 30 minutes. Brush meat loaf with remaining honey-mustard sauce and bake 25–30 minutes until meat is cooked through.

Nutrition per serving: 252 calories, 5.8 g fat, 23 g carbohydrates, 24 g protein, 61 mg cholesterol, <1 g dietary fiber, 253 mg sodium
Exchanges: 3 lean meat, 1½ other carb
Carb Choices: 2

One teaspoon of basil herb blend (available in produce departments) is equivalent to 1 teaspoon of freshly chopped basil or ¼ teaspoon dried basil.

Barbecue Meat Loaf

Easy | **Do Ahead** | **Freeze** | **Serves: 6**

1½ lbs. extra-lean ground beef

¼ cup + 2 tbsp. egg substitute

¾ cup cornflake crumbs

1 tbsp. 1-Step Beef Seasoning

¾ cup barbecue sauce, *divided*

Preheat oven to 350°. Spray 9×5-inch loaf pan with cooking spray. Combine beef, egg substitute, cornflake crumbs, 1-Step Beef Seasoning, and ½ cup barbecue sauce in bowl; mix well. Press mixture into loaf pan; spread remaining barbecue sauce on top. Bake 45–50 minutes until meat loaf is cooked through and no longer pink.

Nutrition per serving: 218 calories, 5.1 g fat, 13 g carbohydrates, 24 g protein, 61 mg cholesterol, <1 g dietary fiber, 537 mg sodium
Exchanges: 3 lean meat, 1 other carb
Carb Choices: 1

Meat
Entrées

Shopping List

Meat/Fish/Poultry
1½ lbs. extra-lean ground beef

Dairy
egg substitute

Packaged
cornflake crumbs

Condiments
barbecue sauce

Seasonings/Spices
1-Step Beef Seasoning

Cut calories from meat loaf recipes by substituting grated potatoes or carrots for a small portion of the ground beef.

Cranberry Upside-Down Meat Loaf

Easy | **Do Ahead** | **Serves: 8**

¼ cup brown sugar

½ cup whole cranberry sauce

2 lb. extra-lean ground beef

¾ cup nonfat half and half

¾ cup seasoned breadcrumbs

½ cup egg substitute

1 tsp. onion powder

Preheat oven to 350°. Spray 9×5-inch loaf pan with cooking spray. Sprinkle sugar in bottom of loaf pan; mash cranberry sauce and spread over sugar. Combine beef, half and half, breadcrumbs, egg substitute, and onion powder in medium bowl; mix thoroughly and shape into loaf. Place in pan. Bake 50–60 minutes until meat is cooked through. Remove from oven and let stand 5–10 minutes; invert onto platter before serving. Spoon any sauce left in the pan onto meat loaf.

Nutrition per serving: 253 calories, 5 g fat, 24 g carbohydrates, 24 g protein, 61 mg cholesterol, 1 g dietary fiber, 45 mg sodium
Exchanges: 3 lean meat, 1½ other carb
Carb Choices: 2

Shopping List

Dairy
6 oz. nonfat half and half
4 oz. egg substitute

Meat/Fish/Poultry
2 lbs. extra-lean ground beef

Canned
16-oz. can whole cranberry sauce

Packaged
seasoned breadcrumbs

Baking Goods
brown sugar

Seasonings/Spices
onion powder

For this recipe you can substitute ¾ cup evaporated skim milk for half and half without affecting cooking results. While skim milk is acceptable, you may need to reduce the amount and add as needed until meat loaf mixture reaches desired consistency.

5-Minute Meat Loaf

Easy | **Do Ahead** | **Freeze** | **Serves: 8**

2 lbs. extra-lean ground beef

1 cup frozen seasoning vegetables, *thawed and drained*

1 tbsp. onion powder

1 cup cracker crumbs

1 cup nonfat sour cream

dash pepper

Preheat oven to 350°. Spray 9×5-inch loaf pan with cooking spray. Combine all ingredients in medium bowl and mix well. Press mixture into loaf pan. Bake 1¼–1½ hours. Let stand 5–10 minutes before removing from pan. Slice and serve or package and freeze to serve later.

Nutrition per serving: 227 calories, 5.7 g fat, 13 g carbohydrates, 25 g protein, 64 mg cholesterol, <1 g dietary fiber, 191 mg sodium
Exchanges: ½ starch, 1 vegetable, 3 lean meat
Carb Choices: 1

Meat Entrées

Shopping List

Dairy
8 oz. nonfat sour cream

Meat/Fish/Poultry
2 lbs. extra-lean ground beef

Frozen
10-oz. pkg. frozen seasoning vegetables

Packaged
cracker crumbs

Seasonings/Spices
onion powder
pepper

Save time chopping, slicing, and dicing with frozen prepared vegetables such as onions, green peppers, and seasoning vegetables (a blend of celery, onions, and green bell peppers).

Meat Loaf Parmesan

Easy | **Do Ahead** | **Freeze** | **Serves: 8**

2 lbs. extra-lean ground beef

¼ cup egg substitute

1¼ cups nonfat Parmesan cheese

¾ cup frozen diced onions, *thawed and drained*

¼ cup frozen diced green bell peppers, *thawed and drained*

1 cup matzo meal

¾ cup nonfat half and half

½ cup ketchup

2 tbsp. horseradish

2 tbsp. lemon juice

Preheat oven to 350°. Line baking sheet with foil and spray with cooking spray. Combine beef, egg substitute, cheese, onions, peppers, matzo meal, and half and half in medium bowl; mix thoroughly and shape into loaf. Place loaf on baking sheet; bake 45–50 minutes. Combine remaining ingredients and mix until creamy and smooth. Spread mixture over meat loaf; bake 15–20 minutes longer until meat is cooked through.

Nutrition per serving: 286 calories, 4.7 g fat, 28 g carbohydrates, 29 g protein, 61 mg cholesterol, 1 g dietary fiber, 336 mg sodium
Exchanges: 1 starch, 1 vegetable, 3 lean meat, ½ other carb
Carb Choices: 2

Shopping List

Dairy	Frozen
egg substitute	12-oz. pkg. frozen diced onions
6 oz. nonfat Parmesan cheese	10-oz. pkg. frozen diced green bell peppers
6 oz. nonfat half and half	
	Packaged
	matzo meal
Meat/Fish/Poultry	
2 lbs. extra-lean ground beef	**Condiments**
	ketchup
	horseradish
	bottled lemon juice

You can substitute cracker crumbs or dry breadcrumbs for matzo meal.

Canadian Bacon and Pineapple Pizza

Easy | **Do Ahead** | **Serves: 5**

1 large lahvosh cracker bread

1 cup nonfat pizza sauce

2 cups nonfat shredded mozzarella cheese

1 5-oz. pkg. Canadian-style bacon

2 16-oz. cans pineapple chunks in juice, *well drained*

Preheat oven to 450°. Line baking sheet or pizza pan with foil and spray with cooking spray. Place lahvosh cracker bread on pan and spread with thin layer of pizza sauce. Sprinkle cheese over sauce; arrange Canadian-style bacon and pineapple chunks on top; bake 12–15 minutes until cheese is melted and cracker bread is lightly browned.

Nutrition per serving: 246 calories, 1.1 g fat, 36 g carbohydrates, 22 g protein, 10 mg cholesterol, 3 g dietary fiber, 806 mg sodium
Exchanges: 1 starch, 1 vegetable, 1 fruit, 2 very lean meat
Carb Choices: 2

Meat Entrées

Shopping List

Meat/Fish/Poultry
5-oz. pkg. Canadian-style bacon

Dairy
8 oz. nonfat shredded mozzarella cheese

Canned
2 16-oz. cans pineapple chunks

Packaged
15¾-oz. pkg. lahvosh cracker bread (largest size)

Condiments
8 oz. nonfat pizza sauce

Canadian-style bacon is a much healthier alternative to regular slab bacon: A 2-ounce serving (four slices) has only 60 calories and 1.5 grams of fat.

Chapter Index

7 Chicken Suppers

Chinese Chicken Salad

Chicken is a lean, healthful meat that is low in calories and high in protein. No wonder it's such a favorite with dieters!

Whatever your health goals, keep in mind that no magic foods exist. The keys to a healthy diet are balance, variety, and moderation. A diet that includes whole grains, fruits, vegetables, meat, and dairy products is essential for good health and weight maintenance.

9 Tips for Healthful Eating

1. To maximize health be sure to eat five servings of vegetables, two to four servings of fruit, and at least three servings of whole grains every day.

2. Determine your ideal weight and focus on maintaining it. Fighting to weigh less than your ideal weight often leads to frustration and overeating. Focus on what you can control rather than trying to control the uncontrollable. You are responsible for the choices you make every day: food, physical activity, and stress-relief.

3. Watch your portions! It's all about control. Skip the supersize, value meals that pack on more calories and fat than you should eat in an entire day.

4. Eat regularly. Skipping meals actually leads to overeating; healthy snacking fills nutritional gaps and keeps hunger at bay.

5. Enjoy your favorite foods in moderation. Any food can fit into a balanced, moderated meal plan.

6. Seek balance rather than perfection. Let your food choices throughout the day guide your healthy eating plan. For instance, if you had a high-calorie, high-fat breakfast, lighten your next few meals. In the end, what really counts is how many calories you take in and how many you expend through physical activity.

7. Track your eating habits for several days to determine whether you overindulge on certain foods, skip meals in an effort to lose weight, or cheat yourself out of essential nutrients. Once you identify the weaknesses, you can make changes.

8. Be patient. Change takes time, but soon small changes will add up to large ones.

9. Get rid of the good food/bad food mind-set. Once you accept a lifestyle based on variety, balance, and moderation, unnecessary feelings of guilt disappear.

Chicken Suppers

Chicken and Vegetable Skillet Meal

Easy | **Serves: 4**

2 6-oz. pkgs. honey roasted
    chicken breast strips

1 16-oz. pkg. frozen broccoli,
    cauliflower, and carrots

2 tbsp. nonfat chicken broth

½ tsp. chili powder

3 tbsp. brown sugar

Combine all ingredients in a large saucepan. Cook over medium-high heat 5–7 minutes. Reduce heat to low, cover, and cook 15 minutes until vegetables are tender and heated through.

Nutrition per serving: 200 calories, 1.7 g fat, 22 g carbohydrates, 24 g protein, 50 mg cholesterol, 4 g dietary fiber, 567 mg sodium
Exchanges: 3 vegetable, 2 very lean meat, ½ other carb
Carb Choices: 1

Shopping List

Meat/Fish/Poultry
2 6-oz. pkgs. honey roasted
    chicken breast strips

Frozen
16-oz. pkg. frozen broccoli,
    cauliflower, and carrots

Canned
nonfat chicken broth

Baking Goods
brown sugar

Seasoning/Spices
chili powder

As an alternative to purchasing precooked chicken breast slices, grill or pan-fry in a nonstick skillet several boneless, skinless chicken breasts that have been seasoned as desired. Cool completely and wrap in plastic wrap; store in a zip-top bag in freezer for up to six months. You can store chicken whole or cut up, ready to add to stir-fries, soups, casseroles, salads, and more.

Chicken Provencal

Easy | Do Ahead | Serves: 6

1½ lbs. boneless, skinless
  chicken breasts

1 16-oz. pkg. frozen pepper
  stir-fry, *thawed and drained*

2 14½-oz. cans Italian-style
  stewed tomatoes,
  lightly drained

2 tsp. Italian seasoning

Preheat oven to 350°. Spray 9×13-inch baking dish with cooking spray. Place chicken in dish; top with remaining ingredients and mix lightly. Cover and bake 45–55 minutes until chicken is tender and cooked through.

Nutrition per serving: 169 calories, 1 g fat, 13 g carbohydrates, 24 g protein, 50 mg cholesterol, 2 g dietary fiber, 418 mg sodium
Exchanges: 2 vegetable, 3 very lean meat
Carb Choices: 1

Chicken
Suppers

Shopping List

Meat/Fish/Poultry
1 ½ lbs. boneless, skinless
  chicken breasts

Frozen
16-oz. pkg. frozen pepper
  stir-fry

Canned
2 14½-oz. cans Italian-style
  stewed tomatoes

Seasonings/Spices
Italian seasoning

Make your own Italian seasoning:

For every 2 tablespoons of Italian seasoning, combine 1 teaspoon each: oregano, marjoram, thyme, basil, rosemary, and sage.

Mediterranean Chicken Bake

Easy | Do Ahead | Serves: 6

1½ lbs. boneless, skinless chicken breasts

3 tbsp. lemon juice, *divided*

1½ tbsp. 1-Step Chicken Seasoning

6 oz. nonfat crumbled feta cheese

chopped fresh parsley (optional)

Preheat oven to 350°. Spray 9×13-inch baking dish with cooking spray. Arrange chicken breasts in dish; drizzle with 1½ tablespoons lemon juice and sprinkle with 1-Step Chicken Seasoning. Top with crumbled feta cheese and drizzle with remaining lemon juice. Bake 25–35 minutes until chicken is cooked through. Garnish with chopped parsley before serving, if desired.

Nutrition per serving: 152 calories, 1 g fat, 4 g carbohydrates, 28 g protein, 50 mg cholesterol, 0 g dietary fiber, 656 mg sodium
Exchanges: 4 very lean meat
Carb Choices: 0

Shopping List

Meat/Fish/Poultry
1½ lbs. boneless, skinless chicken breasts

Dairy
6 oz. nonfat crumbled feta cheese

Condiments
bottled lemon juice

Seasonings/Spices
1-Step Chicken Seasoning

Optional
fresh parsley

Uncooked frozen chicken thaws quickly in the microwave; for best results follow microwave manufacturer's directions.

Sweet and Spicy Chicken with Rice

Easy | Serves: 4

2–3 tbsp. nonfat chicken broth

1 lb. boneless, skinless chicken breast tenders, *cut in half*

2 tbsp. Mexican seasoning

1 16-oz. jar chunky-style salsa with corn and beans

¾ cup apricot preserves

2 cups hot cooked rice

Spray nonstick skillet with cooking spray; add chicken broth and heat over medium-high heat. Add chicken breasts; sprinkle with Mexican seasoning. Cook, stirring frequently, until chicken is cooked through. Combine salsa and apricot preserves in medium bowl; mix well. Pour mixture over chicken; bring to a boil over medium-high heat. Reduce heat to low, cover, and simmer 5–6 minutes until heated through. Serve chicken over cooked rice.

Nutrition per serving: 451 calories, 0.7 g fat, 79 g carbohydrates, 29 g protein, 57 mg cholesterol, 2 g dietary fiber, 1,180 mg sodium
Exchanges: 2½ starch, 1 vegetable, 3 very lean meat, 2 other carb
Carb Choices: 5

Chicken Suppers

Shopping List

Meat/Fish/Poultry
1 lb. boneless, skinless chicken breast tenders

Canned
14-oz. can nonfat chicken broth

Packaged
rice

Condiments
16-oz. jar chunky style salsa with corn and beans
6 oz. apricot preserves

Seasonings/Spices
Mexican seasoning

When purchasing packaged uncooked chicken, select packages with very little or no liquid in the bottom; always avoid torn or leaking packages.

One-Dish Chicken and Vegetable Bake

Easy | Do Ahead | Serves: 6

1 16-oz. pkg. frozen broccoli, cauliflower, and carrots, *thawed and drained*

3 6-oz. pkgs. honey roasted chicken breast strips, *cubed*

1 10¾-oz. can condensed 98% fat-free cream of chicken soup, *undiluted*

1 cup nonfat sour cream

¾ cup nonfat shredded mozzarella cheese

Preheat oven to 375°. Spray 9×13-inch baking dish with cooking spray. Place vegetables and chicken in dish; toss gently to mix. Combine soup and sour cream in small bowl; mix until creamy. Pour soup mixture over vegetables and chicken and toss lightly to coat. Bake 10 minutes; sprinkle with cheese and bake 10–15 minutes until casserole is bubbly hot and cheese is melted.

Nutrition per serving: 229 calories, 2.4 g fat, 17 g carbohydrates, 32 g protein, 51 mg cholesterol, 3 g dietary fiber, 856 mg sodium
Exchanges: 2 vegetable, 4 very lean meat, 1 other carb
Carb Choices: 1

Shopping List

Meat/Fish/Poultry
3 6-oz. pkgs. honey roasted chicken breast strips

Dairy
8 oz. nonfat sour cream
nonfat shredded mozzarella cheese

Frozen
16-oz. pkg. frozen broccoli, cauliflower, and carrots

Canned
10-oz. can condensed 98% fat-free cream of chicken soup

Variation: Substitute your favorite variety pack of frozen vegetables.

Swiss Cheese Chicken

Easy | **Do Ahead** | **Serves: 4**

1 lb. boneless, skinless chicken breasts

¼ cup Shake 'n Bake Italian coating mix

1 15-oz. can seasoned tomato sauce for lasagna

4 oz. nonfat Swiss cheese slices

Preheat oven to 400°. Line baking sheet with foil and spray with cooking spray. Arrange chicken on baking sheet; sprinkle with Italian coating mix. Bake 20 minutes; pour sauce over top and bake 10 minutes. Arrange cheese slices on top; broil on high until cheese is melted.

Nutrition per serving: 206 calories, 1.4 g fat, 13 g carbohydrates, 28 g protein, 63 mg cholesterol, 2 g dietary fiber, 1,597 mg sodium
Exchanges: 1 vegetable, 4 very lean meat, ½ other carb
Carb Choices: 1

Chicken
Suppers

Shopping List

Meat/Fish/Poultry
1 lb. boneless, skinless chicken breasts

Dairy
4 oz. nonfat Swiss cheese slices

Canned
15-oz. can seasoned tomato sauce for lasagna

Packaged
5.75-oz. box Shake 'n Bake Italian coating mix

A chicken's skin color is a result of the type of feed the chicken eats and not a measure of nutritional value, flavor, tenderness, or fat content.

Teriyaki Chicken with a Twist

Easy | **Do Ahead** | **Serves: 4**

1 lb. boneless, skinless chicken breasts

¼ cup Dijon mustard

¼ cup sweet teriyaki sauce

¼ cup Tomato 'n Bacon Parmesano salad topping

3 tbsp. nonfat Parmesan cheese

Preheat oven to 400°. Line baking sheet with foil and spray with cooking spray. Arrange chicken breasts in single layer on baking sheet; brush chicken on both sides with mustard; pour teriyaki sauce over top and turn to coat. Sprinkle chicken with Tomato 'n Bacon Parmesano salad topping and Parmesan cheese. Bake 25–30 minutes until lightly browned and cooked through.

Nutrition per serving: 212 calories, 3.5 g fat, 17 g carbohydrates, 25 g protein, 50 mg cholesterol, 1 g dietary fiber, 1,156 mg sodium
Exchanges: 3 very lean meat, 1 other carb
Carb Choices: 1

Shopping List

Meat/Fish/Poultry
1 lb. boneless, skinless chicken breasts

Dairy
nonfat Parmesan cheese

Packaged
5-oz. pkg. Tomato 'n Bacon Parmesano salad topping

Condiments
Dijon mustard
17-oz. bottle sweet teriyaki sauce

The average American eats more than 80 pounds of chicken each year.

2-Step Italian Chicken

Easy | **Do Ahead** | **Serves: 4**

1 lb. boneless, skinless
   chicken breasts

1 cup nonfat Creamy Italian or
   Caesar salad dressing

¼ cup nonfat Parmesan cheese

Preheat oven to 375°. Spray shallow baking dish with cooking spray. Arrange chicken breasts in dish; pour salad dressing over top and sprinkle with Parmesan cheese. Bake 20–25 minutes until chicken is completely cooked through.

Nutrition per serving: 1,651 calories, 1 g fat, 10 g carbohydrates, 24 g protein, 50 mg cholesterol, 0 g dietary fiber, 827 mg sodium
Exchanges: 3 very lean meat, ½ other carb
Carb Choices: 1

Chicken
Suppers

Shopping List

Meat/Fish/Poultry
1 lb. boneless, skinless
   chicken breasts

Dairy
nonfat Parmesan cheese

Condiments
8 oz. nonfat Italian or
   Caesar salad dressing

When determining how much chicken to purchase, count on ¼ pound boneless, skinless chicken breast per person. If the meat comes on the bone, increase to ½ pound.

Chicken Broccoli Pie

Easy | **Do Ahead** | **Serves: 4**

1 10¾-oz. can condensed 98% fat-free cream of chicken soup

¼ cup skim milk

2 cups cooked rice

1½ cups frozen chopped broccoli, *thawed and drained*

2 6-oz. pkgs. honey roasted chicken breast strips, *cubed*

pepper to taste

¼ cup seasoned breadcrumbs

½ cup nonfat shredded cheddar cheese

Preheat oven to 400°. Spray 9-inch pie plate with cooking spray. Combine soup and milk in small bowl; mix well. Press cooked rice into bottom and sides of pie plate. Top with broccoli and chicken; season with pepper. Pour soup mixture over top. Combine breadcrumbs and cheddar cheese in zip-top bag and shake to mix. Sprinkle cheese mixture on top and bake 20–25 minutes until bubbly hot and golden brown.

Nutrition per serving: 377 calories, 3.4 g fat, 57 g carbohydrates, 33 g protein, 51 mg cholesterol, 5 g dietary fiber, 1,012 mg sodium
Exchanges: 3 starch, 1 vegetable, 3 very lean meat
Carb Choices: 3

Shopping List

Dairy	Canned
skim milk	10¾-oz. can condensed
nonfat shredded cheddar	98% fat-free cream of
cheese	chicken soup

Meat/Fish/Poultry	Packaged
2 6-oz. pkgs. honey	rice
roasted chicken breast	seasoned bread crumbs
strips	
	Seasonings/Spices
Frozen	pepper
16-oz. pkg. frozen	
chopped broccoli	

Do not substitute long grain rice for Minute Rice. Minute Rice is a precooked long grain rice, which means it cooks very quickly and absorbs all the flavors. Minute Rice is ideal for one-dish skillet dinners or casseroles.

Chicken Enchilada Stuffed Potatoes

Easy | Do Ahead | Serves: 4

4 large baking potatoes
  (each about 4 oz.)

1 16-oz. pkg. frozen broccoli,
  corn, and red peppers

1 14½-oz. can diced tomatoes
  with green chiles, *not drained*

2 6-oz. pkgs. Southwestern
  chicken breast strips

1 1.5-oz. packet enchilada
  sauce dry mix

1 cup nonfat shredded
  cheddar cheese

salsa (optional)

Preheat oven to 450°. Prick baking potatoes with fork in several places. Microwave on High for 8–9 minutes per potato. Place in oven and bake 15–20 minutes. While potatoes are cooking, spray large nonstick skillet with cooking spray and heat over medium heat. Add broccoli mixture and cook, stirring frequently, just until vegetables are thawed. Add tomatoes and chicken; sprinkle with enchilada sauce dry mix and toss to coat. Bring to a boil over medium-high heat. Reduce heat to medium, cover, and cook 5–7 minutes until heated through. Line baking sheet with foil and spray with cooking spray. Split potatoes open and lightly mash pulp; top each potato with broccoli-tomato-chicken mixture. Sprinkle ¼ cup cheese on top. Bake in 450° oven for 8–10 minutes until cheese is melted and lightly browned. Serve with salsa, if desired.

Chicken Suppers

Shopping List

Produce
4 large baking potatoes

Meat/Fish/Poultry
2 6-oz. pkgs. Southwestern
  chicken breast strips

Frozen
16-oz. pkg. frozen broccoli,
  corn, and red peppers

Canned
14½-oz. can diced
  tomatoes with green
  chiles

Seasonings/Spices
1.5-oz. packet enchilada
  sauce dry mix

Dairy
nonfat shredded cheddar
  cheese

Optional
salsa

Nutrition per serving: 467 calories, 2.8 g fat, 73 g carbohydrates, 31 g protein, 60 mg cholesterol, 9 g dietary fiber, 2,099 mg sodium
Exchanges: 3 starch, 3 vegetable, 3 very lean meat, 1 other carb
Carb Choices: 5

You can substitute any variety of cooked chicken pieces and season as desired, or make your own with boneless, skinless chicken breasts or tenderloins.

Honey Mustard Baked Chicken Tenderloins

Easy | **Do Ahead** | **Freeze** | **Serves: 4**

1¼ lbs. boneless, skinless chicken breast tenderloins

1 tsp. honey

¼ cup Dijon mustard

¾ tsp. lemon juice

½ cup cornflake crumbs

1 tsp. garlic powder

nonfat Honey-Dijon salad dressing or dip (optional)

Preheat broiler on High heat. Line broiler pan with foil and spray with cooking spray. Arrange chicken tenderloins in a single layer on broiler pan. Combine honey, mustard, and lemon juice in small bowl; mix until creamy and smooth. Brush mixture over chicken tenderloins. Broil 7–8 minutes. Combine cornflake crumbs and garlic powder in zip-top bag; shake to mix. Remove chicken from oven; sprinkle cornflake mixture over chicken (do not turn chicken). Spray the chicken lightly with cooking spray and broil 1–2 minutes until lightly browned and cooked through. Serve with nonfat Honey-Dijon salad dressing or dip, if desired.

Nutrition per serving: 229 calories, 2 g fat, 20 g carbohydrates, 33 g protein, 71 mg cholesterol, 0 g dietary fiber, 585 mg sodium
Exchanges: ½ starch, 4 very lean meat, 1 other carb
Carb Choices: 1

Shopping List

Meat/Fish/Poultry
1¼ lbs. boneless, skinless chicken breast tenderloins

Packaged
21-oz. pkg. cornflake crumbs

Seasonings/Spice
garlic powder

Condiments
honey
Dijon mustard
bottled lemon juice

Optional
nonfat Honey-Dijon salad dressing or dip

For best flavor and food safety, tightly wrap and refrigerate cooked poultry for only one to two days.

Hot Chicken Salad Burritos with Roasted Onion and Garlic Sauce

Easy | Do Ahead | Serves: 6

3 6-oz. pkgs. Southwestern chicken breast strips

1¼ cups nonfat shredded cheddar cheese, *divided*

¾ cup shredded carrots

¼ cup sweet roasted onion and garlic sauce

1 tbsp. onion powder

½ cup nonfat mayonnaise

1 tbsp. diced green chiles

6 98% fat-free flour tortillas

salsa (optional)

Preheat oven to 350°. Spray shallow baking dish with cooking spray. Combine chicken strips, 1 cup cheese, and carrots in medium bowl. Combine roasted onion and garlic sauce, onion powder, mayonnaise, and green chiles; mix well. Add to chicken mixture and toss until coated. Divide filling among tortillas; roll up and place seam sides down in baking dish. Sprinkle remaining cheese on top. Bake 8–10 minutes until cheese is melted and tortillas are lightly browned. Serve with salsa, if desired.

Nutrition per serving: 240 calories, 2 g fat, 33 g carbohydrates, 33 g protein, 50 mg cholesterol, 2 g dietary fiber, 1,306 mg sodium
Exchanges: 1 starch, 4 very lean meat, 1 other carb
Carb Choices: 2

Chicken Suppers

Shopping List

Produce
8-oz. pkg. shredded carrots

Meat/Fish/Poultry
3 6-oz. pkgs. Southwestern chicken breast strips

Dairy
6-oz. pkg. nonfat shredded cheddar cheese

Packaged
17.5-oz. pkg. 98% fat-free flour tortillas

Canned
4-oz. can diced green chiles

Condiments
14-oz. jar sweet roasted onion and garlic sauce
nonfat mayonnaise

Seasonings/Spices
onion powder

Optional
salsa

The following herbs
partner well with poultry: basil, bay leaf, caraway, coriander, cumin, dill, lemon balm, marjoram, mint, rosemary, and tarragon.

Chili Bean and Bacon Pizza

Easy | Do Ahead | Serves: 5

8   slices low-fat turkey bacon,
    cooked and crumbled

2   16-oz. cans chili beans,
    not drained

1   cup frozen diced onions,
    thawed and drained

1   large lahvosh cracker bread

2½ cups nonfat cheddar cheese

Preheat oven to 400°. Line baking sheet with foil and spray with cooking spray. Arrange bacon slices on sheet and bake 8–12 minutes until browned and crisp. Crumble cooked bacon when cool. Combine crumbled bacon, chili beans, and onions in medium bowl; mix well. Spread bacon-bean mixture over cracker bread. Top with cheese. Bake 12–15 minutes until cheese is melted and cracker bread is lightly browned.

Nutrition per serving: 280 calories, 1.4 g fat, 34 g carbohydrates, 30 g protein, 24 mg cholesterol, 0 g dietary fiber, 1,535 mg sodium
Exchanges: 2 starch, 1 vegetable, 3 very lean meat
Carb Choices: 2

Shopping List

Dairy
10 oz. nonfat shredded cheddar
    cheese

Meat/Fish/Poultry
12-oz. pkg. low-fat turkey bacon

Frozen
12-oz. pkg. frozen diced onions

Canned
2 16-oz. cans chili beans

Packaged
15¾-oz. pkg. lahvosh cracker
    bread

Turkey bacon provides a healthful savings: three slices of regular cooked bacon contains 109 calories and 10 grams of fat (90% of calories from fat!).

p. 175 Sweet and Spicy Chicken with Rice

Chicken Provencal p. 173

p. 177 Swiss Cheese Chicken

Chicken Broccoli Pie p. 180

Honey Mustard Baked Chicken Tenderloins p. 182

Chicken Enchilada Stuffed Potatoes p. 181

Chinese Chicken Salad

Easy | **Do Ahead** | **Serves: 6**

1 8-oz. pkg. shredded cabbage

1 8-oz. pkg. shredded lettuce

1 8-oz. pkg. stringless sugar
   snap peas

1 cup canned sliced water
   chestnuts, *drained*

½ cup diced bell pepper

3 6-oz. pkgs. honey roasted
   chicken breast strips

¾ cup nonfat French or Catalina
   salad dressing

2 tbsp. slivered almonds
   (optional)

Combine all ingredients except salad dressing and optional almonds in large bowl and toss to mix. Cover and refrigerate 1–2 hours. Pour salad dressing over top and toss to mix. Garnish with almonds, if desired.

Nutrition per serving: 209 calories, 1.6 g fat, 20 g carbohydrates, 24 g protein, 50 mg cholesterol, 1 g dietary fiber, 648 mg sodium
Exchanges: 3 vegetable, 3 very lean meat, ½ other carb
Carb Choices: 1

To retain juices and keep chicken from drying out when cooking, turn chicken with tongs instead of a fork.

Chicken
Suppers

Shopping List

Produce
8-oz. pkg. shredded
   cabbage
8-oz. pkg. shredded
   lettuce
8-oz. pkg. stringless
   sugar snap peas
7 oz. pkg. diced bell peppers

Meat/Fish/Poultry
3 6-oz. pkgs. honey
   roasted chicken
   breast strips

Canned
8-oz. can sliced water
   chestnuts

Condiments
nonfat French or
   Catalina salad dressing

Optional
slivered almonds

Chapter Index

8 Fish Dinners

Fish and Vegetable Packet Meal

The average American eats only 15 pounds of fish and shellfish a year, compared to a whopping 165 pounds of beef, chicken, and pork. Experts advise families to eat fish at least once a week to reap its low-fat, high-protein benefits. Here are some cooking tips.

1. Many different kinds of fish taste delicious cooked the same way, with only minor allowances for thickness.

2. Fish is best cooked quickly with high heat.

3. Cook fish at 450°F for 10 minutes per inch thickness, turning the fish halfway through cooking time.

4. Add 5 minutes if you are cooking fish in foil or sauce.

5. Double the cooking time (20 minutes per inch) for frozen fish if you haven't defrosted it.

6. Fish is done when it flakes easily with a fork and loses its translucent or raw appearance.

Best Cooking Methods for Fish Fillets, Steaks, Stuffed or Whole

Cooking Method	Best for...
Baking	Whole, whole stuffed, fillets, stuffed fillets, steaks, fish chunks
Broiling	Steaks, whole fish, split whole fish, fillets
Grilling	Steaks (i.e., salmon, halibut, swordfish, tuna)
Microwaving	Flat or rolled fillets
Pan-Frying	Fillets or breaded fillets
Poaching	Whole fish, fillets, or steaks
Sear-Roasting	Thick steaks
Steaming	Whole fish, chunks, steaks, stuffed fillets
Stir-Frying	Fish pieces or chunks usually cooked with vegetables

Fish Dinners

Parmesan-Coated Fish Fillets

Easy | Do Ahead | Serves: 4

½ cup egg substitute

2 tbsp. lemon juice

¾ cup cornflake crumbs

¼ cup Parmesan cheese

1 tsp. garlic powder

2 tsp. dried parsley flakes

1 lb. halibut or orange roughy fillets, ¼–½ inch thick

Preheat oven to 350°. Line baking sheet with foil and spray with cooking spray. Combine egg substitute and lemon juice in bowl; mix well. Combine cornflake crumbs, Parmesan cheese, garlic powder, and parsley flakes in shallow dish; mix well. Dip fillets in egg mixture; roll in crumb mixture to coat. Arrange fish in single layer on baking sheet; spray lightly with cooking spray. Bake 10–15 minutes until coating is lightly browned and fish flakes easily with a fork.

Nutrition per serving: 173 calories, 0.8 g fat, 16 g carbohydrates, 23 g protein, 23 mg cholesterol, 0 g dietary fiber, 388 mg sodium
Exchanges: 1 starch, 3 very lean meat
Carb Choices: 1

Shopping List

Meat/Fish/Poultry
1 lb. halibut or orange roughy fillets

Dairy
4 oz. egg substitute
nonfat Parmesan cheese

Packaged
cornflake crumbs

Condiments
bottled lemon juice

Seasonings/Spices
garlic powder
dried parsley flakes

Avoid buying fish that smells "fishy." It should have a subtle smell associated with the water it came from.

Baked Halibut with Citrus Cilantro Sauce

Easy | **Do Ahead** | **Serves: 4**

1 lb. halibut steaks

1½ tsp. onion powder

½ tsp. garlic powder

½ cup citrus grill marinade
  with orange juice

2 tbsp. chopped fresh cilantro

Spray shallow baking dish with cooking spray. Place halibut in dish; sprinkle with onion and garlic powders. Pour marinade over fish and turn to coat. Cover and refrigerate 30 minutes. Preheat oven to 400°. Cover baking dish with foil and bake 15 minutes; remove foil and bake 5 10 minutes until fish flakes easily with a fork. Garnish with fresh chopped cilantro and serve.

Nutrition per serving: 178 calories, 2.6 g fat, 9 g carbohydrates, 24 g protein, 36 mg cholesterol, 0 g dietary fiber, 313 mg sodium
Exchanges: 3 very lean meat, ½ other carb
Carb Choices: 1

Fish
Dinners

Shopping List

Produce
fresh cilantro

Meat/Fish/Poultry
1 lb. halibut steaks

Condiments
16 oz. bottle citrus grill
  marinade with orange juice

Seasonings/Spices
onion powder
garlic powder

Three good reasons to eat fish regularly:
It may reduce the risk of heart disease, lower blood pressure, and help improve certain inflammatory conditions such as arthritis.

Red Snapper with Tequila Lime Marinade

Easy | **Serves: 6**

1½ lbs. red snapper fillets

1 cup tequila lime with lime juice marinade, *divided*

2 tbsp. chopped fresh parsley

lime wedges for garnish (optional)

Place fillets in shallow dish; pour ¾ cup marinade over top. Cover and refrigerate 30 minutes. Preheat broiler on High heat. Line broiler pan or baking sheet with foil and spray with cooking spray. Arrange fillets on baking sheet; brush with remaining marinade and broil 6–8 minutes until fish flakes easily with a fork. Sprinkle with fresh parsley and, if desired, garnish with lime wedges.

Nutrition per serving: 181 calories, 1.5 g fat, 11 g carbohydrates, 23 g protein, 42 mg cholesterol, 0 g dietary fiber, 499 mg sodium
Exchanges: 3 very lean meat, 1 other carb
Carb Choices: 1

Shopping List

Produce
fresh parsley

Meat/Fish/Poultry
1½ lbs. red snapper fillets

Condiments
tequila lime with lime juice marinade

Optional
lime

Fish steaks and fillets lend themselves well to broiling. For fish that's 1 inch thick or less, place broiler pan 2 to 4 inches from heat source; for thicker pieces, place pan 5 to 6 inches from heat source. Follow the 10-minute cooking rule (10 minutes for every inch of thickness) and turn fish after half the total cooking time.

Fish and Vegetable Packet Meal

Easy | Do Ahead | Serves: 4

1 lb. cod, flounder, or sole fillets

1 16-oz. pkg. frozen broccoli stir-fry, *thawed and drained*

1 tsp. celery seeds

pepper

¼ cup nonfat chicken broth

Preheat oven to 450°. Cut four 12-inch square pieces of heavy-duty foil and spray with cooking spray. Place fish fillets on sprayed side of foil; divide stir-fry vegetables and spoon on top of fish. Sprinkle with celery seeds and pepper; drizzle 1 tablespoon broth over top of each. Fold sides of foil and wrap tightly to seal. Place packets on baking sheet and bake 20–25 minutes until fish flakes easily with a fork and vegetables are tender.

Nutrition per serving: 122 calories, 0.8 g fat, 5 g carbohydrates, 23 g protein, 41 mg cholesterol, 1 g dietary fiber, 152 mg sodium
Exchanges: 1 vegetable, 3 very lean meat
Carb Choices: 0

Fish Dinners

Shopping List

Meat/Fish/Poultry
1 lb. cod, flounder, or sole fish fillets

Frozen
16-oz. pkg. frozen broccoli stir-fry

Canned
nonfat chicken broth

Seasonings/Spices
dried celery seeds
pepper

Cod, a flaky white fish with a mild, sweet flavor, is often used in chowders and stews. A 4½-ounce serving has merely 134 calories and 1 gram of fat.

Salmon with Orange Glaze

Easy | Serves: 4

¼ cup orange marmalade

¼ cup light soy sauce

2 tsp. white wine vinegar

¼ tsp. garlic powder

¼ tsp. ground ginger

⅛ tsp. cayenne pepper

1 lb. salmon fillets

Combine all ingredients except salmon in zip-top bag and mix well. Place salmon in bag and toss lightly until coated. Seal bag and refrigerate 15–20 minutes. Preheat broiler on High heat. Line broiler pan with foil and spray with cooking spray. Remove salmon from marinade and place on pan. Brush with marinade and broil 7 minutes; turn salmon over, brush with marinade, and broil 5–6 minutes until fish flakes easily with a fork.

Nutrition per serving: 197 calories, 3.9 g fat, 16 g carbohydrates, 24 g protein, 59 mg cholesterol, <1 g dietary fiber, 678 mg sodium
Exchanges: 3 lean meat, 1 other carb
Carb Choices: 1

Shopping List

Meat/Fish/Poultry
1 lb. salmon fillets

Condiments
orange marmalade
light soy sauce
white wine vinegar

Seasonings/Spices
garlic powder
ground ginger
cayenne pepper

The most popular and widely available salmon is farm-raised Atlantic salmon. While wild Atlantic salmon is virtually extinct, wild Pacific salmon is still available.

Parmesan Halibut with Vegetables

Easy | **Serves: 4**

1 lb. halibut fillets

1 16-oz. pkg. frozen broccoli, cauliflower, and carrots

1 tsp. lemon-pepper seasoning

½ cup tomato sauce

½ cup water

¼ cup nonfat Parmesan cheese

Preheat oven to 400°. Line baking sheet with foil and spray with cooking spray. Arrange fish fillets on baking sheet; top with vegetables and sprinkle with lemon-pepper seasoning. Combine tomato sauce and water in small cup; mix well. Pour sauce over fish and sprinkle with Parmesan cheese. Bake 15–20 minutes until fish flakes easily with a fork.

Nutrition per serving: 178 calories, 2.8 g fat, 10 g carbohydrates, 28 g protein, 36 mg cholesterol, 4 g dietary fiber, 326 mg sodium
Exchanges: 2 vegetable, 4 very lean meat
Carb Choices: 1

Fish Dinners

Shopping List

Meat/Fish/Poultry
1 lb. halibut fillets

Frozen
16-oz. pkg. frozen broccoli, cauliflower, and carrots

Dairy
nonfat Parmesan cheese

Canned
8-oz. can tomato sauce

Seasonings/Spices
lemon-pepper seasoning

Flaky, milky-white halibut is best prepared with subtle flavors that don't overwhelm its delicate taste and texture.

Tilapia with Melon Salsa

Easy | **Do Ahead** | **Serves: 4**

2 cups diced cantaloupe

2 cups diced honeydew melon

1 cup diced mango

¼ cup diced green chiles

½ cup bottled lime juice

½ cup rice vinegar

½ cup minced fresh cilantro

1 lb. tilapia fillets

¼ cup 30-Minute Lemon-Pepper Marinade for Chicken, Meat, or Fish

Combine cantaloupe, honeydew melon, mango, green chiles, lime juice, rice vinegar, and cilantro in medium bowl; toss until well mixed. Cover and refrigerate 1–2 hours. Place tilapia fillets in shallow dish; pour marinade over top, cover, and refrigerate 30–45 minutes. Preheat broiler on High heat. Line broiler pan with foil and spray with cooking spray. Arrange tilapia on foil; broil 8 minutes until fish flakes easily with a fork. Serve melon salsa with fish.

Nutrition per serving: 205 calories, 1.7 g fat, 32 g carbohydrates, 22 g protein, 49 mg cholesterol, 3 g dietary fiber, 616 mg sodium
Exchanges: 2 fruit, 3 very lean meat
Carb Choices: 2

Shopping List

Produce

2-lb. cantaloupe (or packaged diced cantaloupe)

2-lb. honeydew melon (or packaged diced honeydew melon)

1 mango

fresh cilantro

Meat/Fish/Poultry

1 lb. tilapia fillets

Canned

4-oz. can diced green chiles

Condiments

30-Minute Lemon-Pepper Marinade for Chicken, Meat, or Fish

bottled lime juice

rice vinegar

Tilapia is a favorite even with those who claim not to like fish. Similar to cod, tilapia has a firm texture and mild flavor.

Swordfish with Orange-Soy Sauce

Easy | **Serves: 4**

1 lb. swordfish steaks

1 cup light soy sauce

1 cup orange juice

¼ cup finely chopped
    orange peel

2 tbsp. cornstarch

Line broiler pan with foil and spray with cooking spray. Arrange swordfish on foil; broil 10–14 minutes until fish flakes easily with a fork, turning once. Combine soy sauce, orange juice, and orange peel in small saucepan; bring to a low boil over medium heat. Reduce heat to low and cook 5 minutes. Remove 2 tablespoons sauce and place in small cup; add cornstarch and mix until blended. Return mixture to saucepan and cook, stirring constantly, until thickened and heated through. Serve sauce over swordfish fillets.

Nutrition per serving: 219 calories, 4.6 g fat, 16 g carbohydrates, 29 g protein, 44 mg cholesterol, 1 g dietary fiber, 2,215 mg sodium
Exchanges: 1 fruit, 4 very lean meat
Carb Choices: 1

Fish
Dinners

Shopping List

Produce
orange

Meat/Fish/Poultry
1 lb. swordfish fillets

Refrigerated
8 oz. orange juice

Baking Goods
cornstarch

Condiments
8 oz. light soy sauce

Although swordfish became an endangered species in the early 1990s, the market is slowly recovering. Usually sold as "steaks," swordfish is known for its mild flavor and meaty texture.

Snappy Snapper Packet

Easy | Do Ahead | Serves: 4

1 lb. red snapper fillets

½ tsp. garlic powder

⅓ cup chunky-style salsa

¾ tsp. bottled lime juice

Preheat oven to 350°. Line baking sheet with foil and spray with cooking spray. Arrange fillets on foil; sprinkle with garlic powder. Spoon salsa over top and drizzle with lime juice. Wrap foil around fillets, fold seam to seal, and bake 15–20 minutes until fish flakes easily with a fork.

Nutrition per serving: 120 calories, 1.5 g fat, 1 g carbohydrates, 23 g protein, 42 mg cholesterol, <1 g dietary fiber, 177 mg sodium
Exchanges: ½ vegetable, 3 very lean meat
Carb Choices: 0

Shopping List

Meat/Fish/Poultry
1 lb. red snapper fillets

Condiments
chunky-style salsa
bottled lime juice

Seasonings/Spices
garlic powder

Within the large snapper family, the American red snapper is a favorite among people due to its pronounced sweet flavor. Although other snapper varieties may not be quite as sweet as American snapper, they can be easily substituted.

Sweet and Sour Fish Fillets

Easy | Do Ahead | Serves: 4

1 cup frozen pepper stir-fry

1 10-oz. pkg. frozen sugar snap peas

1 cup sweet and sour sauce

1 lb. orange roughy or flounder fillets

Spray large nonstick skillet with cooking spray and heat over medium-high heat. Add pepper stir-fry and sugar snap peas; cook, stirring frequently, until vegetables are crisp-tender. Remove from skillet; set aside and wrap with foil to keep warm. Respray skillet with cooking spray; add sweet and sour sauce. Cook over medium heat just until mixture begins to bubble. Place fish fillets in sauce, spooning sauce over top to cover. Cover skillet and cook 5–7 minutes until fish flakes easily with a fork. Serve sweet and sour fillets over vegetables; spoon sauce from skillet over top.

Nutrition per serving: 192 calories, 0.8 g fat, 20 g carbohydrates, 19 g protein, 23 mg cholesterol, <1 g dietary fiber, 276 mg sodium
Exchanges: 1 vegetable, 3 very lean meat, 1 other carb
Carb Choices: 1

Fish Dinners

Shopping List

Meat/Fish/Poultry

1 lb. orange roughy or flounder fillets

Frozen

16-oz. pkg. frozen pepper stir-fry
10-oz. pkg. frozen sugar snap peas

Condiments

8-oz. bottle sweet and sour sauce (or seasoning packet prepared according to directions)

Flounder is a flaky white fish that needs very little to enhance its delicate flavor.

Fish-Fry with Ratatouille

Easy | **Serves: 4**

1½ lbs. mahi-mahi or swordfish fillets, *cut into 1-inch chunks*

2 tbsp. nonfat vegetable or chicken broth

1½ tsp. bottled minced garlic

1 16-oz. pkg. frozen pepper stir-fry

2 14½-oz. cans stewed tomatoes with bell pepper and onion, *lightly drained*

Spray large nonstick skillet with cooking spray; add fish chunks and cook, stirring frequently, 3–4 minutes. Remove from skillet and set aside. Add broth to skillet and heat over medium-high heat. Add garlic, pepper stir-fry, and tomatoes; bring to a boil over high heat. Reduce heat to low and simmer, stirring occasionally, until vegetables are tender. Stir in cooked fish and toss to mix; heat through 2–3 minutes and serve.

Nutrition per serving: 240 calories, 1.8 g fat, 22 g carbohydrates, 35 g protein, 122 mg cholesterol, 3 g dietary fiber, 721 mg sodium
Exchanges: 4 vegetable, 4 very lean meat
Carb Choices: 1

Shopping List

Meat/Fish/Poultry
1½ lbs. mahi-mahi or swordfish fillets

Frozen
16-oz. pkg. frozen pepper stir-fry

Canned
2 14½-oz. cans stewed tomatoes with bell pepper and onion
nonfat vegetable or chicken broth

Seasonings/Spices
minced garlic

Mahi-mahi, originally called dophinfish (though not related to the dolphin), goes well with fruity or spicy sauces. Highly versatile, it's great grilled, broiled, pan-fried, or braised.

Sesame-Soy Ahi Tuna

Easy | Serves: 6

1½ lbs. ahi tuna steaks

½ cup Honey Soy Marinade for seafood, *divided*

2 tbsp. sesame seeds

Preheat broiler on High heat. Line broiler pan with foil and spray with cooking spray. Arrange tuna steaks on pan; brush with ¼ cup of the marinade. Broil 3–4 minutes; turn steaks over, brush with remaining marinade, sprinkle with sesame seeds, and broil 3–4 minutes until rare to medium-rare (or to desired doneness).

Nutrition per serving: 180 calories, 2.5 g fat, 10 g carbohydrates, 27g protein, 51 mg cholesterol, <1 g dietary fiber, 562 mg sodium
Exchanges: 4 very lean meat, ½ other carb
Carb Choices: 1

Fish Dinners

Shopping List

Meat/Fish/Poultry
1½ lbs. ahi tuna steaks

Condiments
9.6-oz. bottle Honey Soy Marinade for seafood

Seasonings/Spices
sesame seeds

Ideal for grilling or searing, tuna is best when seared on the outside and almost raw on the inside. If overcooked, tuna steaks become dry, tough, and chewy.

Broiled Salmon-Stuffed Tomatoes

Easy | **Do Ahead** | **Serves: 6**

3 large tomatoes

2 7.1-oz. pouches premium skinless and boneless pink salmon

¼ cup diced celery

3 tbsp. nonfat mayonnaise

1½ tsp. Dijon mustard

¼ cup + 2 tbsp. nonfat Parmesan cheese

Preheat broiler on High heat. Line baking sheet with foil and spray with cooking spray. Cut tomatoes in half and scoop out pulp, leaving a ½-inch shell. Combine salmon, celery, mayonnaise, and mustard in medium bowl; mix well. Fill tomato shells with salmon mixture; sprinkle each with 1 tablespoon Parmesan cheese. Broil 3–4 minutes until bubbly hot and lightly browned.

Nutrition per serving: 137 calories, 4.4 g fat, 8 g carbohydrates, 16 g protein, 37 mg cholesterol, 1 g dietary fiber, 501 mg sodium
Exchanges: 1 vegetable, 2 lean meat
Carb Choices: 1

Shopping List

Produce
3 large tomatoes
celery

Dairy
nonfat Parmesan cheese

Packaged
2 7.1-oz. pouches premium skinless and boneless pink salmon

Condiments
nonfat mayonnaise
Dijon mustard

For best results for Broiled Salmon-Stuffed Tomatoes, place the baking sheet 5–6 inches away from the heat source when broiling.

Seafood Kabobs

Easy | Do Ahead | Serves: 4

2 zucchini, *cut into ¼-inch rounds*

2 cups cherry tomatoes

½ lb. large sea scallops

½ lb. ahi tuna, *cut into 1-inch chunks*

½ lb. large uncooked shrimp, *peeled and deveined*

1 cup lemon-pepper marinade with lemon juice, *divided*

Shopping List

Produce
2 zucchini
1 pint cherry tomatoes

Meat/Fish/Poultry
½ lb. large sea scallops
½ lb. ahi tuna
½ lb. large shrimp, peeled and deveined

Condiments
lemon-pepper marinade with lemon juice

Combine zucchini, tomatoes, scallops, tuna, and shrimp in 9×13-inch baking dish. Pour ¾ cup marinade over top and turn to coat. Cover dish and refrigerate 30 minutes. Preheat broiler on High heat. Line broiler or baking sheet with foil and spray with cooking spray. Drain seafood, zucchini, and tomatoes, discarding marinade. Alternately thread metal skewers with seafood, zucchini, and tomatoes. Brush kabobs with 2 tablespoons of the remaining marinade; broil 2–3 minutes. Turn kabobs over, brush with remaining marinade, and broil 2–3 minutes until shrimp are pink, scallops are white, and ahi tuna is cooked to taste.

Nutrition per serving: 270 calories, 2.7 g fat, 22 g carbohydrates, 37 g protein, 132 mg cholesterol, 3 g dietary fiber, 1,739 mg sodium
Exchanges: 1 vegetable, 5 very lean meat, 1 other carb
Carb Choices: 1

Fish Dinners

Purchasing fish fillets or steaks is the easiest and best way to buy fish. Check for freshness: Fish flesh should feel firm and should spring back when you touch it.

Shrimp Creole

Easy | **Serves: 6**

2 tbsp. nonfat chicken broth

1 16-oz. pkg. frozen pepper stir-fry

½ cup frozen seasoning vegetables

1 28-oz. can diced tomatoes, *drained*

1 cup frozen peas, *thawed and drained*

1½ lbs. cooked baby shrimp, *peeled and deveined*

1 tsp. chili powder

4 strips extra-lean turkey bacon, *cooked and crumbled*

3 cups hot cooked rice

Spray large nonstick skillet or Dutch oven with cooking spray. Add chicken broth and heat over medium-high heat. Add frozen pepper stir-fry and seasoning vegetables; cook, stirring occasionally, until vegetables are thawed. Add diced tomatoes; bring to a boil over high heat. Reduce heat to low and simmer 5–10 minutes until slightly thickened. Add peas, shrimp, and chili powder; cook, stirring frequently, 5–10 minutes until heated through. Fold in crumbled bacon and serve with cooked rice.

Nutrition per serving: 297 calories, 2 g fat, 42 g carbohydrates, 26 g protein, 184 mg cholesterol, 4 g dietary fiber, 534 mg sodium
Exchanges: 2 starch, 3 vegetable, 2 very lean meat
Carb Choices: 3

Shopping List

Meat/Fish/Poultry	Canned
1½ lbs. cooked baby shrimp	28-oz. can diced tomatoes
1.25-lb. pkg. extra-lean turkey bacon	nonfat chicken broth
	Packaged
	rice
Frozen	
16-oz. pkg. frozen pepper stir-fry	**Seasonings/Spices**
10-oz. pkg. frozen seasoning vegetables	chili powder
10-oz. pkg. frozen peas	

Frozen seasoning vegetables are a "must-have" for every freezer; this mixture of onions, celery, and bell peppers is an easy, flavorful addition to almost any dish.

Shrimp Stir-Fry

Easy | **Serves: 4**

1 tbsp. nonfat vegetable broth

1 16-oz. pkg. frozen sugar snap stir-fry

1 cup sweet and spicy stir-fry seasoning

¾ lb. uncooked medium shrimp, *peeled and deveined (thaw if frozen)*

1 8-oz. can pineapple chunks in juice, *well drained*

2 cups cooked rice

Spray large nonstick skillet with cooking spray; add broth and heat over medium-high heat. Add stir-fry vegetables; cook, stirring frequently, 3–4 minutes until tender. Add stir-fry seasonings and shrimp; cook 3–4 minutes until shrimp are pink and cooked through. Stir in pineapple; heat through. Serve over cooked rice.

Nutrition per serving: 401 calories, 1.7 g fat, 67 g carbohydrates, 23 g protein, 131 mg cholesterol, 4 g dietary fiber, 1,076 mg sodium
Exchanges: 2 starch, 1 vegetable, 1 fruit, 3 very lean meat, 1 other carb
Carb Choices: 4½

Fish Dinners

Shopping List

Meat/Fish/Poultry
¾ lb. medium shrimp

Frozen
16-oz. pkg. frozen sugar snap stir-fry

Canned
14-oz. can nonfat vegetable broth
8-oz. can pineapple chunks in juice

Packaged
rice

Condiments
16-oz. bottle sweet and spicy stir-fry seasoning

Sugar snap stir-fry is a bag of frozen vegetables that includes sugar snap peas, carrots, onions, and mushrooms.

Honey Dijon Fish Kabobs

1   16-oz. pkg. precooked
    roasted onion potato
    cubes

2   small zucchini,
    sliced ¾–1 inch thick

1   lb. halibut fillets, *cut into
    1¼–1½-inch pieces*

¾   cup Dijon and honey
    marinade with lemon juice

Preheat broiler on High heat. Line broiler pan with foil and spray with cooking spray. Alternately thread potato cubes, zucchini, and fish on metal skewers and place in single layer on pan. Brush kabobs generously with marinade on both sides. Broil 5–6 inches from heat for 3 minutes, brushing several times with marinade; discard any remaining marinade. Broil 5–9 minutes longer until fish flakes easily with a fork and vegetables are tender.

Nutrition per serving: 252 calories, 2.6 g fat, 28 g carbohydrates, 27 g protein, 36 mg cholesterol, 4 g dietary fiber, 299 mg sodium
Exchanges: 1½ starch, 2 vegetable, 2 very lean meat
Carb Choices: 2

Shopping List

Produce
16-oz. pkg. precooked roasted
   onion potato cubes
2 small zucchini

Meat/Fish/Poultry
1 lb. halibut fillets

Condiments
Dijon and honey marinade
   with lemon juice

Save the fish department for one of your last stops at the grocery store. For best results take fish directly home and refrigerate immediately. Freeze or cook it within 24 hours. Keep the fish as cold as possible by storing it in the coldest part of your refrigerator.

Shrimp, Pineapple, and Mushroom Pita Pizzas

Easy | **Do Ahead** | **Serves: 4**

4 whole pita breads

3 cups nonfat shredded
   mozzarella cheese

1 6-oz. can crabmeat,
   drained and flaked

1 6-oz. can baby shrimp,
   drained

½ cup canned crushed
   pineapple in juice, *drained*

1 cup sliced mushrooms

½ cup diced bell peppers

Preheat oven to 450°. Line baking sheet(s) with foil and spray with cooking spray. Arrange pitas in a single layer on baking sheet(s). Top each pita with ¾ cup cheese. Arrange crabmeat, shrimp, pineapple, mushrooms, and peppers on top and bake 10–12 minutes until cheese is melted and pitas are lightly browned.

Nutrition per serving: 353 calories, 1.5 g fat, 28 g carbohydrates, 50 g protein, 126 mg cholesterol, 1 g dietary fiber, 1,105 mg sodium
Exchanges: 1 starch, 1 vegetable, ½ fruit, 6 very lean meat
Carb Choices: 2

Fish Dinners

Shopping List

Produce
bell pepper
8 oz. sliced mushrooms

Dairy
12 oz. nonfat shredded
   mozzarella cheese

Canned
6-oz. can crabmeat
6 oz. can baby shrimp
8-oz. can crushed pineapple
   in juice

Packaged
pita bread

You can make this pizza on the crust of your choice: low-fat flour tortillas, baked pizza shells (e.g., Boboli), lahvosh cracker bread, or thawed frozen bread dough.

Fish Tacos

1 tbsp. + 1 cup nonfat chicken or vegetable broth, *divided*

½ cup frozen diced onions

1 tsp. crushed garlic

2 14½-oz. cans petite-cut diced tomatoes with green chiles, *well drained*

½ tsp. ground cumin

1½ lbs. halibut fillets

1½ tsp. bottled lime juice

6 98% fat-free flour tortillas

Spray large nonstick skillet with cooking spray; add 1 tablespoon broth and heat over medium-high heat. Add onions and garlic; cook, stirring frequently, until tender. Add drained tomatoes, remaining broth, and cumin; bring to a boil over high heat. Reduce heat to low. Add halibut; sprinkle with lime juice. Cook over low heat 15–20 minutes until fish flakes easily with a fork. Remove fish; cut into bite-size pieces. Return fish to skillet and mix with other ingredients. Wrap tortillas in paper towels and microwave on High 30–45 seconds per tortilla. Spread fish mixture down center of each tortilla, roll up, and serve immediately.

Nutrition per serving: 273 calories, 3.3 g fat, 30 g carbohydrates, 29 g protein, 36 mg cholesterol, 2 g dietary fiber, 1,091 mg sodium
Exchanges: 1 starch, 3 vegetable, 3 very lean meat
Carb Choices: 2

Shopping List

Meat/Fish/Poultry
1½ lbs. halibut fillets

Frozen
12-oz. pkg. frozen diced onions

Canned
2 14½-oz. cans petite-cut diced tomatoes with green chiles
14-oz. can nonfat chicken or vegetable broth

Packaged
17.5-oz. pkg. 98% fat-free flour tortillas

Condiments
bottled lime juice

Seasonings/Spices
ground cumin
crushed garlic

A raw 6-ounce fish fillet or steak usually yields about a 4½-ounce serving when cooked.

Tuna Stuffed Tomatoes

Easy | Do Ahead | Serves: 4

2 7.1-oz. pouches
  chunk light tuna

2 cups Salad Confetti (or a
  combination of chopped
  carrots, broccoli, radishes,
  cauliflower, and celery)

2 cups cooked rice

2 tbsp. nonfat mayonnaise

2 tsp. honey Dijon mustard

4 large beefsteak tomatoes,
  tops removed and seeded

Combine tuna, Salad Confetti, and rice in medium bowl; toss to mix. Combine mayonnaise and mustard in small cup and blend well. Add to tuna mixture and toss to mix. Fill tomato cups with tuna mixture and serve.

Nutrition per serving: 335 calories, 1.2 g fat, 43 g carbohydrates, 34 g protein, 18 mg cholesterol, 3 g dietary fiber, 838 mg sodium
Exchanges: 1½ starch, 3 vegetable, 4 very lean meat
Carb Choices: 3

Fish
Dinners

Shopping List

Produce
2 7-oz. containers Salad Confetti
4 large beefsteak tomatoes

Packaged
2 7.1-oz. pouches
  chunk light tuna
rice

Condiments
nonfat mayonnaise
honey Dijon mustard

Choosing cans or pouches of sealed light tuna packed in water instead of oil-packed tuna saves 61 calories and 5.4 grams of fat per 2-ounce serving.

Chapter Index

9 Meatless Meals

4-Bean Chili-Stuffed Potatoes

Even meat lovers can enjoy and benefit from meatless meals. Designate one or two nights a week for dinners that include a variety of flavorful, nutritious fruits and vegetables. You may decide to go meatless more often.

Are you ready to make the move? Selecting meatless meals once or twice a week can be beneficial to your health. The goal is to make gradual changes to your diet that are not only nutritionally sound but include foods you enjoy. Meatless meals include a wide variety of foods: whole grains, legumes, vegetables, fruits, nuts, and seeds. Trying out new foods can provide nutritional benefits and enhance your eating enjoyment.

Meatless meals, as well as any other types of meals, should focus on aspects that promote healthy eating. Here are some guidelines to keep in mind.

- Choose a variety of foods.

- Consider healthful foods to include rather than foods to avoid.

- Stop worrying about protein intake. Grains, beans, vegetables, and nuts all provide protein. As long as you eat a varied diet with sufficient calories, you will meet daily protein needs.

- Watch the fat! Claims of health benefits do not mean a food is fat-, sugar-, or cholesterol-free.

Meatless Meals

9 Perfectly Good Reasons
to Include More Meatless Meals in Your Menu Plan

A diet rich in fruits and vegetables plays a key role in reducing the risk or incidence of...

1. **major causes** of illness and death.

2. **gastrointestinal and smoking-related cancers** including lung, colon, stomach, mouth, larynx, esophagus, and bladder.

3. **heart disease.** Increasing intake of beans, peas, oats, and barley, rich in soluble fiber, can help lower blood cholesterol. Folic acid, found in fruits and vegetables, lowers blood levels of homocysteine; these foods are also rich sources of phytochemicals that protect the heart.

4. **stroke.**

5. **diverticulosis and constipation.**

6. **macular degeneration.**

7. **neural tube birth defects.**

8. **diabetes.**

9. **foodborne illness.**

Baked Orzo with Vegetables and Beans

Easy | Do Ahead | Serves: 6

¾ cup egg substitute

2 tbsp. cracker crumbs

1½ tbsp. nonfat Parmesan cheese

1 14½-oz. can diced tomatoes with garlic and onions, *drained*

1 10-oz. pkg. frozen chopped broccoli or spinach, *thawed and drained*

1 15-oz. can garbanzo beans, *rinsed and drained*

4 cups cooked orzo pasta

Preheat oven to 350°. Spray 3-quart casserole with cooking spray. Combine all ingredients in casserole and mix well. Bake, uncovered, 25–30 minutes until golden brown and bubbly hot.

Nutrition per serving: 256 calories, 1.4 g fat, 48 g carbohydrates, 13 g protein, <1 mg cholesterol, 3 g dietary fiber, 431 mg sodium
Exchanges: 2 starch, 4 vegetable
Carb Choices: 3

Shopping List

Dairy
6 oz. egg substitute
nonfat Parmesan cheese

Frozen
10-oz. pkg. frozen chopped broccoli or spinach

Canned
14½-oz. can diced tomatoes with garlic and onions
15-oz. can garbanzo beans

Packaged
cracker crumbs
8-oz. pkg. orzo pasta

The word "vegetarian" came about in 1847, created by the Vegetarian Society of the United Kingdom. Vegetarian practices, however, trace back to ancient Hindu teaching and figures like the Greek mathematician and philosopher Pythagoras.

Stovetop "Sausage" Lasagna

Easy | Serves: 6

1 14-oz. pkg. Gimme Lean sausage-style

1 10-oz. pkg. frozen diced green bell peppers

½ cup diced frozen onions

1 4-oz. can sliced mushrooms, *drained*

2½ cups water

6 oz. uncooked mini lasagna noodles

¾ tsp. Italian seasoning

1 26-oz. jar nonfat pasta sauce (any variety)

1½ cups nonfat shredded mozzarella cheese

2 tbsp. nonfat Parmesan cheese

Spray Dutch oven with cooking spray and heat over medium-high heat. Add "sausage," bell peppers, onions, and mushrooms; cook, stirring frequently, until "sausage" is crumbled and vegetables are tender. Add water, noodles, Italian seasoning, and pasta sauce; bring to a boil over high heat. Reduce heat to medium-low and cook 10–15 minutes until lasagna noodles are tender. Sprinkle cheeses over top and toss lightly to mix. Heat until mozzarella cheese begins to melt.

Nutrition per serving: 284 calories, 1.2 g fat, 39 g carbohydrates, 25 g protein, 0 mg cholesterol, 3 g dietary fiber, 991 mg sodium
Exchanges: 1 starch, 4 vegetable, 3 very lean meat
Carb Choices: 3

Meatless Meals

Low-fat cooking is easy when you use high-quality nonstick cookware. Use it and you won't need to add oil or fat to stove-top cooking.

Shopping List

Meat/Fish/Poultry	Canned
14-oz. pkg. Gimme Lean sausage-style	4-oz. can sliced mushrooms
	Packaged
Dairy	6-oz. pkg. mini lasagna noodles
6 oz. nonfat shredded mozzarella cheese	
nonfat Parmesan cheese	**Condiments**
	26-oz. jar nonfat pasta sauce (any variety)
Frozen	
10-oz. pkg. frozen diced green bell peppers	**Seasonings/Spice**
12-oz. pkg. frozen diced onions	Italian seasoning

Cheese Enchilada Casserole

Easy | **Serves: 6**

2 cups nonfat enchilada sauce

12 low-fat white corn tortillas

2 cups frozen chopped broccoli,
thawed and well drained

1 cup frozen diced onions,
thawed and drained

2 cups frozen chopped spinach,
thawed and drained

1 11-oz. can Mexicorn, *drained*

2½ cups nonfat shredded
cheddar cheese

Preheat oven to 350°. Spray 9×13-inch baking dish with cooking spray. Spread ½ cup enchilada sauce in dish; arrange half the tortillas (overlapping, if necessary) on top of sauce. Top with half of the remaining enchilada sauce. Combine broccoli, onions, spinach, and Mexicorn in medium bowl; spread vegetable mixture on tortillas; top with 1¼ cups cheese. Place remaining tortillas on top and spread with remaining enchilada sauce. Sprinkle remaining cheese on top. Bake 25–30 minutes until browned and heated through. Remove from oven and let stand 5 minutes before serving.

Nutrition per serving: 320 calories, 0.7 g fat, 57 g carbohydrates, 23 g protein, 0 mg cholesterol, 10 g dietary fiber, 1,138 mg sodium
Exchanges: 2½ starch, 3 vegetable, 1 very lean meat
Carb Choices: 4

Shopping List

Dairy
6 oz. nonfat shredded
cheddar cheese

Frozen
16-oz. pkg. frozen chopped
broccoli
12-oz. pkg. frozen diced
onions
16-oz. pkg. frozen chopped
spinach

Canned
11-oz. can Mexicorn

Packaged
8.5-oz. pkg. low-fat white
corn tortillas

Condiments
16- to 17.5-oz. can or jar
nonfat enchilada sauce

Don't equate meatless meals with protein-deficient meals. If you choose the right combination of foods, they will provide all the nutrients you need!

Layered Eggplant Parmesan

1½ lbs. eggplant,
cut into ½-inch slices

1 tsp. onion powder

1½ tsp. garlic powder

2 cups nonfat pasta sauce

¼ cup nonfat Parmesan cheese

1½ cups nonfat shredded
mozzarella cheese

Preheat broiler on High heat. Line baking sheet with foil and arrange eggplant slices in single layer; sprinkle with onion and garlic powders and spray lightly with cooking spray. Broil 4–5 minutes per side until lightly browned. Turn oven to 350°. Spray 9×13-inch baking dish with cooking spray. Arrange half the eggplant slices in bottom of dish; top with 1 cup pasta sauce, 2 tablespoons Parmesan cheese, and ¾ cup mozzarella cheese; repeat layers. Bake 25–30 minutes until cheese is melted and casserole is bubbly hot. Let stand 3–5 minutes before serving.

Nutrition per serving: 111 calories, 0.2 g fat, 14 g carbohydrates, 12 g protein, 0 mg cholesterol, 0 g dietary fiber, 468 mg sodium
Exchanges: 3 vegetable, 1 very lean meat
Carb Choices: 1

Meatless
Meals

Shopping List

Produce
1½ lbs. eggplant

Dairy
nonfat Parmesan cheese
6 oz. nonfat shredded
mozzarella cheese

Condiments
16-oz. jar or can nonfat
pasta sauce

Seasonings/Spice
onion powder
garlic powder

This is a wonderful low-fat alternative to fat-laden meat lasagna.

Vegetable Pie

Easy | Do Ahead | Serves: 6

1   16-oz. pkg. frozen broccoli,
    cauliflower, and carrots,
    thawed and drained

½   cup frozen diced onions,
    thawed and drained

3   cups nonfat shredded cheddar
    cheese, *divided*

1⅓ cup skim milk

¾   cup Garden Vegetable Egg
    Beaters

¾   cup reduced-fat baking mix

1   tsp. Mrs. Dash seasoning

Preheat oven to 400°. Spray 10-inch pie plate with cooking spray. Combine broccoli, cauliflower, carrots, onions, and 2 cups cheese in pie plate and carefully toss to mix. Combine milk, Egg Beaters, baking mix, and Mrs. Dash seasoning in medium bowl; beat with electric mixer until blended and smooth. Pour mixture over vegetables and cheese. Bake 25–35 minutes until knife inserted in center comes out clean. Remove from oven; top with remaining cheese and bake 3–5 minutes until cheese is melted and lightly browned.

Nutrition per serving: 224 calories, 0.4 g fat, 32 g carbohydrates, 24 g protein, 1 mg cholesterol, 2 g dietary fiber, 958 mg sodium
Exchanges: 1 starch, 3 vegetable, 2 very lean meat
Carb Choices: 2

Shopping List

Dairy
12 oz. nonfat shredded
    cheddar cheese
16 oz. skim milk
8 oz. Garden Vegetable
    Egg Beaters

Frozen
16-oz. pkg. frozen broccoli,
    cauliflower, and carrots
12-oz. pkg. frozen diced onions

Packaged
2 lb. 8-oz. pkg. reduced-fat
    baking mix

Seasonings/Spice
Mrs. Dash seasoning

Variation: Substitute different vegetable combinations and substitute nonfat mozzarella for part or all of the cheese.

Bean and Corn Tacos **p. 240**

4-Bean Chili-Stuffed Potatoes p. 235

p. 241 Mexican Pizza

Cheese Enchilada Casserole p. 222

p. 238 2-Step Vegetarian Tostadas

Garden Vegetable Frittata with Potatoes p. 234

Vegetarian Chili Skillet Meal

Easy | Serves: 4

1 tbsp. nonfat vegetable broth

½ cup frozen diced onions

1 16-oz. pkg. frozen broccoli, cauliflower, and carrots

1 8-oz. can low-sodium tomato sauce

1 tsp. chili powder

½ tsp. sugar

⅛ tsp. red pepper flakes

1 16-oz. can chili beans, *drained*

1¼ cups nonfat shredded cheddar cheese

2 cups cooked couscous

Spray large nonstick skillet with cooking spray; add broth and heat over medium-high heat. Add onions and frozen vegetables; cook, stirring frequently, 7–8 minutes until vegetables are tender. Add tomato sauce, chili powder, sugar, and red pepper flakes. Bring to a boil over high heat; reduce heat to low and simmer 8–10 minutes. Add beans; heat 5 minutes. Sprinkle cheese over top, toss lightly, and cook 2–3 minutes until cheese is melted. Serve over cooked couscous.

Nutrition per serving: 326 calories, 1.3 g fat, 68 g carbohydrates, 21 g protein, 0 mg cholesterol, 15 g dietary fiber, 848 mg sodium
Exchanges: 3 starch, 3 vegetable, ½ very lean meat
Carb Choices: 5

Meatless Meals

Shopping List

Dairy
nonfat shredded cheddar cheese

Frozen
16-oz. pkg. frozen broccoli, cauliflower, and carrots
12-oz. pkg. frozen chopped onions

Canned
8-oz. can low-sodium tomato sauce
16-oz. can chili beans
nonfat vegetable broth

Packaged
couscous
sugar

Seasonings/Spice
chili powder
red pepper flakes

Dried herbs and spices
lose their flavor and potency after about a year. It's best to buy them in the smallest possible amounts and store them in tightly closed bottles in a cool, dry place out of direct light.

Garden Vegetable Frittata with Potatoes

Easy | **Serves: 4**

1 tbsp. nonfat vegetable broth

1½ cups frozen pepper stir-fry,
   thawed and drained

1 cup shredded potatoes (*if frozen, thawed and drained*)

1 cup frozen chopped spinach,
   thawed and drained

1 tsp. Italian seasoning

1 cup Garden Vegetable
   Egg Beaters

1 tbsp. nonfat cottage cheese

½ cup nonfat shredded
   cheddar cheese (optional)

Spray large nonstick skillet with cooking spray. Add broth and heat over medium-high heat. Add pepper stir-fry, potatoes, spinach, and Italian seasoning; cook, stirring frequently, until potatoes are lightly browned and vegetables are crisp-tender. Beat Egg Beaters and cottage cheese with electric mixer until frothy and blended; pour egg mixture over vegetables. Cover skillet and cook until eggs are completely set; lift eggs with spatula several times while cooking to let uncooked portion run underneath. Sprinkle with cheddar cheese, if desired; cover skillet and cook over medium until cheese is melted.

Nutrition per serving: 91 calories, 0.1 g fat, 14 g carbohydrates, 9 g protein, 0 mg cholesterol, 2 g dietary fiber, 243 mg sodium
Exchanges: ½ starch, 1 vegetable, 1 very lean meat
Carb Choices: 1

Shopping List

Produce
18-oz. pkg. shredded potatoes
   (or frozen shredded
   potatoes)

Dairy
8 oz. Garden Vegetable
   Egg Beaters
nonfat cottage cheese

Frozen
16-oz. pkg. frozen pepper
   stir-fry
10-oz. pkg. frozen chopped
   spinach

Canned
nonfat vegetable broth

Seasonings/Spice
Italian seasoning

Optional
nonfat shredded cheddar
   cheese

Learn to read and use nutrition labels correctly so you can make healthier choices. When you're in the habit of reading labels, you can make sure calories, fat, and cholesterol levels fit within your limits.

4-Bean Chili-Stuffed Potatoes

Easy | **Serves: 2**

2 large baking potatoes
(each about 4 oz.)

1 15-oz. can vegetable garden
4 bean chili

¼ cup chopped green onions

1 cup nonfat shredded cheddar
cheese

nonfat sour cream (optional)

Pierce potatoes in several places with a fork. Microwave on High for 9 minutes per potato. Preheat oven to 450°. Place potatoes in oven 10–15 minutes. Remove from oven and cool 5 minutes. Cut potatoes in half lengthwise, but do not cut all the way through. Fluff potato pulp with a fork, keeping it in shell. Top potatoes with chili, green onions, and cheese. Bake 10–12 minutes until cheese is melted and lightly browned. Carnish with nonfat sour cream, if desired.

Nutrition per serving: 482 calories, 1.1 g fat, 87 g carbohydrates, 29 g protein, 0 mg cholesterol, 12 g dietary fiber, 1,321 mg sodium
Exchanges: 5½ starch, 1 very lean meat
Carb Choices: 6

Meatless
Meals

Shopping List

Produce
2 large baking potatoes
green onions

Dairy
4 oz. nonfat shredded
cheddar cheese

Canned
15-oz. can vegetable garden
4-bean chili

Optional
nonfat sour cream

Potatoes and lettuce are the two most popular fresh vegetables in the United States.

Vegetarian Fajitas

Easy | **Serves: 4**

1   16-oz. pkg. frozen pepper
    stir-fry

1   11-oz. can Mexicorn, *drained*

1   14½-oz. can petite-cut diced
    tomatoes with green chiles,
    well drained

4   98% fat-free flour tortillas

    nonfat sour cream and/or

    salsa (optional)

Spray large nonstick skillet with cooking spray and heat over medium heat. Add pepper stir-fry and cook, stirring frequently, until vegetables are softened. Add Mexicorn and tomatoes; cook over medium heat until completely heated through. Wrap tortillas in paper towels and microwave on High for 15–30 seconds per tortilla until warmed. Spoon fajita mixture down center of tortillas; roll and serve with nonfat sour cream and/or salsa, if desired.

Nutrition per serving: 228 calories, 1 g fat, 49 g carbohydrates, 8 g protein, 0 mg cholesterol, 5 g dietary fiber, 1,029 mg sodium
Exchanges: 2 starch, 3 vegetable
Carb Choices: 3

Shopping List

Frozen
16-oz. pkg. frozen pepper
    stir-fry

Canned
11-oz. can Mexicorn
14½-oz. can petite-cut diced
    tomatoes with green chiles

Packaged
17.5-oz. pkg. 98% fat-free
    flour tortillas

Optional
nonfat sour cream
salsa

To avoid overcooking frozen vegetables, thaw them first by placing them in a colander and running water through them until they separate and the ice crystals melt. Cook for 2½ minutes—no more!

Vegetarian Burritos

Easy | **Serves: 6**

1 tbsp. nonfat vegetable broth

¾ cup shredded carrots

¾ cup shredded zucchini

1 cup frozen diced onions,
  thawed and drained

3 cups cooked rice

¾ cup nonfat shredded cheddar
  cheese

¼ cup diced green chiles, *drained*

¾ cup nonfat sour cream

6 98% fat-free flour tortillas

1¼ cups shredded lettuce

1½ cups chunky-style salsa,
  lightly drained

  additional salsa (optional)

Spray large nonstick skillet with cooking spray; add broth and heat over medium-high heat. Add carrots, zucchini, and onions; cook, stirring frequently, until vegetables are tender. Drain any liquid from skillet. Stir in cooked rice, cheese, and green chiles; cook over medium heat, stirring constantly, until cheese is mostly melted. Remove skillet from heat and stir in sour cream; mix well. Wrap tortillas in paper towels and microwave on High for 15–30 seconds per tortilla. Spoon vegetable mixture down center of each tortilla; top with ¼ cup shredded lettuce and ¼ cup drained chunky-style salsa. Wrap and serve with additional salsa, if desired.

Meatless Meals

Nutrition per serving: 331 calories, 0.9 g fat, 63 g carbohydrates, 14 protein, 0 mg cholesterol, 4 g dietary fiber, 901 mg sodium
Exchanges: 3 starch, 4 vegetable
Carb Choices: 4

Shopping List

Produce
8-oz. pkg. shredded carrots
1 zucchini
8-oz. pkg. shredded lettuce

Dairy
nonfat shredded cheddar
  cheese
6 oz. nonfat sour cream

Frozen
12-oz. pkg. frozen diced onions

Canned
nonfat vegetable broth
4-oz. can diced green chiles

Packaged
17.5-oz. pkg. 98% fat-free
  flour tortillas
rice

Condiments
12–16-oz. jar chunky-style
  salsa

To save time, freeze leftover sides, pasta, and beans in meal-size portions and use them in your favorite dishes. Simply thaw, microwave, or reheat on the stove.

2-Step Vegetarian Tostadas

Easy | Serves: 4

14 oz. Gimme Lean ground beef-style

1 tbsp. onion powder

1 tsp. garlic powder

1 14½-oz. can seasoned diced tomato sauce for tacos

8 white corn tortillas

garnishes: shredded lettuce, chopped tomatoes, diced onions, and diced green chiles (optional)

1 cup nonfat shredded cheddar cheese

1 cup salsa

Preheat oven to 450°. Spray large nonstick skillet with cooking spray and heat over medium-high heat. Add Gimme Lean "beef"; sprinkle with onion and garlic powders. Cook, stirring frequently, until "beef" is browned and crumbled. Add tomato sauce; bring to a boil over medium-high heat. Reduce heat to low and simmer, uncovered, 5 minutes. Place tortillas on oven rack and heat 30–45 seconds until lightly crisp. Arrange tortillas on plates (2 tortillas per person); top with "beef" mixture and garnish as desired. Top each tostada with ¼ cup shredded cheese. Serve with salsa.

Nutrition per serving: 321 calories, 2.4 g fat, 47 g carbohydrates, 29 g protein, 0 mg cholesterol, 9 g dietary fiber, 1,795 mg sodium
Exchanges: 2½ starch, 2 vegetable, 2 very lean meat
Carb Choices: 3

Shopping List

Produce	Condiments
14 oz. Gimme Lean ground beef-style	8 oz. salsa
Dairy	**Seasonings/Spice**
4 oz. nonfat shredded cheddar cheese	onion powder
	garlic powder
Canned	**Optional**
14½-oz. can seasoned diced tomato sauce for tacos	shredded lettuce
	tomato
	diced onions
	4-oz. can diced green chiles
Packaged	
8.5-oz. pkg. white corn tortillas	

You can enjoy these vegetarian tostadas guilt–free! Two typical fast-food beef, bean, and cheese tostadas would pack on 668 calories, 34 grams of fat, and 150 milligrams of cholesterol.

Tortilla Chili Wraps

Easy | **Serves: 4**

4   98% fat-free flour tortillas

1   cup nonfat shredded
     cheddar cheese

¼   cup canned diced green
     chiles

2   15-oz. cans garden
     vegetable 4-bean chili

     nonfat sour cream, chopped
     green onions, or salsa
     (optional)

Shopping List

Dairy
nonfat shredded
   cheddar cheese

Canned
4-oz. can diced
   green chiles
2 15-oz. cans garden
   vegetable 4-bean chili

Packaged
17.5-oz. pkg. 98% fat-free
   flour tortillas

Optional
nonfat sour cream
green onions
salsa

Preheat oven to 400°. Line baking sheet with foil and spray with cooking spray. Sprinkle each tortilla with ¼ cup cheese and 1 tablespoon green chiles. Roll tortillas tightly and place seam sides down on baking sheet. Cover with foil and bake 10 minutes. Pour chili into microwave-safe bowl and heat on High 5–6 minutes until bubbly hot. Pour hot chili over cooked tortilla rolls and serve. Garnish with nonfat sour cream, chopped green onions, or salsa, if desired.

Nutrition per serving: 339 calories, 1.3 g fat, 58 g carbohydrates, 21 g protein, 0 mg cholesterol, 8 g dietary fiber, 1,469 mg sodium
Exchanges: 4 starch, 1 very lean meat
Carb Choices: 4

Meatless Meals

Did you know? On average, one bean burrito at a Mexican restaurant has 14 grams of fat!

Bean and Corn Tacos

2 tsp. nonfat vegetable broth

2 cups frozen pepper stir-fry

2 tbsp. taco seasoning

1 cup whole kernel corn, *drained*

½ cup canned black beans, *rinsed and drained*

½ cup chili beans, *rinsed and drained*

1 8-oz. can low-sodium tomato sauce

6 10-inch 98% fat-free flour tortillas, *warmed*

1 cup shredded lettuce

¾ cup nonfat shredded cheddar cheese

¾ cup chunky-style salsa

Spray large nonstick skillet with cooking spray. Add vegetable broth and heat over medium-high heat. Add pepper stir-fry and taco seasoning; cook, stirring frequently, 2–3 minutes until peppers and onions are softened. Add corn, black beans, chili beans, and tomato sauce; bring to a boil over high heat. Reduce heat to low and simmer 20–25 minutes until thickened. Spoon bean mixture onto tortillas; garnish with shredded lettuce, cheese, and salsa, as desired.

Nutrition per serving: 241 calories, 0.6g fat, 45 g carbohydrates, 12 g protein, 0 mg cholesterol, 4 g dietary fiber, 1,050 mg sodium
Exchanges: 2 starch, 3 vegetable
Carb Choices: 3

Add variety to vegetarian meals by including a wide assortment of fruits, vegetables, grains, and beans.

Shopping List

Produce	15-oz. can chili beans
8-oz. pkg. shredded lettuce	8-oz. can low-sodium tomato sauce
Dairy	
nonfat shredded cheddar cheese	**Packaged**
	17.5-oz. pkg. 98% fat-free flour tortillas
Frozen	
16-oz. pkg. frozen pepper stir-fry	**Condiments**
	chunky-style salsa
Canned	**Seasonings/Spice**
nonfat vegetable broth	taco seasoning packet
11-oz. can whole kernel corn	
15-oz. can black beans	

Mexican Pizza

Easy | **Do Ahead** | **Serves: 5**

1 whole lahvosh cracker bread

14 oz. Gimme Lean ground beef-style

1 11-oz. can Mexicorn, *drained*

1 16-oz. pkg. frozen pepper stir-fry

1 15-oz. can nonfat refried beans

1½ tsp. roasted minced garlic

1½ cups chunky-style salsa, *divided*

1 14½-oz. can petite-cut diced tomatoes with jalapeños, *well drained*

2 cups nonfat shredded cheddar cheese

Preheat oven to 400°. Spray large foil sheet with cooking spray; place lahvosh cracker bread on sheet. Spray large nonstick skillet with cooking spray and heat over medium-high heat. Add "beef" to skillet and cook, stirring frequently, until browned and crumbled. Add corn and peppers to "beef" and heat 5–8 minutes. Combine refried beans and garlic in small bowl; mix well. Spread bean mixture onto lahvosh. Top with ¾ cup salsa, "beef" mixture, and remaining salsa. Top with diced tomatoes and cheese. Bake 15–18 minutes until cheese is lightly browned and pizza is heated through.

Meatless Meals

Nutrition per serving: 476 calories, 0.6 g fat, 69 g carbohydrates, 39 g protein, 0 mg cholesterol, 14 g dietary fiber, 2,894 mg sodium
Exchanges: 4 starch, 2 vegetable, 3 very lean meat
Carb Choices: 5

Shopping List

Produce
14 oz. Gimme Lean ground beef-style
4-oz. jar roasted minced garlic

Frozen
16-oz. pkg. pepper stir-fry

Dairy
8 oz. nonfat shredded cheddar cheese

Canned
11-oz. can Mexicorn
14½-oz. can petite-cut diced tomatoes with jalapeños
15-oz. can nonfat refried beans

Packaged
15¾-oz. lahvosh cracker bread

Condiments
12 oz. chunky-style salsa

Gimme Lean "meat" products are excellent vegetarian alternatives to beef—you can substitute them for ground beef in most recipes.

241

Whole Wheat Onion-Sausage Pizza

Easy | Do Ahead | Serves: 5

1 14-oz. pkg. Gimme Lean sausage-style

½ cup diced onions

2 14½-oz. cans diced tomatoes with garlic and onion, *drained*

¾ cup nonfat pizza or pasta sauce

1 large whole wheat lahvosh cracker bread

2½ cups nonfat mozzarella cheese, *divided*

2 tbsp. nonfat Parmesan cheese

Preheat oven to 450°. Line large baking sheet or pizza pan with foil and spray with cooking spray. Spray large nonstick skillet with cooking spray and heat over medium-high heat. Add Gimme Lean sausage and onions. Cook, stirring frequently, until "sausage" is browned and crumbled. Remove skillet from heat; add tomatoes and mix well. Spread pizza or pasta sauce in a thin layer over cracker bread. Top with 2 cups mozzarella cheese. Arrange "sausage"-tomato mixture over cheese. Sprinkle remaining mozzarella and the Parmesan cheese on top. Bake 12–15 minutes until cracker bread is lightly browned and cheese is melted.

Nutrition per serving: 225 calories, 0 g fat, 17 g carbohydrates, 33 g protein, 0 mg cholesterol, 4 g dietary fiber, 1,255 mg sodium
Exchanges: ½ starch, 2 vegetable, 4 very lean meat
Carb Choices: 1

Shopping List

Produce
14 oz. Gimme Lean sausage-style
7-oz. container diced onions

Dairy
10 oz. nonfat shredded mozzarella cheese
nonfat Parmesan cheese

Canned
6 oz. nonfat pizza or pasta sauce
2 14½-oz. cans diced tomatoes with garlic and onion

Packaged
15¾-oz. pkg. whole wheat lahvosh cracker bread (largest size)

Microwaving vegetables is easy and healthful; it locks in vitamins using very little or no water.

Whole Wheat Vegetarian Pizza

Easy | **Do Ahead** | **Serves: 5**

1 large whole wheat lahvosh cracker bread

½–¾ cup nonfat pizza sauce

1½ cups nonfat shredded mozzarella cheese, *divided*

1 cup nonfat shredded cheddar cheese

1 16-oz. pkg. broccoli and cauliflower florets

1 cup frozen chopped spinach, *thawed and drained*

1½ cups frozen pepper stir-fry, *thawed and drained*

1 cup sliced mushrooms

1 cup diced red onions

1 14½-oz. can Italian diced tomatoes with garlic, oregano, and basil, *well drained*

Store mushrooms in a paper bag to keep them white longer.

Preheat oven to 450°. Line baking sheet or pizza pan with foil and spray with cooking spray. Place lahvosh cracker bread on pan; spread pizza sauce in a thin layer over bread. Sprinkle 1 cup mozzarella and 1 cup cheddar cheese over sauce. Place broccoli and cauliflower florets in microwave-safe dish; cover and microwave on High 5–6 minutes until crisp-tender. Arrange broccoli, cauliflower, spinach, pepper stir-fry, mushrooms, and red onions on pizza. Top with tomatoes; sprinkle with remaining mozzarella cheese. Bake 15–18 minutes until cheese is melted and lightly browned. Let stand 3–5 minutes before serving.

Meatless Meals

Nutrition per serving: 190 calories, 0.5 g fat, 21 g carbohydrates, 24 g protein, 0 mg cholesterol, 6 g dietary fiber, 757 mg sodium
Exchanges: 1 starch, 2 vegetable, 2 very lean meat
Carb Choices: 1

Shopping List

Produce
16-oz. pkg. broccoli and cauliflower florets
8 oz. sliced mushrooms
7-oz. container diced red onions

Dairy
6 oz. nonfat shredded mozzarella cheese
4 oz. nonfat shredded cheddar cheese

Frozen
10-oz. pkg. frozen chopped spinach

16-oz. pkg. frozen pepper stir-fry

Canned
6-oz. can pizza sauce (or 2 Boboli sauce packets)
14-½-oz. can Italian diced tomatoes with garlic, oregano, and basil

Packaged
15¾-oz. pkg. whole wheat lahvosh cracker bread (largest size)

243

Chapter Index

10 Pasta and Rice

Rotini with Chicken and Vegetables

Ever wonder which type of pasta to use with your favorite sauce? Generally thin, delicate pastas, such as angel hair, fare best with light, thin sauces. Thicker shapes, such as fettuccini, work well with heavier sauces. Pair shapely pastas that have holes or ridges, such as mostaccioli, with chunky meat or vegetable sauces.

Type of noodle	Used in	Recommended
Alphabet	Soups	Thin marinara sauce
Angel hair (Capellini)	Soups, salads, stir-fry meals	Thin, delicate sauce
Bow ties (Farfalle)	Soups, salads	Any sauce
Ditalini	Casseroles, soups, salads, stir-fry meals	Any sauce
Fettuccine	Main dishes, soups, salads	Thick sauce
Fusilli	Soups, salads, casseroles	Any sauce
Jumbo shells	Stuffed with cheese, meat, or vegetables	Thick sauce
Linguine	Salads, stir-fry meals	Any sauce
Macaroni	Soups, salads, stir-fry dishes, casseroles	Any sauce
Manicotti	Stuffed and baked	Thick sauce
Medium shells	Soups, salads, casseroles	Any sauce
Orzo	Soups, casseroles	Any sauce
Penne (Mostaccioli)	Salads, casseroles, stir-fry meals	Chunky sauce
Rigatoni	Casseroles	Chunkiest meat sauce
Rotini	Salads, baked casseroles, stir-fry meals	Any sauce
Spaghetti	Soups, casseroles, stir-fry meals	Any sauce
Wagon wheels	Soups, salads, casseroles, stir-fry meals	Chunkier sauce
Ziti	Salads, casseroles, stir-fry meals	Chunky sauce

Pasta
and
Rice

Pasta Dos and Don'ts

- Do use at least 1 quart of water for every 4 ounces of dry pasta.
- Do bring the water to a vigorous boil.
- Do NOT add pasta to water before it boils.
- Do NOT add oil to cooked pasta; doing so keeps sauce from sticking.
- Do stir pasta in boiling water with a wooden spoon; this ensures even cooking and prevents pasta from sticking together or to bottom of pan.
- Do test pasta after 4 minutes and continue cooking just until tender.
- Do NOT rely on package directions; cooking times vary depending on shape and size of pasta.

- Do remember that pasta continues to cook after removed from water.
- Do cook pasta ingredients that you'll use in baked dishes for one-third the normal cooking time. Boil only until flexible but still firm.
- Do drain pasta in a colander and shake to remove excess water.
- Do NOT rinse pasta after cooking unless the recipe recommends it.
- Do rinse lasagna noodles after cooking so they separate without tearing.
- Do return cooked and drained pasta to cooking pan to keep warm or toss it with sauce and place in a preheated serving dish.

Penne Pasta Skillet Meal

Easy | **Serves: 4**

1 lb. extra-lean ground beef

1½ tbsp. onion powder

½ tsp. garlic powder

1 15-oz. can seasoned diced
   tomato sauce for lasagna

¾ cup water

1½ cups uncooked penne pasta

2 cups nonfat shredded
   cheddar cheese

2 tbsp. nonfat Parmesan cheese

Spray large nonstick skillet with cooking spray and heat over medium-high heat. Add ground beef and season with onion and garlic powders. Cook, stirring frequently, until beef is crumbled and browned. Add tomato sauce, water, and penne pasta. Cover and cook 13–15 minutes until pasta is tender. Sprinkle cheddar cheese over top; cover and cook over medium-low heat until cheese is melted. Sprinkle with Parmesan cheese and serve immediately.

Nutrition per serving: 426 calories, 5.4 g fat, 44 g carbohydrates, 45 g protein, 61 mg cholesterol, 2 g dietary fiber, 1,231 mg sodium
Exchanges: 2½ starch, 1 vegetable, 4 lean meat
Carb Choices: 3

Shopping List

Meat/Fish/Poultry
1 lb. extra-lean ground beef

Dairy
8 oz. nonfat shredded cheddar
   cheese
nonfat Parmesan cheese

Canned
15-oz. can seasoned diced
   tomato sauce for lasagna

Packaged
8-oz. pkg. penne pasta

Seasonings/Spices
onion powder
garlic powder

Four ounces of uncooked pasta equals 2½ cups cooked macaroni, shells, rotini, cavatelli, wheels, penne, or ziti.

Cinci-Chili Pasta

Easy | **Do Ahead** | **Serves: 4**

½ lb. extra-lean ground beef

1 cup frozen diced onions

¼ cup frozen diced green bell
    peppers

2 14½-oz. cans stewed
    tomatoes with bell pepper
    and onion, *do not drain*

1 15-oz. can kidney beans,
    do not drain

1 8-oz. can tomato sauce

1 tbsp. chili powder

1 8-oz. pkg. spaghetti, *cooked
    and drained*

    nonfat shredded cheddar
    cheese, diced onions
    (optional)

Spray large saucepan or Dutch oven with cooking spray and
heat over medium-high heat. Add ground beef, 1 cup onions,
and green bell peppers. Cook, stirring frequently, until beef is
browned and crumbled and vegetables are tender. Stir in
tomatoes, beans, tomato sauce, and chili powder; bring to a
boil over high heat. Reduce heat to medium-low and cook,
stirring occasionally, 10–15 minutes. Serve meat mixture over
cooked spaghetti; garnish with cheese and additional onions,
if desired.

Nutrition per serving: 469 calories, 4.3 g fat, 82 g carbohydrates, 27 g protein,
30 mg cholesterol, 8 g dietary fiber, 1,244 mg sodium
Exchanges: 4½ starch, 2 vegetable, 2 very lean meat
Carb Choices: 5

Pasta
and
Rice

As a general rule of thumb, always use 4 times
the amount of water than pasta.

Shopping List

Meat/Fish/Poultry	
½ lb. extra-lean ground beef	15-oz. can kidney beans
	8-oz. can tomato sauce
Frozen	**Packaged**
12-oz. pkg. frozen diced onions	8-oz. pkg. spaghetti
10-oz. pkg. frozen diced green bell peppers	**Seasonings/Spices**
	chili powder
Canned	**Optional**
2 14½-oz. cans stewed tomatoes with bell pepper and onion	nonfat shredded cheddar cheese
	diced onions

Sweet and Spicy Pasta with Chicken and Stir-Fry Vegetables

Easy | Serves: 6

6 oz. uncooked angel hair pasta

1 tbsp. nonfat vegetable broth

1½ cups shredded carrots

1 8-oz. pkg. stringless sugar snap peas

1 8-oz. pkg. shredded cabbage

3 6-oz. pkgs. chicken breast strips

1 cup sweet and spicy stir-fry seasoning

Prepare pasta according to package directions; drain and keep warm. Spray large nonstick skillet with cooking spray; add broth and heat over medium-high heat. Add carrots, sugar snap peas, and cabbage; cook, stirring frequently, until vegetables are tender. Add chicken; pour stir-fry seasoning over vegetables and chicken. Cook, stirring constantly, until vegetables and chicken are heated through. Serve over cooked angel hair pasta.

Nutrition per serving: 315 calories, 2.1 g fat, 46 g carbohydrates, 25 g protein, 50 mg cholesterol, 4 g dietary fiber, 1,092 mg sodium
Exchanges: 1 starch, 3 vegetable, 3 very lean meat, 1 other carb
Carb Choices: 3

Shopping List

Produce
8-oz. pkg. shredded carrots
8-oz. pkg. stringless sugar snap peas
8-oz. pkg. shredded cabbage

Meat/Fish/Poultry
3 6-oz. pkgs. chicken breast strips

Canned
nonfat vegetable broth

Packaged
6 oz. angel hair pasta

Condiments
16-oz. bottle sweet and spicy stir-fry seasoning

Package directions for cooking dried pasta are merely a guideline. For best results, test pasta for doneness after about 4 minutes by tasting it. Pasta cooking times will vary depending on shape and thickness.

Rotini with Chicken and Vegetables

Easy | **Serves: 6**

3½ cups nonfat chicken broth

1 tsp. garlic powder

1 12-oz. pkg. uncooked rotini pasta

1 16-oz. pkg. frozen broccoli, cauliflower, and carrots

3 6-oz. pkgs. grilled chicken breast strips

3 tbsp. nonfat Parmesan cheese

Combine chicken broth and garlic powder in large saucepan; bring to a boil over high heat. Add pasta; reduce heat to medium and cook 9–10 minutes until tender. Add vegetables; bring to a boil over high heat; reduce heat to medium and cook until vegetables are tender. Stir in chicken and cook 5 minutes until heated through. Spoon pasta onto platter and sprinkle with Parmesan cheese.

Nutrition per serving: 359 calories, 2.6 g fat, 52 g carbohydrates, 31 g protein, 50 mg cholesterol, 2 g dietary fiber, 943 mg sodium
Exchanges: 3 starch, 1 vegetable, 3 very lean meat
Carb Choices: 3

Pasta and Rice

Shopping List

Meat/Fish/Poultry
3 6-oz. pkgs. grilled chicken breast strips

Dairy
nonfat Parmesan cheese

Frozen
16-oz. pkg. frozen broccoli, cauliflower, and carrots

Canned
2 14-oz. cans nonfat chicken broth

Packaged
12-oz. pkg. rotini pasta

Seasonings/Spices
garlic powder

When substituting one pasta for another, try to use one with similar characteristics. Match the shapes of pasta to the sauce. Flat pastas are best with thin sauces, while other shapes may be best with chunkier sauces.

Chicken Tetrazzini

Average | **Do Ahead** | **Freeze** | **Serves: 6**

1 12-oz. pkg. spaghetti,
   cooked and drained

1 4-oz. can sliced mushrooms,
   drain and reserve liquid

3 6-oz. pkgs. grilled chicken
   breast strips, *cut in thirds*

2 cups nonfat chicken broth,
   divided

¼ cup flour

   dash pepper

1 cup nonfat half and half

¾ cup nonfat Parmesan cheese,
   divided

Preheat oven to 350°. Spray 9×13-inch baking dish with cooking spray. Toss cooked spaghetti, mushrooms, and chicken in baking dish. Spray medium saucepan with cooking spray; add ¼ cup broth and heat over medium-low heat. Stir in flour and pepper; cook, stirring constantly, until bubbly. Remove pan from heat; stir in remaining broth, half and half, and half the reserved mushroom liquid (discard the other half).Continue cooking over medium-high heat until mixture comes to a boil; cook, stirring constantly, 1–2 minutes until sauce is thickened. Pour sauce over spaghetti mixture, sprinkle with ¼ cup Parmesan cheese, and toss thoroughly. Sprinkle remaining cheese over top and bake 45–55 minutes until bubbly hot and lightly browned on top.

Nutrition per serving: 405 calories, 2.5 g fat, 61 g carbohydrates, 33 g protein, 50 mg cholesterol, <1 g dietary fiber, 806 mg sodium
Exchanges: 2 starch, 2 vegetable, 3 very lean meat, 1 other carb
Carb Choices: 4

Shopping List

Meat/Fish/Poultry	Packaged
3 6-oz. pkgs. grilled chicken breast strips	12-oz. pkg. spaghetti
	Baking goods
Dairy	flour
8 oz. nonfat half and half	
nonfat Parmesan cheese	**Seasonings/Spices**
	pepper
Canned	
4-oz. can sliced mushrooms	
16 oz. nonfat chicken broth	

When boiling pasta to be used as part of a dish that requires further cooking, undercook it by one-third of the cooking time specified on the package.

Angel Hair Pasta Salad with Shrimp

Easy | **Do Ahead** | **Serves: 8**

1 16-oz. pkg. angel hair pasta, *cooked, drained, and rinsed under cold water*

1 12-oz. pkg. frozen cooked baby shrimp, *peeled and deveined*

¾ cup chopped green onions

1¼ cups nonfat Ranch salad dressing, *divided*

¼ cup nonfat Parmesan cheese (optional)

Combine cooked pasta, shrimp, green onions, and 1 cup salad dressing; toss carefully to mix. Cover and refrigerate at least 1 hour before serving. Add remaining dressing just before serving and toss lightly to mix. Sprinkle with Parmesan cheese, if desired.

Nutrition per serving: 299 calories, 1.7 g fat, 52 g carbohydrates, 16 g protein, 66 mg cholesterol, 2 g dietary fiber, 401 mg sodium
Exchanges: 2½ starch, 2 very lean meat, 1 other carb
Carb Choices: 3

Pasta and Rice

Shopping List

Produce
green onions

Frozen
12-oz. pkg. frozen cooked baby shrimp

Packaged
16-oz. pkg. angel hair pasta

Condiments
12 oz. nonfat Ranch salad dressing

Optional
nonfat Parmesan cheese

When heating water to a boil, use a lid to reduce the time it takes.

Shrimp and Eggplant Caesar Linguine

Easy | **Serves: 4**

8 oz. pkg. uncooked linguine

¼ cup fat-free creamy Caesar salad dressing

1½ cups trimmed and peeled asparagus pieces

¾ cup frozen pepper stir-fry

1 cup diced eggplant

1 lb. large uncooked shrimp, *peeled and deveined*

2 tsp. dried parsley flakes

¼ cup white wine

nonfat Parmesan cheese

(optional)

Cook linguini according to package directions; drain and keep warm. Spray large nonstick skillet with cooking spray; add salad dressing to skillet and heat over medium-high heat. Add asparagus, peppers, and eggplant. Cook, stirring frequently, until vegetables are crisp-tender. Add shrimp, parsley, and wine; cook, stirring frequently, until shrimp is cooked through. Toss shrimp mixture with linguine; serve with Parmesan cheese, if desired.

Nutrition per serving: 261 calories, 2.7 g fat, 28 g carbohydrates, 28 g protein, 175 mg cholesterol, 3 g dietary fiber, 311 mg sodium
Exchanges: 1 starch, 3 vegetable, 3 very lean meat
Carb Choices: 2

Shopping List

Produce	Condiments
8 oz. asparagus spears	fat-free creamy Caesar
¼ lb. eggplant	salad dressing
Meat/Fish/Poultry	**Other**
1 lb. large uncooked shrimp	white wine
	Seasonings/Spice
Frozen	dried parsley flakes
16-oz. pkg. frozen pepper stir-fry	
	Optional
	nonfat Parmesan cheese
Packaged	
8 oz. linguine	

Four ounces of uncooked or 1-inch-diameter bunch of dry pasta will equal 2 cups cooked spaghetti, angel hair pasta, vermicelli, or linguine.

Shrimp Scampi Pasta

Easy | **Serves: 8**

- 1 8-oz. pkg. uncooked angel hair pasta
- 2 tbsp. cornstarch
- 1¾ cups nonfat chicken or vegetable broth
- 2 tsp. bottled minced garlic
- 1 tbsp. dried parsley flakes
- 2 tbsp. bottled lemon juice
- dash Tabasco sauce
- 1 lb. uncooked medium shrimp, *peeled and deveined*
- 2 tbsp. nonfat Parmesan cheese

Prepare pasta according to package directions; drain and keep warm. While pasta is cooking, prepare sauce. Spray medium saucepan with cooking spray. Add cornstarch, broth, garlic, parsley, lemon juice, and Tabasco; mix well. Bring to a boil over high heat, stirring frequently, and cook until mixture thickens. Add shrimp; cook 4–5 minutes until shrimp turn pink. Spoon shrimp and sauce over angel hair pasta and toss lightly. Sprinkle with Parmesan cheese and serve.

Nutrition per serving: 184 calories, 1.6g fat, 25 g carbohydrates, 16 g protein, 87 mg cholesterol, 1 g dietary fiber, 268 mg sodium
Exchanges: 1½ starch, 2 very lean meat
Carb Choices: 2

Pasta and Rice

Shopping List

Meat/Fish/Poultry
1 lb. medium shrimp

Dairy
nonfat Parmesan cheese

Canned
14-oz. can nonfat chicken or vegetable broth

Packaged
8-oz. pkg. angel hair pasta

Baking Goods
cornstarch

Condiments
bottled lemon juice
Tabasco sauce

Seasonings/Spices
bottled minced garlic
dried parsley flakes

Do not add pasta to water before it boils. Pasta quickly breaks down in tepid water as the starch dissolves; boiling water is essential to "set" the outside of the pasta and prevent it from sticking together.

Macaroni and Cheese in Minutes

Easy | **Serves: 4**

1 8-oz. pkg. uncooked elbow macaroni

1½ cups nonfat shredded cheddar cheese

½ cup nonfat shredded mozzarella cheese

1 cup skim milk

1½ tsp. prepared mustard

dash pepper

Cook pasta according to package directions; drain and keep warm. Spray large saucepan with cooking spray; add remaining ingredients and cook over low heat, stirring constantly, until cheese is melted and sauce is thickened. Add cooked macaroni and toss to coat.

Nutrition per serving: 327 calories, 1.3 g fat, 49 g carbohydrates, 26 protein, 1 mg cholesterol, 0 g dietary fiber, 557 mg sodium
Exchanges: 2½ starch, ½ milk, 2 very lean meat
Carb Choices: 3

Shopping List

Dairy
6 oz. nonfat shredded
    cheddar cheese
nonfat shredded mozzarella
    cheese
8 oz. skim milk

Packaged
8-oz. pkg. elbow macaroni

Condiments
prepared mustard (regular,
    spicy, or Dijon)

Seasonings/Spices
pepper

When cooking pasta or rice (brown, long grain, or wild), cook extra. Freeze 1-cup servings in sealed zip-lock bags. It heats quickly in the microwave for quick meals.

Penne with Spinach-Cheese Sauce

Easy | **Serves: 6**

1 12-oz. pkg. uncooked penne pasta

1 tbsp. nonfat chicken or vegetable broth

1 tsp. minced garlic

1 16-oz. pkg. frozen chopped spinach, *thawed and drained*

1 cup nonfat cottage cheese

1 cup nonfat half and half

2 tsp. Italian seasoning

¾ cup nonfat Parmesan cheese

Cook pasta according to package directions; drain and keep warm. Spray large nonstick skillet with cooking spray; add broth and heat over medium-high heat. Add garlic and spinach; cook, stirring frequently, 3–4 minutes until tender. Combine cottage cheese, half and half, and Italian seasoning in blender; process until smooth. Gradually add to skillet, stirring to blend with garlic and spinach. Bring to a boil over high heat; reduce heat to low and cook 10–15 minutes until heated through. Add cooked pasta and toss to coat; sprinkle with Parmesan cheese and serve.

Nutrition per serving: 295 calories, 1 g fat, 56 g carbohydrates, 15 g protein, 1 mg cholesterol, 2 g dietary fiber, 198 mg sodium
Exchanges: 2 starch, 2 vegetable, 1 other carb
Carb Choices: 4

Pasta and Rice

Shopping List

Dairy
8 oz. nonfat cottage cheese
8 oz. nonfat half and half
nonfat Parmesan cheese

Frozen
10-oz. pkg. frozen chopped spinach

Canned
nonfat chicken or vegetable broth

Packaged
12-oz. pkg. penne pasta

Seasonings/Spices
minced garlic
Italian seasoning

Making sure you have enough water is essential to preparing perfect pasta. Pasta releases a starchy substance while cooking; if there is not enough water to dilute the starch, the pasta will be sticky.

Penne with Creamy Pasta Sauce

Easy | **Serves: 8**

1 8-oz. pkg. uncooked
   penne pasta

1 26-oz. jar nonfat pasta sauce
   (any variety)

½ cup nonfat half and half

½ cup nonfat Parmesan cheese

Cook pasta according to package directions; drain and keep warm. Combine pasta sauce and half and half in medium saucepan; cook over medium heat, stirring frequently, until mixture is heated through and thickened. Pour over pasta and toss to mix; sprinkle with Parmesan cheese and serve.

Nutrition per serving: 163 calories, 0.4 g fat, 32 g carbohydrates, 6 g protein, 0 mg cholesterol, 0 g dietary fiber, 330 mg sodium
Exchanges: 1 starch, 2 vegetable, ½ other carb
Carb Choices: 2

Shopping List

Dairy
4 oz. nonfat half and half
nonfat Parmesan cheese

Packaged
8-oz. pkg. penne pasta

Condiments
26-oz. jar nonfat pasta sauce
   (any variety)

Use at least 1 quart of water for every 4 ounces of dry pasta. Bring the water to a vigorous boil, add pasta all at once, and cook, uncovered, at a rolling boil for the recommended cooking time.

Garden Vegetable Pasta Bake

Easy | **Do Ahead** | **Freeze** | **Serves: 6**

½ cup Garden Vegetable
   Egg Beaters

¾ cup nonfat Parmesan cheese

½ cup nonfat half and half
   dash pepper

2 cups cooked rigatoni

1 15½-oz. can diced tomatoes
   with garlic, oregano, and
   basil, *well drained*

1½ cups nonfat shredded
   mozzarella cheese

Preheat oven to 400°. Spray 11×7-inch baking dish with cooking spray. Combine Egg Beaters, Parmesan cheese, half and half, and pepper in medium bowl; mix well. Stir in pasta and toss to coat. Spread pasta mixture into baking dish; top with diced tomatoes and sprinkle with cheese. Spray foil sheet with cooking spray; cover baking dish and bake 25 minutes. Remove foil and bake 5–7 minutes until cheese is lightly browned. Serve immediately.

Nutrition per serving: 175 calories, 0.2 g fat, 22 g carbohydrates, 18 protein, 0 mg cholesterol, 1 g dietary fiber, 468 mg sodium
Exchanges: 1 starch, 1 vegetable, 2 very lean meat
Carb Choices: 1

Pasta
and
Rice

Shopping List

Dairy
4 oz. Garden Vegetable Egg
   Beaters
3 oz. nonfat Parmesan cheese
4 oz. nonfat half and half
6 oz. nonfat shredded
   mozzarella cheese

Canned
15¼-oz. can diced tomatoes
   with garlic, oregano, and basil

Packaged
8 oz. rigatoni

Seasonings/Spices
pepper

Most dried pasta doubles in volume when cooked. For accuracy, measure dried pasta by weight rather than by cup; cooked pasta can be measured by volume.

Brown Rice Primavera

Easy | Serves: 4

2 tbsp. nonfat chicken or vegetable broth

2 cups diced eggplant

1 medium zucchini, *sliced*

½ cup frozen diced green bell peppers, *thawed and drained*

2 tsp. onion powder

2 cups uncooked instant brown rice

1¾ cups water

1 14½-oz. can petite-cut diced tomatoes with garlic, oregano, and basil, *drained*

1 6-oz. pkg. crumbled nonfat feta cheese

Spray large nonstick skillet with cooking spray; add broth and heat over medium-high heat. Add eggplant, zucchini, and peppers; sprinkle with onion powder. Cook, stirring frequently, 6–8 minutes until vegetables are tender. Add brown rice and water; bring to a boil over high heat. Reduce heat to medium-low, cover, and cook 5 minutes until liquid is absorbed and rice is tender. Stir in tomatoes and cheese; mix lightly, cover, and cook over low heat 5–6 minutes until heated through.

Nutrition per serving: 173 calories, 0.3 g fat, 30 g carbohydrates, 13 g protein, 0 mg cholesterol, 3 g dietary fiber, 875 mg sodium
Exchanges: 1½ starch, 2 vegetable
Carb Choices: 2

Shopping List

Produce	**Canned**
1 medium eggplant	nonfat chicken or vegetable
1 medium zucchini	broth
	14½-oz. can petite-cut
Dairy	diced tomatoes with garlic,
6-oz. pkg. crumbled nonfat	oregano, and basil
feta cheese	
	Packaged
Frozen	instant brown rice
10-oz. pkg. frozen diced green	
bell peppers	**Seasonings/Spices**
	onion powder

For fluffier rice, make sure there is a little bit of liquid in the bottom of the pot when your rice is finished cooking; then, let the rice rest for a few minutes before fluffing with a fork.

Baked Macaroni

Average | Do Ahead | Serves: 6

¼ cup nonfat chicken broth

¼ cup frozen diced onions

¼ cup frozen diced green bell
  peppers

1 tsp. Mexican seasoning

1 cup uncooked elbow
  macaroni or small
  shell pasta

1¼ cups nonfat shredded
  cheddar cheese

1 16-oz. can whole kernel
  corn, *drained*

1 16-oz. can cream-style corn

dash pepper

Spray nonstick skillet with cooking spray; add broth and heat over medium-high heat. Add onions and bell peppers; sprinkle with Mexican seasoning and cook, stirring frequently, until vegetables are softened. Preheat oven to 350°. Spray 2-quart casserole with cooking spray; combine onion mixture with remaining ingredients and toss to mix. Bake 55–60 minutes until heated through, stirring every 15 minutes.

Nutrition per serving: 220 calories, 0.6 g fat, 45 g carbohydrates, 13 g protein, 0 mg cholesterol, 3 g dietary fiber, 526 mg sodium
Exchanges: 3 starch
Carb Choices: 3

Pasta
and
Rice

Shopping List

Dairy
8 oz. nonfat shredded
  cheddar cheese

Frozen
12-oz. pkg. frozen diced
  onions
10-oz. pkg. frozen diced
  green bell peppers

Canned
16-oz. can whole kernel corn
16-oz. can cream-style corn
nonfat chicken broth

Packaged
8-oz. pkg. elbow macaroni or
  small shell pasta

Seasonings/Spices
Mexican seasoning
pepper

The best pasta is made of 100% semolina because it retains its shape and firmness while cooking. When purchasing dried pasta, be sure to look for semolina in the ingredients.

Baked Linguine with Broccoli

Easy | Do Ahead | Serves: 4

¼ cup Garden Vegetable
Egg Beaters

½ cup nonfat shredded
mozzarella cheese

¾ cup nonfat sour cream

1 10-oz. pkg. frozen chopped
broccoli, *thawed and
drained*

6 oz. uncooked linguine, *cooked
and drained*

1¾ cups nonfat pasta sauce
(any variety)

2 tbsp. nonfat Parmesan cheese

Preheat oven to 350°. Spray 1½-quart baking dish with cooking spray. Combine Egg Beaters, cheese, sour cream, and broccoli in medium bowl; mix well. Fold in cooked linguine and toss carefully. Spoon linguine mixture into baking dish; top with pasta sauce and toss lightly. Bake 20–25 minutes until bubbly hot; sprinkle with Parmesan cheese and bake 5 minutes longer until lightly browned. Remove from oven and let stand 3–5 minutes before serving.

Nutrition per serving: 282 calories, 0.8 g fat, 47 g carbohydrates, 18 g protein, 0 mg cholesterol, 4 g dietary fiber, 520 mg sodium
Exchanges: 2 starch, 3 vegetable, 1 very lean meat
Carb Choices: 3

Shopping List

Dairy
Garden Vegetable Egg Beaters
nonfat shredded mozzarella
cheese
6 oz. nonfat sour cream
nonfat Parmesan cheese

Frozen
10-oz. pkg. frozen chopped
broccoli

Packaged
6 oz. linguine

Condiments
14-oz. jar nonfat pasta sauce
(any variety)

If you want to spice up a jar of pasta sauce, add any of the following ingredients for variety: sautéed garlic, mushrooms, or bell peppers; basil or red pepper flakes; or nonfat half and half to make a creamy red sauce.

Southwest Vegetable Pasta Bake

Easy | **Do Ahead** | **Serves: 6**

6 cups cooked rotini or rotelle pasta

4 cups chunky-style salsa, *lightly drained*

2½ cups nonfat shredded cheddar cheese, *divided*

1 cup nonfat cottage cheese

1 16-oz. can chili beans, *drained*

1 11-oz. can Mexicorn, *drained*

Preheat oven to 375°. Spray 9×13-inch baking dish with cooking spray. Combine cooked pasta, salsa, 1¼ cups cheddar cheese, cottage cheese, chili beans, and Mexicorn in baking dish; mix well. Sprinkle remaining cheddar cheese on top and bake 25–30 minutes until cheese is lightly browned and casserole is bubbly hot. Let stand 3–5 minutes before serving.

Nutrition per serving: 415 calories, 1.7 g fat, 79 g carbohydrates, 27 g protein, 1 mg cholesterol, 8 g dietary fiber, 1,797 mg sodium
Exchanges: 4 starch, 3 vegetable, 1 very lean meat
Carb Choices: 5

Pasta and Rice

Shopping List

Dairy
10 oz. nonfat shredded cheddar cheese
8 oz. nonfat cottage cheese

Canned
16-oz. can chili beans
11-oz. can Mexicorn

Packaged
12 oz. rotini or rotelle pasta

Condiments
2 16-oz. jars chunky-style salsa

After adding pasta to boiling water, stir with a wooden spoon to prevent pasta from sticking together or to the bottom of the pan. Stir frequently while cooking to ensure even cooking.

Orange Rice

1¾ cups nonfat chicken broth

¾ cup orange marmalade

1 tbsp. Dijon mustard

2 cups uncooked instant rice

¼ cup chopped Mandarin oranges

Combine chicken broth, marmalade, and mustard in medium saucepan; bring to a boil over high heat. Add rice and mix lightly. Reduce heat to low, cover, and simmer 5 minutes until cooked through. Stir in oranges and heat 2–3 minutes. Serve immediately with chicken or fish.

Nutrition per serving: 356 calories, 0.3 g fat, 82 g carbohydrates, 5 g protein, 0 mg cholesterol, 2 g dietary fiber, 411 mg sodium
Exchanges: 3 starch, 2 fruit
Carb Choices: 5

Shopping List

Canned
14-oz. can nonfat chicken broth
8-oz. can Mandarin oranges

Packaged
instant rice

Condiments
6 oz. orange marmalade
Dijon mustard

To boost flavor and nutrition of rice, cook it in liquid reserved from cooking vegetables.

Lemon Rice Pilaf

Easy | **Serves: 4**

3 cups nonfat chicken broth

2 tbsp. chopped green onions

1 tsp. grated lemon peel

½ tsp. garlic powder

⅛ tsp. pepper

1 cup uncooked long grain rice
(*not instant*)

1 cup canned sliced water
chestnuts, *diced*

Combine chicken broth, green onions, lemon peel, garlic powder, and pepper in large saucepan; bring to a boil over high heat. Add rice; reduce heat to low, cover, and simmer 20 minutes. Stir in diced water chestnuts and continue cooking until most of the liquid is absorbed.

Nutrition per serving: 201 calories, 0.7 g fat, 42 g carbohydrates, 6 g protein, 0 mg cholesterol, <1 g dietary fiber, 592 mg sodium
Exchanges: 2½ starch, 1 vegetable
Carb Choices: 3

Pasta
and
Rice

Shopping List

Produce
green onions
lemon

Canned
24 oz. nonfat chicken broth
6-oz. can sliced water chestnuts

Packaged
long grain rice (not instant)

Seasonings/Spices
garlic powder
pepper

For fluffier, whiter rice, add one teaspoon of lemon juice per quart of water.

Confetti Pasta Salad

Easy | Do Ahead | Serves: 4

1½ cups rotini pasta, *cooked, drained, and rinsed under cold water*

2½ cups Salad Confetti mix

¼ cup grape tomatoes

½ cup nonfat creamy Caesar salad dressing

¼ cup nonfat Parmesan cheese

Combine cooked pasta with Salad Confetti and tomatoes; drizzle dressing over top and toss to coat. Cover and refrigerate 1–2 hours before serving. Sprinkle with Parmesan cheese just before serving.

Nutrition per serving: 221 calories, 0.6 g fat, 45 g carbohydrates, 9 g protein, 0 mg cholesterol, 1 g dietary fiber, 67 mg sodium
Exchanges: 1 starch, 3 vegetable, 1 other carb
Carb Choices: 3

Shopping List

Produce
2 7-oz. containers Salad Confetti mix
grape tomatoes

Dairy
nonfat Parmesan cheese

Packaged
8-oz. pkg. rotini pasta

Condiments
nonfat creamy Caesar salad dressing

The only time you should rinse pasta after draining is when you are going to use it in a cold dish, or when you are not going to add sauce and serve immediately. If it is necessary to rinse pasta, rinse under cold water to stop the cooking process and drain well.

Risotto

Easy | **Serves: 6**

2 tbsp. + 3½ cups nonfat chicken or vegetable broth, *divided*

1 cup uncooked long grain rice (not instant)

1½ tsp. bottled minced garlic

3 tbsp. nonfat Parmesan cheese

1 tbsp. chopped fresh parsley (optional)

Spray large nonstick skillet with cooking spray; add 2 tablespoons broth and heat over medium-high heat. Add rice and garlic; cook, stirring constantly, 2–3 minutes until lightly browned. Add ½ cup broth; cook over medium heat until liquid is absorbed. Add remaining broth ¼ cup at a time, cooking until liquid is absorbed. Add additional broth as needed until rice is creamy. Stir in cheese; cook until cheese is melted and heated through. Garnish with parsley; if desired.

Nutrition per serving: 131 calories, 0.1 g fat, 26 g carbohydrates, 5 g protein, 0 mg cholesterol, <1 dietary fiber, 497 mg sodium
Exchanges: 1½ starch
Carb Choices: 2

Pasta and Rice

Shopping List

Dairy
nonfat Parmesan cheese

Canned
3 14-oz. cans nonfat chicken or vegetable broth

Packaged
long grain rice (not instant)

Seasonings/Spices
bottled minced garlic

Optional
fresh parsley

Eat like the Italians! In Italy, risotto is served in the center of warmed, individual shallow bowls and eaten from around the edges, continuously spreading rice from the center.

Sun-Dried Tomato Couscous

Easy | **Serves: 4**

2½ cups nonfat chicken or vegetable broth, *divided*

½ cup frozen diced onions

2 tsp. bottled minced garlic

3 tbsp. chopped sun-dried tomatoes (not packed in oil)

1⅓ cups uncooked couscous

2 tsp. dried basil, *crushed*

Spray large saucepan with cooking spray; add ¼ cup broth and heat over medium-high heat. Add onions and garlic; cook, stirring frequently, until onions are tender. Stir in sun-dried tomatoes; cook 1–2 minutes. Add remaining broth; bring to a boil over high heat. Stir in couscous and basil. Remove saucepan from heat, cover, and let stand 5 minutes until liquid is absorbed. Fluff with a fork before serving.

Nutrition per serving: 256 calories, 0.7 g fat, 51 g carbohydrates, 10 g protein, 0 mg cholesterol, 10 g dietary fiber, 498 mg sodium
Exchanges: 3 starch, 1 vegetable
Carb Choices: 3

Shopping List

Frozen
12-oz. pkg. frozen diced onions

Canned
2 14-oz. cans nonfat chicken broth

Packaged
couscous
5-oz. pkg. sun-dried tomatoes (not packed in oil)

Seasonings/Spices
bottled minced garlic
dried basil

Couscous is the perfect rush-hour ingredient; it cooks up light and fluffy by absorbing boiling liquid after it's removed from the heat.

Vegetarian Couscous

Easy | **Serves: 4**

2 cups water

1⅓ cups uncooked couscous

1 28-oz. jar nonfat pasta sauce
(any variety)

1 15-oz. can cannellini beans,
drained

⅛ tsp. crushed red pepper

2 tbsp. nonfat Parmesan
cheese

Pour water into large saucepan; bring to a boil over high heat. Stir in couscous, cover, and remove pan from heat. Let stand 5 minutes until liquid is absorbed and couscous is tender. Combine pasta sauce, beans, and pepper in microwave-safe dish; microwave on High 5–6 minutes until bubbly hot. Pour sauce over cooked couscous and toss to coat; sprinkle with Parmesan cheese and serve.

Nutrition per serving: 430 calories, 0.8 g fat, 85 g carbohydrates, 18 g protein, 0 mg cholesterol, 4 g dietary fiber, 642 mg sodium
Exchanges: 5 starch, 2 vegetable
Carb Choices: 6

Pasta
and
Rice

Shopping List

Dairy
nonfat Parmesan cheese

Canned
15-oz. can cannellini beans

Packaged
couscous

Condiments
28-oz. jar nonfat pasta sauce
(any variety)

Seasonings/Spices
crushed red pepper

Couscous is a North African-style pasta
that is ready in 5 minutes. The tiny pasta, made with semolina wheat, tastes similar to Italian pasta.

Chapter Index

11 Simple Sides

Pineapple Berry Salad

Adding spices to fresh, frozen, or canned vegetables is the easiest and quickest way to prepare a side dish. A little bit of flavor goes a long way. Mix and match for the best side dishes yet! Simple rule of thumb: 1 tablespoon fresh herbs or packaged herb blends equals 1 teaspoon dried herb.

Vegetables	Best Spice Selection
Artichokes	Thyme
Asparagus	Basil, caraway, dill, tarragon
Beets	Ginger, ground cloves, thyme
Broccoli	Dill, oregano, rosemary, tarragon
Brussels sprouts	Dill, paprika, sage, thyme
Cabbage	Caraway, cumin, dill, oregano, savory
Carrots	Allspice, cinnamon, dill, ginger, ground cloves, mint, nutmeg, thyme
Cauliflower	Chili powder, cumin, curry, dill, nutmeg, tarragon
Celery	Dill, marjoram, thyme
Corn	Basil, chili powder, cilantro, cumin, nutmeg
Cucumber	Cayenne pepper, dill
Eggplant	Allspice, basil, curry, marjoram, oregano, sage
Green beans	Basil, nutmeg, marjoram, sesame seeds, tarragon, thyme
Lima beans	Oregano, sage, savory, tarragon, thyme
Mushrooms	Oregano, rosemary, savory, tarragon, thyme
Onions	Chili powder, nutmeg, oregano, whole cloves
Peas	Cilantro, dill, ginger, marjoram, mint, nutmeg, savory, sesame seeds, thyme
Peppers, bell	Basil, marjoram, oregano
Potatoes	Bay leaf, chives, dill, marjoram, paprika, parsley, rosemary, thyme
Spinach	Allspice, cinnamon, rosemary
Squash/Pumpkin	Allspice, basil, cinnamon, ginger, ground cloves, sage
Sweet potatoes	Cinnamon, ground cloves, nutmeg, thyme
Tomatoes	Basil, bay leaf, cilantro, parsley, oregano, sage, tarragon, thyme
Zucchini	Basil, marjoram, mint, oregano

Simple
Sides

Broccoli-Cheese Bake

Easy | **Do Ahead** | **Serves: 6**

1 20-oz. pkg. frozen chopped broccoli, *thawed and drained*

2 cups nonfat cottage cheese

½ cup egg substitute

½ cup nonfat Parmesan cheese

Preheat oven to 375°. Spray 9-inch pie plate or 8-inch baking dish with cooking spray. Combine all ingredients in baking dish and mix well. Bake 25–30 minutes until lightly browned and cooked through. Let stand 5 minutes before cutting.

Nutrition per serving: 70 calories, 0.1 g fat, 9 g carbohydrates, 10 g protein, 2 mg cholesterol, 4 g dietary fiber, 204 mg sodium
Exchanges: 2 vegetable, 1 very lean meat
Carb Choices: 1

Shopping List

Dairy
16 oz. nonfat cottage cheese
4 oz. egg substitute
nonfat Parmesan cheese

Frozen
20-oz. pkg. frozen chopped broccoli

One of the easiest ways to cut calories but preserve flavors you crave is to select lower fat versions of salad dressings and sauces.

Cornflake Crumb Corn Casserole

Easy | Do Ahead | Serves: 6

½ cup egg substitute

½ cup + 2 tbsp. nonfat half and half

2 15¼-oz. cans whole kernel corn, *drained*

2 cups nonfat shredded cheddar cheese

1 cup cornflake crumbs, *divided*

I Can't Believe It's Not Butter spray

Preheat oven to 350°. Spray 11-inch shallow baking dish with cooking spray. Combine egg substitute, half and half, corn, cheese, and ½ cup cornflake crumbs in medium bowl; mix well. Pour mixture into baking dish. Sprinkle with remaining cornflake crumbs and spray with "butter" spray (5–8 sprays). Bake 25–30 minutes until bubbly hot and lightly browned.

Nutrition per serving: 257 calories, 0.1 g fat, 47 g carbohydrates, 18 g protein, 0 mg cholesterol, 3 g dietary fiber, 601 mg sodium
Exchanges: 3 starch, 1 very lean meat
Carb Choices: 3

Simple Sides

Shopping List

Dairy
4 oz. egg substitute
nonfat half and half
8 oz. nonfat shredded
  cheddar cheese
I Can't Believe It's Not
  Butter spray

Canned
2 15¼-oz. cans whole
  kernel corn

Packaged
cornflake crumbs

While you can substitute breadcrumbs for the cornflake crumbs, the flavor won't be quite as sweet.

Rosemary Garlic Mashed Potatoes

Easy | Serves: 8

7 cups rosemary and garlic
diced potatoes

1½ tsp. garlic powder

1½ cups nonfat sour cream

1 cup nonfat chicken broth,
warmed

pepper to taste

2 tbsp. chopped green onions
(optional)

Combine potatoes and garlic powder in large saucepan; add enough water to completely cover potatoes. Bring to a boil over high heat; reduce heat to low, cover, and simmer 10–15 minutes until tender. Drain potatoes in colander. Place potatoes in large bowl; mash well. Add sour cream and chicken broth; beat with electric mixer until creamy and smooth. Season with pepper; garnish with chopped green onions, if desired.

Nutrition per serving: 139 calories, 0 g fat, 27 g carbohydrates, 6 g protein, 0 mg cholesterol, 3 g dietary fiber, 351 mg sodium
Exchanges: 1½ starch
Carb Choices: 2

Shopping List

Produce
4 16-oz. pkgs. rosemary and
garlic diced potatoes

Dairy
12 oz. nonfat sour cream

Canned
14-oz. can nonfat chicken broth

Seasonings/Spices
garlic powder
pepper

Optional
green onions

You can substitute any precooked diced potatoes, or boil, peel, and dice your own potatoes; season and prepare as directed.

Super Stuffed Potatoes

Easy | Do Ahead | Serves: 4

4 large baking potatoes (each about 4 oz.)

1 cup nonfat sour cream

¾ cup nonfat shredded cheddar cheese

3 tbsp. chopped green onions

2 tbsp. Tomato 'n Bacon Parmesano salad topping

Shopping List

Produce
4 large baking potatoes
green onions

Dairy
8 oz. nonfat sour cream
nonfat shredded cheddar cheese

Packaged
5-oz. pkg. Tomato 'n Bacon Parmesano salad topping

Prick baking potatoes with a fork in several places. Microwave on High for 9 minutes per potato. Preheat oven to 500°. Place microwaved potatoes in oven 10–15 minutes until skin is browned. Remove from oven and let cool 5–10 minutes. Reduce oven temperature to 450°. Cut a ¼-inch slice from the top of each potato; carefully scoop out pulp and place in medium bowl. Mash pulp with fork; add sour cream, cheddar cheese, and onions; mix well. Spoon potato mixture back into potato shells; sprinkle with 1½ teaspoons Tomato 'n Bacon Parmesano salad topping. Line baking sheet with foil and spray with cooking spray; place stuffed potatoes on baking sheet. Bake 12–15 minutes until cheese is melted and potatoes are heated through. If prepared ahead, keep potato mixture in bowl; microwave on High 2–3 minutes to heat through. Stuff potatoes and proceed as directed.

Simple Sides

Nutrition per serving: 307 calories, 0.7 g fat, 57 g carbohydrates, 15 protein, 0 mg cholesterol, 6 g dietary fiber, 279 mg sodium
Exchanges: 3 starch, 1 very lean meat, ½ other carb
Carb Choices: 4

Baked potato meals are one of the greatest fast food options—you can top your tater with just about anything from meat and cheese to veggies and fresh herbs.

Cranberry Corn Bread Dressing

Easy | Do Ahead | Serves: 12

½ cup + 14-oz. can nonfat chicken or vegetable broth, *divided*

2 cups frozen seasoning vegetables

1 16-oz. pkg. corn bread dressing mix

2 6-oz. pkg. dried cranberries

2 tbsp. dried parsley flakes

1 tsp. dried rosemary

dash pepper

Spray large nonstick skillet or Dutch oven with cooking spray; add ½ cup broth and heat over medium-high heat. Add frozen seasoning vegetables; cook, stirring frequently, until vegetables are tender. Stir in remaining broth and bring to a boil over high heat. Remove skillet from burner; stir in remaining ingredients and mix well. Preheat oven to 350°. Spray 9×13-inch baking dish with cooking spray. Spoon dressing into baking dish and bake 30–45 minutes until lightly browned.

Nutrition per serving: 243 calories, 1.4 g fat, 53 g carbohydrates, 5 g protein, <1 mg cholesterol, 2 g dietary fiber, 808 mg sodium
Exchanges: 2 starch, 1 vegetable, 1 fruit
Carb Choices: 4

Shopping List

Frozen
10-oz. pkg. frozen seasoning vegetables

Canned
3 14-oz. cans nonfat chicken or vegetable broth

Packaged
16-oz pkg. corn bread dressing mix
2 6-oz. pkgs. dried cranberries

Seasonings/Spices
dried parsley flakes
dried rosemary
pepper

Many supermarkets carry seasoning packages in the produce section, especially during holiday season. Not having to slice, dice, mince, or chop saves lots of time in the kitchen.

Corn Pudding

Easy | **Serves: 6**

¾ cup egg substitute

1 cup nonfat half and half

2 tbsp. sugar

1 15½-oz. can white whole kernel corn, *drained*

1 tsp. onion powder

⅛ tsp. cinnamon

Preheat oven to 350°. Spray 1-quart casserole with cooking spray. Combine all ingredients in casserole dish and mix well. Place casserole in larger pan filled with 1-inch of hot water. Bake 1 hour until cooked through.

Nutrition per serving: 117 calories, 0.7 g fat, 24 g carbohydrates, 5 g protein, 0 mg cholesterol, 1 g dietary fiber, 327 mg sodium
Exchanges: 1 starch, ½ other carb
Carb Choices: 1

Simple Sides

Shopping List

Dairy
6 oz. egg substitute
8 oz. nonfat half and half

Canned
15½-oz. can white whole kernel corn

Baking Goods
sugar

Seasonings/Spices
onion powder
cinnamon

White corn, often referred to as shoepeg corn, has small, narrow kernels with a distinct sweet flavor. Use yellow and white corn kernels interchangeably; you can also try this recipe with frozen corn kernels rather than canned. Simply thaw and drain frozen kernels before preparing recipe.

Creamed Mexicorn

3 oz. nonfat cream cheese, *softened*

1 11-oz. can Mexicorn, *drained*

Spray small saucepan with cooking spray. Add cream cheese; cook over low heat, stirring frequently, until cheese is creamy and melted. Stir in Mexicorn and cook until heated through. Serve immediately.

Nutrition per serving: 74 calories, 0.4 g fat, 16 g carbohydrates, 4 g protein, 0 mg cholesterol, 2 g dietary fiber, 404 mg sodium
Exchanges: 1 starch
Carb Choices: 1

Shopping List

Dairy
3 oz. nonfat cream cheese

Canned
11-oz. can Mexicorn

Most canned corn is prepared from yellow or golden varieties.

Almost From Scratch Baked Beans

Easy | **Do Ahead** | **Serves: 4**

½ cup vegetarian baked beans,
   lightly drained

½ cup canned black beans,
   rinsed and drained

½ cup canned cannellini beans,
   rinsed and drained

½ cup canned red kidney beans,
   rinsed and drained

1 tbsp. onion powder

3 tbsp. barbecue sauce

3 tbsp. brown sugar

2 tsp. prepared mustard

Preheat oven to 400°. Spray oven-proof and microwave-safe baking dish with cooking spray. Combine all ingredients in dish and mix well. Cover and microwave on High 3–4 minutes. Place casserole in oven and bake, uncovered, 25–30 minutes until bubbly hot.

Nutrition per serving: 186 calories, 0.6 g fat, 39 g carbohydrates, 8 g protein, 0 mg cholesterol, 5 g dietary fiber, 570 mg sodium
Exchanges: 2 starach, ½ other carb
Carb Choices: 3

Simple
Sides

Shopping List

Canned
15-oz. can vegetarian
   baked beans
15-oz. can black beans
15-oz. can cannellini beans
15-oz. can red kidney beans

Baking Goods
brown sugar

Condiments
barbecue sauce
prepared mustard

Seasonings/Spices
onion powder

Canned baked beans are generally processed in tomato sauce or brown sugar and molasses; vegetarian styles are usually lowest in calories and fat.

Cheddar Hash Browns

Easy | Do Ahead | Serves: 6

¾ cup skim milk

½ cup nonfat vegetable broth, *divided*

¼ tsp. garlic powder

1 1-lb. 4-oz. pkg. Southwest-style hash brown potatoes

2 cups nonfat shredded cheddar cheese

Combine milk, ¼ cup + 2 tablespoons broth, and garlic powder in large bowl; mix well. Stir in hash browns. Spray large nonstick skillet with cooking spray; add remaining broth to skillet and heat over medium-high heat. Add hash brown mixture; cook, stirring frequently, over medium heat until heated through. Stir in cheese and cook 3–4 minutes, stirring constantly. Preheat oven to 350°. Spray 1½- to 2-quart baking dish with cooking spray. Transfer potatoes to baking dish and bake, uncovered, 40–45 minutes until lightly browned and bubbly hot.

Nutrition per serving: 121 calories, 0.1 g fat, 15 g carbohydrates, 13 g protein, 1 mg cholesterol, 1 g dietary fiber, 454 mg sodium
Exchanges: 1 starch, 1 very lean meat
Carb Choices: 1

Shopping List

Produce
1-lb. 4-oz. pkg. Southwest-style hash brown potatoes

Dairy
8 oz. nonfat shredded cheddar cheese
6 oz. skim milk

Canned
nonfat vegetable broth

Seasonings/Spices
onion powder

You can substitute chicken broth for the vegetable broth without affecting the finished result.

Chili Spice Sweet Potato Fries

Easy | **Do Ahead** | **Serves: 4**

½ cup nonfat Parmesan cheese

1 tsp. chili powder

2 large sweet potatoes,
   cut into ½-inch sticks

Preheat oven to 450°. Line baking sheet with foil and spray with cooking spray. Combine Parmesan cheese and chili powder in large zip-top bag. Add potato sticks, toss to coat, and arrange in a single layer on baking sheet. Bake 10–15 minutes; turn potatoes and bake 10–12 minutes more until golden brown and crisp.

Nutrition per serving: 120 calories, 0.2 g fat, 25 g carbohydrates, 6 g protein, 0 mg cholesterol, 3 g dietary fiber, 105 mg sodium
Exchanges: 1½ starch
Carb Choices: 2

Simple
Sides

Shopping List

Produce
2 large sweet potatoes

Dairy
nonfat Parmesan cheese

Seasonings/Spices
chili powder

You'll never want fast food fries again after savoring these tender, crisp, sweet potato fries.

Sweet 'n Tangy Carrots

Easy | **Serves: 4**

1 16-oz. pkg. frozen sliced
   carrots

½ tsp. cinnamon

¾ cup pineapple juice

Spray microwave-safe dish with cooking spray. Place carrots in dish; sprinkle with cinnamon and pour pineapple juice over top. Microwave on High 2–3 minutes; turn dish and microwave 3–4 minutes until carrots are tender.

Nutrition per serving: 68 calories, 0.1 g fat, 16 g carbohydrates, 2 g protein, 0 mg cholesterol, 4 g dietary fiber, 67 mg sodium
Exchanges: 1 vegetable, ½ fruit
Carb Choices: 1

Shopping List

Frozen
16-oz. pkg. frozen sliced carrots

Canned
pineapple juice

Seasonings/Spices
cinnamon

When purchasing frozen vegetables, select packages that feel firm. To assure good quality, use vegetables immediately after defrosting.

Carrot Potato Pancakes

Easy | **Do Ahead** | **Serves: 6**

1 8-oz. pkg. shredded carrots

1 18-oz. pkg. shredded
   potatoes

1 tbsp. onion powder

1 tbsp. basil herb blend

¼ cup seasoned breadcrumbs

¼ cup nonfat Parmesan cheese

¼ cup + 2 tbsp. egg substitute

   I Can't Believe It's Not
      Butter spray

Preheat oven to 400°. Line baking sheet with foil and spray with cooking spray. Place shredded carrots and potatoes in colander and press out all the moisture. Transfer to a large bowl; add onion powder, herb blend, breadcrumbs, and Parmesan cheese and mix well. Stir in egg substitute and mix. Using ¼ cup measure, drop vegetable mixture onto baking sheet; carefully flatten with spatula. Lightly spray pancakes with "butter" spray. Bake 5–6 minutes; turn pancakes over and bake 5–6 minutes until browned and crisp.

Nutrition per serving: 133 calories, 0.3 g fat, 28 g carbohydrates, 6 g protein, 0 mg cholesterol, 3 g dietary fiber, 124 mg sodium
Exchanges: 1 starch, 2 vegetable
Carb Choices: 2

Simple
Sides

Shopping List

Produce
8-oz. pkg. shredded carrots
18-oz. pkg. shredded potatoes
basil herb blend

Dairy
I Can't Believe It's Not Butter spray
nonfat Parmesan cheese
egg substitute

Packaged
seasoned breadcrumbs

Seasonings/Spices
onion powder

All out of breadcrumbs? You can substitute cracker crumbs, crushed croutons, crushed stuffing, cornflake crumbs, or matzo meal.

Pearl Potatoes with Onions and Herbs

Easy | Serves: 6

1 18-oz. pkg. garden herb
    pearl potatoes

1 tbsp. 1-Step Garlic Herb
    Chicken Seasoning

¼ cup dried minced onions

Preheat oven to 450°. Line baking sheet with foil and spray with cooking spray. Spread potatoes in a single layer on baking sheet; sprinkle with 1-Step Garlic Herb seasoning and minced onions. Bake 20–25 minutes until lightly browned and crisp.

Nutrition per serving: 101 calories, 0 g fat, 22 g carbohydrates, 2 g protein, 0 mg cholesterol, 2 g dietary fiber, 250 mg sodium
Exchanges: 1 starch
Carb Choices: 1

Shopping List

Produce
18-oz. pkg. garden herb pearl
    potatoes

Seasonings/Spices
1-Step Garlic Herb Chicken
    Seasoning
dried minced onions

One-Step Garlic Herb Chicken seasoning is a combination of garlic-toasted wheat crumbs and a variety of seasonings.

Cinnamon Spice Baby Carrots

Easy | Serves: 6

2 16-oz. bags frozen baby
   carrots, *cooked and
   drained*

¼ cup brown sugar

1 tbsp. cornstarch

⅔ cup water

½ tsp. cinnamon

½ cup raisins

2 tsp. white wine vinegar

Cook carrots according to package directions; drain and keep warm. Combine brown sugar, cornstarch, water, and cinnamon in small saucepan; mix until sugar and cornstarch are dissolved. Stir in raisins and vinegar. Cook over medium heat, stirring constantly, until sauce becomes thick and raisins are plump. Pour sauce over cooked baby carrots and serve immediately.

Nutrition per serving: 141 calories, 0.3 g fat, 35 g carbohydrates, 2 g protein, 0 mg cholesterol, 5 g dietary fiber, 57 mg sodium
Exchanges: 3 vegetable, ½ fruit, ½ other carb
Carb Choices: 2

Simple Sides

Shopping List

Frozen
2 16-oz. pkgs. frozen baby
   carrots

Baking Goods
raisins
brown sugar
cornstarch

Condiments
white wine vinegar

Seasonings/Spice
cinnamon

You can substitute fresh baby carrots for frozen ones, but plan on an extended cooking time.

Lemon Parmesan Broccoli Florets

Easy | **Serves: 4**

¾ lb. packaged broccoli florets

water

2 tbsp. + 2 tsp. seasoned
  breadcrumbs

1 tbsp. + 1 tsp. nonfat
  Parmesan cheese

1 tbsp. bottled lemon juice

Preheat oven to 450°. Spray glass microwave-safe and oven-proof dish with cooking spray; add broccoli florets, drizzle with water, and microwave on High 3–4 minutes until crisp-tender. Combine breadcrumbs and Parmesan cheese and mix well; sprinkle over broccoli and drizzle with lemon juice. Bake 12–15 minutes until breadcrumbs are lightly browned.

Nutrition per serving: 46 calories, 0.5 g fat, 8 g carbohydrates, 4 g protein, 0 mg cholesterol, 3 g dietary fiber, 69 mg sodium
Exchanges: 2 vegetable
Carb Choices: 1

Shopping List

Produce
¾ lb. broccoli florets

Dairy
nonfat Parmesan cheese

Packaged
seasoned breadcrumbs

Condiments
bottled lemon juice

You can season homemade breadcrumbs with salt, herbs, garlic powder, onion powder, and/or lemon peel, if you wish.

Hot Spinach Salad

Easy | **Serves: 4**

- 2 9-oz. pkgs. fresh spinach leaves, *chopped*
- 1 7-oz. container diced tri-pepper mix
- 1½ cups grape tomatoes
- 2 8-oz. pkgs. sliced mushrooms, *divided*
- ¾ cup nonfat Italian salad dressing (not creamy)
- ½ cup chopped green onions
- 6 tbsp. Tomato 'n Bacon Parmesano salad topping

Combine spinach, peppers, tomatoes, and 2 cups sliced mushrooms in large bowl; toss to mix. For dressing, spray large nonstick skillet with cooking spray and heat over medium-high heat. Add remaining mushrooms; cook, stirring frequently, 4–5 minutes until softened. Add salad dressing and green onions to skillet; cook, stirring constantly, about 1 minute just until heated. Pour dressing over spinach salad mix; sprinkle with salad topping and serve immediately.

Nutrition per serving: 160 calories, 2.6 g fat, 26 g carbohydrates, 9 g protein, 0 mg cholesterol, 8 g dietary fiber, 346 mg sodium
Exchanges: 3 vegetable, 1 other carb
Carb Choices: 2

Simple Sides

Shopping List

Produce
2 9-oz. pkgs. fresh spinach leaves
7-oz. container diced tri-pepper mix
1 pint grape tomatoes
2 8-oz. pkgs. sliced mushrooms
¼ lb. green onions

Packaged
5-oz. pkg. Tomato 'n Bacon Parmesano salad topping

Condiments
6 oz. nonfat Italian salad dressing (not creamy)

Save money by purchasing whole bell peppers and chopping them yourself.

Mexicorn Tomato Salad

Easy | Do Ahead | Serves: 6

¹⁄₃ cup nonfat Italian salad dressing

3 tbsp. basil herb blend

2 14½-oz. cans diced tomatoes with basil, garlic, and oregano, *well drained and patted dry*

2 11-oz. cans Mexicorn, *drained*

fresh basil leaves (optional)

Combine salad dressing and basil herb blend; mix well. Place well-drained tomatoes in medium bowl; pour salad dressing mix over top and toss lightly. Stir in Mexicorn and mix lightly. Serve immediately or cover and refrigerate several hours. Garnish with fresh basil leaves, if desired.

Nutrition per serving: 115 calories, 0.5 g fat, 25 g carbohydrates, 4 g protein, 0 mg cholesterol, 3 g dietary fiber, 629 mg sodium
Exchanges: 1 starch, 2 vegetable
Carb Choices: 0

Shopping List

Produce
basil herb blend

Canned
2 14½-oz. cans diced tomatoes with basil, garlic, and oregano
2 11-oz. cans Mexicorn

Condiments
nonfat Italian salad dressing

Optional
fresh basil leaves

Canned vegetables are great timesavers that preserve taste and nutrients. Check the cans carefully though–bulging or swelling cans indicate spoilage.

Garden Ranch Salad

Easy | **Serves: 4**

1 16-oz. pkg. broccoli and cauliflower florets, *chopped*

¾ cup grape tomatoes, *cut in half*

2 tbsp. nonfat Parmesan cheese

½ cup nonfat Ranch salad dressing

Combine chopped broccoli and cauliflower with tomatoes in medium bowl; sprinkle with Parmesan cheese. Pour salad dressing over top and toss to coat.

Nutrition per serving: 75 calories, 0.4 g fat, 15 g carbohydrates, 4 g protein, 0 mg cholesterol, 3 g dietary fiber, 319 mg sodium
Exchanges: 3 vegetable
Carb Choices: 1

Simple Sides

Shopping List

Produce
16 oz. pkg. broccoli and cauliflower florets
grape tomatoes

Dairy
nonfat Parmesan cheese

Condiments
nonfat Ranch salad dressing

Save tons of calories and fat by switching to nonfat salad dressing. You can save almost 110 calories and 17 grams of fat per 2-tablespoon serving.

Corn, Tomato, and Onion Salad with Red Wine Vinaigrette

Easy | **Do Ahead** | **Serves: 4**

1 11-oz. can Mexicorn, *drained*

2 14½-oz. cans petite-cut diced tomatoes with roasted garlic and sweet onion, *well drained*

⅓ cup fat-free red wine vinegar salad dressing

Combine Mexicorn and tomatoes in medium bowl; pour dressing over top and toss to mix. Cover and refrigerate at least 1 hour before serving.

Nutrition per serving: 114 calories, 0.4 g fat, 24 g carbohydrates, 4 g protein, 0 mg cholesterol, 3 g dietary fiber, 673 mg sodium
Exchanges: 1 starch, 2 vegetable
Carb Choices: 2

Shopping List

Canned

11-oz. can Mexicorn
2 14½-oz. cans petite-cut diced tomatoes with roasted garlic and sweet onion

Condiments

12-oz. bottle fat-free red wine vinegar salad dressing

Don't just pour on the dressing. Toss your salad before you take the first bite. By making sure food is coated, you won't overload on dressing.

Creamy Cucumber Salad

Easy | **Do Ahead** | **Serves: 6**

3 large cucumbers, *peeled and sliced thin*

1 small onion, *sliced thin*

8 oz. nonfat sour cream

2 tbsp. sugar

pepper to taste

Combine cucumber and onion slices in medium bowl. Combine sour cream and sugar; mix well. Pour sour cream mixture over cucumber and onions; mix lightly and season with pepper to taste. Cover and refrigerate until ready to serve.

Nutrition per serving: 72 calories, 0.2 g fat, 14 g carbohydrates, 4 protein, 0 mg cholesterol, 2 dietary fiber, 28 mg sodium
Exchanges: 0
Carb Choices: 0

Simple Sides

Shopping List

Produce
3 large cucumbers
1 small onion

Dairy
8 oz. nonfat sour cream

Baking Goods
sugar

Seasonings/Spice
pepper

Cut sugar intake by substituting 2 tablespoons Splenda for granulated sugar.

Pineapple Berry Salad

Easy | **Serves: 4**

2 10-oz. pkgs. Lafayette or
   spring mix salad

1 16-oz. can pineapple
   chunks in juice, *drain and
   reserve 2 tbsp. juice*

1 6-oz. pkg. Dried Berries 'n
   Cherries

½ cup nonfat honey Dijon
   salad dressing

Combine lettuce, pineapple chunks, and dried fruit in large bowl; toss to mix. Combine salad dressing with reserved pineapple juice and mix well. Pour dressing over salad and toss to coat. Dressing can be made ahead and refrigerated 1–2 days, if desired.

Nutrition per serving: 263 calories, 0.8 g fat, 60 g carbohydrates, 4 g protein, 0 mg cholesterol, 5 g dietary fiber, 133 mg sodium
Exchanges: 3 vegetable, 3 fruit
Carb Choices: 4

Shopping List

Produce
2 10-oz. pkgs. Lafayette or
   spring mix salad

Canned
16-oz. can pineapple chunks
   in juice

Packaged
6-oz. pkg. Dried Berries 'n
   Cherries

Condiments
nonfat honey Dijon salad
   dressing

You can substitute any packaged salad blend, or stop at your supermarket salad bar for prepared items.

Couscous Salad with Dried Fruit

Easy | Do Ahead | Serves: 6

1½ cups nonfat chicken broth

1 cup uncooked quick-cooking couscous

1 6-oz. pkg. Dried Berries 'n Cherries

1 7-oz. container Salad Confetti mix

¾ cup nonfat raspberry vinaigrette salad dressing

2 tbsp. slivered toasted almonds

Pour chicken broth into medium saucepan; bring to a boil over high heat. Add couscous; immediately remove from heat, cover, and let stand 5 minutes. Stir couscous with a fork until grains are fluffy. Set aside and let cool 10–15 minutes. Combine cooked couscous, dried fruit, and Salad Confetti in medium bowl; drizzle salad dressing over top and toss to coat. Garnish with toasted almonds. This salad can be served immediately or refrigerated several hours before serving.

Nutrition per serving: 537 calories, 2.2 g fat, 1.9 g carbohydrates, 7 g protein, 0 mg cholesterol, 11 g dietary fiber, 331 mg sodium
Exchanges: 3 starch, 2 vegetable, 4 fruit
Carb Choices: 8

Simple Sides

Shopping List

Produce
7-oz. container Salad
    Confetti mix

Canned
15-oz. can nonfat chicken broth

Packaged
6-oz. pkg. Dried Berries 'n
    Cherries
slivered toasted almonds
quick-cooking couscous

Condiments
8 oz. nonfat raspberry
    vinaigrette salad dressing

Turn this salad into a perfect meatless meal by using vegetable broth in place of chicken broth; add chopped vegetables and substitute other dried fruits, as desired.

Chapter Index

12 Snacks for Kids

After School Snack Mix

Snacking is an important part of healthful eating plans and can help children, teens, and adults meet energy and nutrient needs. Though some believe that snacking undermines the nutritional quality of diets and is contributing to the rise in obesity, it's WHAT you snack on that counts!

Selecting nutritional snacks eliminates worry over empty calories that simply fill up your stomach. Unrestricted access to snacks can lead to overindulgence of calories and fat, but scheduled snacking can provide health benefits while staving off hunger. According to the National Dairy Council, "Healthy snacking during childhood and adolescence can help support adequate growth and development, and may help lay the foundation for lifelong healthful eating behaviors." While there are no purely good or purely bad foods, the best snack choices include a variety of foods from the USDA Food Guide Pyramid's five food groups. Make minimal selections from the top (fats, oils, sweets). Look for foods without trans fats; those foods with 2 grams or more fiber; whole, unprocessed foods; and snacks with a variety of nutrients.

20 Super Snacks in Seconds

1. Whole grain cereal with low-fat milk
2. English muffin with 1 ounce nonfat cheese
3. 6 ounces of nonfat yogurt sprinkled with 1 tablespoon wheat germ
4. Carrot, celery, and cucumber sticks with nonfat ranch salad dressing or salsa
5. 1 small cooked sweet potato sprinkled with Butter Buds or sprayed lightly with I Can't Believe It's Not Butter spray
6. 3 cups air-popped popcorn seasoned with Butter Buds, chili powder, Mexican seasoning, or nonfat Parmesan cheese
7. Baked tortilla chips with nonfat bean dip
8. Pretzel rods or sticks with mustard
9. Whole grain crackers with low-fat cheese
10. Mini rice cakes spread with peanut butter
11. Apple slices with nonfat caramel dip or peanut butter
12. Fresh or dried fruits—whole or cut and made into fruit kabobs
13. Frozen bananas dipped in nonfat chocolate syrup
14. Applesauce or a pudding cup
15. Animal crackers
16. Whole grain bagel with fruit preserves
17. Fresh fruit smoothies
18. Cup sugar-free Jell-O with 2 tablespoons nonfat Cool Whip
19. Cup nonfat pudding layered with 2 crumbled graham crackers and a tablespoon of Cool Whip on top
20. Cup cottage cheese sprinkled with cinnamon

Snacks for Kids

After School Snack Mix

Easy | **Do Ahead** | **Serves: 4**

4 cups Chex cereal

1 6-oz. pkg. Dried Berries 'n Cherries

½ cup chopped dried apricots

1 cup miniature pretzels

3 tbsp. miniature chocolate chips

Combine all ingredients in large zip-top bag and shake until mixed. Keep stored in sealed container or zip-top bag for up to 2 weeks.

Nutrition per serving: 388 calories, 3.7 g fat, 83 g carbohydrates, 6 g protein, 2 mg cholesterol, 3 g dietary fiber, 250 mg sodium
Exchanges: 6 other carb
Carb Choices: 6

Shopping List

Packaged
Chex cereal
6-oz. pkg. Dried Berries 'n Cherries
dried apricots
miniature pretzels (sticks, circles, or any other shape)

Baking Goods
miniature chocolate chips

Steer clear of ready-to-eat popcorn.
A study by the Center for Science in the Public Interest found that a medium-size bucket of movie popcorn contains as much as 650 calories and 43 grams of fat. Top it with butter and the values rise to 910 calories and 71 grams of fat.

Tropical Banana Split Treat

Easy | **Serves: 4**

4 bananas, *split in half*

½ cup apricot preserves

½ cup nonfat Cool Whip, *thawed*

1 cup dried tropical fruit
   medley mix

Place one banana (cut in half lengthwise) on each plate or dish. Spread 1 tablespoon preserves on each banana half. Top each half with 1 tablespoon Cool Whip and sprinkle with 2 tablespoons tropical fruit medley mix.

Nutrition per serving: 332 calories, 0.7 g fat, 83 g carbohydrates, 2 g protein, 0 mg cholesterol, 4 g dietary fiber, 10 mg sodium
Exchanges: 5 fruit
Carb Choices: 6

Snacks for Kids

Shopping List

Produce
4 bananas

Frozen
8-oz. container nonfat Cool Whip

Packaged
8 oz. pkg. dried tropical fruit
   medley mix

Condiments
apricot preserves

Healthful snacks can help fill any nutritional gaps in your daily diet.

Favorite Fruits and Dip with Chocolate Syrup

Easy | **Do Ahead** | **Serves: 4**

½ cup marshmallow crème

1 8-oz. pkg. nonfat cream cheese, *softened*

½ cup double chocolate sundae syrup

½ pint strawberries, *cleaned and hulled*

1 apple, *sliced thin*

1 pear, *sliced thin*

1 8-oz. container Fruit Natural Peach Chunks, *drained*

Combine marshmallow crème and cream cheese in medium bowl; blend until smooth and creamy. Pour chocolate syrup in small cup. Arrange fruit on platter; serve with cream dip and chocolate syrup.

Nutrition per serving: 252 calories, 0.4 g fat, 55 g carbohydrates, 8 g protein, 0 mg cholesterol, 4 g dietary fiber, 387 mg sodium
Exchanges: 3 fruit, ½ other carb
Carb Choices: 4

Shopping List

Produce
½ pint strawberries
1 apple
1 pear
8-oz. container Fruit Natural Peach Chunks

Dairy
8-oz. pkg. nonfat cream cheese

Dessert Toppings
7-oz. jar marshmallow crème
15-oz bottle double chocolate sundae syrup

Make the shift from snacks with empty calories to those that offer the goodness of fruits, vegetables, and whole grains.

After School Snack Mix p. 294

Pizza Potato Slices **p. 317**

p. 307 Fruit and Marshmallow Salad

Banana Mango Smoothie p. 314

p. 319 Mini Pepperoni Pizzas

Cinnamon-Sugar Tortilla Strips p. 311

Peanut Butter and Banana Waffle Snack

Easy | **Serves: 4**

4 fat-free frozen waffles

2 tbsp. reduced-fat peanut butter

1 tbsp. + 1 tsp. sugar-free seedless blackberry jam (or other sugar-free preserve of choice)

2 bananas, *sliced thin*

Toast waffles until lightly browned. Spread each waffle with 1½ teaspoons peanut butter, 1 teaspoon jam, and top with sliced bananas.

Nutrition per serving: 146 calories, 0.8 g fat, 32 g carbohydrates, 5 g protein, 0 mg cholesterol, 1 g dietary fiber, 194 mg sodium
Exchanges: 1 starch, 1 fruit, ½ very lean meat
Carb Choices: 2

Snacks for Kids

Shopping List

Produce
2 bananas

Frozen
10.2-oz. pkg. frozen fat-free waffles

Spreads
reduced-fat peanut butter
sugar-free seedless blackberry jam (or other sugar-free preserves of choice)

Beware: Fat-free products are not calorie-free. Portion control counts with everything.

Pineapple Banana-Berry Pops

Easy | Do Ahead | Serves: 12

1 8-oz. container nonfat
    strawberry-banana yogurt

½ cup skim milk

½ cup pineapple juice

1 banana

1 cup frozen sliced strawberries,
    thawed and drained

Combine all ingredients in food processor or blender; process or blend until smooth and creamy. Pour into twelve 3-ounce paper cups and arrange on baking sheet. Freeze 10–15 minutes; cover with plastic wrap. Insert popsicle sticks through plastic wrap in center and freeze at least 6 hours or overnight. Remove cup and plastic wrap before serving.

Nutrition per serving: 46 calories, 0.1 g fat, 11 g carbohydrates, 1 g protein, 0 mg cholesterol, 2 g dietary fiber, 18 mg sodium
Exchanges: 1 fruit
Carb Choices: 1

Shopping List

Produce
1 banana

Dairy
4 oz. skim milk
8-oz. container nonfat
    strawberry-banana yogurt

Frozen
10-oz. pkg. sliced strawberries

Canned
6-oz. can pineapple juice

Fruits are excellent snack choices;
their sugar contents satisfy taste without excessive calories or fat.

Fruit and Marshmallow Salad

Easy | Do Ahead | Serves: 6

4 cups packaged coleslaw mix

½ cup chopped dried apricots

1 Granny Smith apple, *cored and chopped*

½ cup green or red seedless grapes

1 cup miniature marshmallows

1¼ cups nonfat vanilla yogurt

Combine coleslaw mix, apricots, chopped apple, grapes, and marshmallows in medium bowl; toss to mix. Pour yogurt over top and toss until ingredients are coated and well mixed. Cover and refrigerate 1 hour before serving.

Nutrition per serving: 111 calories, 0.2 g fat, 26 g carbohydrates, 3 g protein, 1 mg cholesterol, 3 g dietary fiber, 338 mg sodium
Exchanges: 1 vegetable, 1 fruit, ½ other carb
Carb Choices: 2

Snacks for Kids

Shopping List

Produce
2 8-oz. pkgs. coleslaw mix
Granny Smith apple
green or red seedless grapes

Dairy
10 oz. nonfat vanilla yogurt

Packaged
dried apricots
miniature marshmallows

A study of children's primetime television revealed that less than 5% of 222 food commercials available to kids during Saturday morning cartoons promoted "reasonably nutritious" products.

Carrot Raisin Salad

1 cup nonfat vanilla yogurt

1 8-oz. can crushed pineapple in juice, *drained*

1 8-oz. pkg. shredded carrots

½ cup raisins

Combine yogurt and pineapple in small bowl; mix well. Combine carrots and raisins in medium bowl; pour yogurt-pineapple dressing over top and toss until coated. Cover and refrigerate until ready to serve.

Nutrition per serving: 271 calories, 0.4 g fat, 65 g carbohydrates, 7 g protein, 3 mg cholesterol, 6 g dietary fiber, 116 mg sodium
Exchanges: 2 vegetable, 3 fruit, ½ milk
Carb Choices: 4

Shopping List

Dairy
nonfat vanilla yogurt

Produce
8-oz. pkg. shredded carrots

Canned
8-oz. can crushed pineapple in juice

Packaged
raisins

According to the National Cancer Institute, 25% of school-age children do not consume one serving a day of vegetables, and for those who eat vegetables, French fries constitute one-fourth of all vegetables eaten.

Graham Sandwich Snacks

Easy | **Do Ahead** | **Serves: 4**

¼ cup miniature chocolate chips

¾ cup nonfat Cool Whip, *thawed*

12 squares low-fat honey
    graham crackers

Fold chocolate chips into Cool Whip. Spread each of 6 graham cracker squares with 2 tablespoons Cool Whip mixture and top with remaining cracker squares. Line baking sheet with foil; arrange graham sandwiches in a single layer; freeze 3–4 hours. Wrap sandwiches in freezer-safe wrap and store in zip-top bag. Sandwiches will keep in freezer for up to 1 week.

Nutrition per serving: 130 calories, 4 g fat, 22 g carbohydrates, 2 g protein, 0 mg cholesterol, 1 g dietary fiber, 14 mg sodium
Exchanges: 1 fat, 1 other carb
Carb Choices: 1

Snacks for Kids

Shopping List

Frozen
8-oz. container nonfat Cool Whip

Packaged
14.4-oz. pkg. low-fat honey
    graham crackers

Baking goods
miniature chocolate chips

According to the Snack Food Association, the typical American consumes more than 22 pounds of snack foods each year.

Chocolate-Chocolate Chip Cookies

Easy | Do Ahead | Freeze | Serves: 24

1 18-oz. pkg. fat-free fudge
    brownie mix

½ cup nonfat vanilla yogurt

2 tbsp. egg substitute

3 tbsp. miniature chocolate chips

   powdered sugar

Preheat oven to 350°. Line baking sheet with foil and spray with cooking spray. Combine brownie mix, yogurt, egg substitute, and chocolate chips; mix until ingredients are moistened. Drop dough by tablespoons onto baking sheet; bake 12–15 minutes until lightly browned. Cool completely; roll cookies in powdered sugar to coat.

Nutrition per serving: 91 calories, 0.4 g fat, 20 g carbohydrates, 1 g protein, <1 mg cholesterol, <1 g dietary fiber, 128 mg sodium
Exchanges: 1 other carb
Carb Choices: 1

Shopping List

Dairy
4-oz. nonfat vanilla yogurt
egg substitute

Baking Goods
18-oz. pkg. fat-free fudge
   brownie mix
miniature chocolate chips
powdered sugar

Don't displace nutritious foods

with sugary treats; balanced meal plans can include special treats without sacrificing nutrition.

Cinnamon-Sugar Tortilla Strips

Easy | **Do Ahead** | **Serves: 4**

2 10-inch 98% fat-free flour
   tortillas, *cut into strips*

   I Can't Believe It's Not Butter
   spray

¼ cup sugar

¾ tsp. cinnamon

Preheat oven to 400°. Line baking sheet with foil and spray with cooking spray. Arrange tortilla strips in a single layer on baking sheet; spray with "butter" spray. Combine sugar and cinnamon in small cup and mix well; sprinkle cinnamon-sugar mixture over tortillas. Bake 6–8 minutes until crisp. Cool 5 minutes before serving or cool completely before storing in zip-top bags.

Nutrition per serving: 106 calories, 0.2 g fat, 24 g carbohydrates, 2 g protein, 0 mg cholesterol, 1 g dietary fiber, 170 mg sodium
Exchanges: 1 starch, ½ other carb
Carb Choices: 2

Snacks for Kids

Shopping List

Dairy
I Can't Believe It's Not Butter
   spray

Packaged
17.5-oz. pkg. 98% fat-free flour
   tortillas

Baking Goods
sugar

Seasonings/Spices
cinnamon

With 8-10 grams of fat per ounce, traditional potato, taco, and tortilla chips are among the most fat-laden snacks. Beware of "lite" varieties, which are not always a nutritional bargain.

Pineapple Pumpkin Sundae

Easy | **Serves: 6**

4 cups nonfat frozen vanilla ice cream or yogurt, *softened*

1¾ cups canned pumpkin pie mix (not canned pumpkin puree)

¾ cup pineapple dessert topping

Combine ice cream and pumpkin pie mix in large bowl; mix until blended smooth. Cover and freeze 2 hours; remove from freezer, beat with mixer until creamy and smooth, and return to freezer for at least 2 hours or until firm. For each serving, top ½ cup pumpkin ice cream with 2 tablespoons pineapple dessert topping and serve immediately.

Nutrition per serving: 146 calories, 0.1 g fat, 32 g carbohydrates, 5 g protein, 5 mg cholesterol, 1 g dietary fiber, 73 mg sodium
Exchanges: 2 other carb
Carb Choices: 2

Shopping List

Frozen
1 quart nonfat frozen vanilla ice cream or yogurt

Canned
30-oz. can pumpkin pie mix (not canned pumpkin puree)

Condiments
12-oz. jar pineapple dessert topping

It's not only important to have the right snacks, but to have them in the right location. Keep kids' snacks on easy-to-reach pantry or refrigerator shelves.

Funfetti Pineapple Cupcakes

Easy | **Do Ahead** | **Freeze** | **Serves: 24**

1   18.9-oz. pkg. Funfetti Premium Cake Mix

4   egg whites

1¼   cup water

⅓   cup canned crushed pineapple in juice, *do not drain*

Preheat oven to 350°. Spray muffin tins with cooking spray. Combine all the ingredients in a medium bowl; beat with electric mixer until creamy and smooth. Fill muffin cups with batter. Bake 20–23 minutes until lightly browned on top. Cool slightly; remove from pan; cool completely.

Nutrition per serving: 97 calories, 2 g fat, 19 g carbohydrates, 2 g protein, 0 mg cholesterol, 0 g dietary fiber, 165 mg sodium
Exchanges: 1 other carb
Carb Choices: 1

Snacks for Kids

Shopping List

Dairy
whole eggs

Canned
8-oz. can crushed pineapple in juice

Baking Goods
18.9-oz. pkg. Funfetti Premium Cake Mix

Save money–snack smarter! Americans spend almost $4 billion a year on cookies and more than $8 billion on potato chips, pretzels, corn chips, and tortilla chips.

Banana Mango Smoothie

Easy | **Serves: 2**

2 bananas, *sliced and frozen*

⅔ cup frozen mango slices

1 12-oz. can mango nectar

8 oz. nonfat vanilla yogurt

Combine all ingredients in blender and process until smooth and creamy. Serve immediately.

Nutrition per serving: 292 calories, 0.9 g fat, 70 g carbohydrates, 6 g protein, 3 mg cholesterol, 4 g dietary fiber, 82 mg sodium
Exchanges: 4 fruit, 1 other carb
Carb Choices: 5

Shopping List

Produce
2 bananas

Dairy
8 oz. nonfat vanilla yogurt

Frozen
16-oz. pkg. frozen mango slices

Canned
12-oz. can mango nectar

The American Heart Association estimates that 36% of children and teens have high cholesterol. Elevated cholesterol levels often carry over into adulthood, increasing the risk of heart disease and stroke.

Pumpkin Smoothie

Easy | **Serves: 4**

1½ cups nonfat half and half

1 15-oz. can canned pumpkin puree (not pumpkin pie mix), *chilled*

1 cup nonfat frozen vanilla yogurt or ice cream, *softened*

2 tbsp. sugar

¾ tsp. cinnamon, *divided*

⅛ tsp. nutmeg

½ cup nonfat Cool Whip, *thawed*

Combine half and half, pumpkin, yogurt, sugar, ¼ teaspoon cinnamon, and the nutmeg in food processor or blender; process or blend until smooth and creamy. Divide among 4 glasses; top each with 2 tablespoons Cool Whip and sprinkle with the remaining cinnamon.

Nutrition per serving: 180 calories, 0.3 g fat, 39 g carbohydrates, 3 g protein, 0 mg cholesterol, 2 g dietary fiber, 38 mg sodium
Exchanges: 2½ other carb
Carb Choices: 3

Snacks for Kids

Shopping List

Dairy
12 oz. nonfat half and half

Frozen
8 oz. nonfat frozen vanilla yogurt or ice cream
8-oz. container nonfat Cool Whip

Canned
15-oz. can pumpkin puree (not pumpkin pie mix)

Baking Goods
sugar

Seasonings/Spices
cinnamon
nutmeg

Keep your kitchen stocked with healthy snack choices. Studies show that snacks are most frequently chosen because of availability rather than preference.

Pretzel Rods

Easy | **Do Ahead** | **Freeze** | **Serves: 36**

1 lb. frozen fat-free roll
    dough, *thawed*

½ cup egg substitute

2 tbsp. water

    coarse salt *(Kosher salt)*

Preheat oven to 350°. Line baking sheet with foil and spray with cooking spray. Roll each piece of dough into 1-inch-thick rod. Arrange in single layer on baking sheet. Combine egg substitute and water in small cup; brush mixture onto rods. Sprinkle with coarse salt and bake 12–15 minutes until golden brown. Pretzel rods can be frozen and reheated in microwave oven (15–30 seconds on High).

Nutrition per serving: 37 calories, 0 g fat, 7 g carbohydrates, 2 g protein, 0 mg cholesterol, <1 dietary fiber, 67 mg sodium
Exchanges: ½ starch
Carb Choices: 0

Shopping List

Frozen
1 lb. frozen fat-free roll dough

Dairy
4 oz. egg substitute

Seasonings/Spices
coarse salt (Kosher salt)

Pretzels are the fastest growing snack food in the United States. Much lower in fat than traditional chips, pretzels come in a variety of shapes and sizes.

Pizza Potato Slices

Easy | **Serves: 4**

1 1-lb. 4-oz. pkg. sliced home fries

¾ cup pizza sauce

2 cups nonfat shredded mozzarella cheese

2 tbsp. nonfat Parmesan cheese

Preheat oven to 450°. Line baking sheet with foil and spray with cooking spray. Arrange home fries on baking sheet in single layer. Bake 10–15 minutes until lightly browned. Spread pizza sauce over potatoes and sprinkle with mozzarella and Parmesan cheeses. Bake 5–10 minutes until cheese is melted.

Nutrition per serving: 255 calories, 0.1 g fat, 36 g carbohydrates, 23 g protein, 0 mg cholesterol, 3 g dietary fiber, 637 mg sodium
Exchanges: 2 starch, 1 vegetable, 2 very lean meat
Carb Choices: 2

Snacks for Kids

Shopping List

Produce
1 lb. 4-oz. pkg. sliced home fries

Dairy
8 oz. nonfat shredded mozzarella cheese
nonfat Parmesan cheese

Canned
15-oz. can pizza sauce

Americans are snacking more than ever.
Studies estimate that the average person snacks over 200 times a year. How often you snack is less important than what you snack on!

Barbecue Chicken Pizza

Easy | **Do Ahead** | **Freeze** | **Serves: 4**

2 6-inch Italian bread shells

½ cup barbecue sauce

1 cup nonfat shredded
   mozzarella cheese

2 6-oz. pkgs. grilled chicken
   breast strips

   red onion slices (optional)

Preheat oven to 450°. Line baking sheet with foil and spray with cooking spray. Arrange bread shells on baking sheet in single layer. Spread each shell with ¼ cup barbecue sauce; top each with ½ cup nonfat shredded mozzarella cheese and 1 package grilled chicken breast strips. Arrange red onion slices with chicken, if desired.

Nutrition per serving: 329 calories, 5 g fat, 32 g carbohydrates, 36 g protein, 50 mg cholesterol, 1 g dietary fiber, 247 mg sodium
Exchanges: 1 starch, 5 lean meat, 1 other carb
Carb Choices: 2

Shopping List

Dairy
4 oz. nonfat shredded
   mozzarella cheese

Meat/Fish/Poultry
2 6-oz. pkgs. grilled chicken
   breast strips

Packaged
6-inch Italian bread shells
   (e.g., Boboli)

Condiments
barbecue sauce

Optional
red onion

American kids typically eat 5 to 10 times the amount of sodium they require. You can help alleviate the problem by substituting a serving of Barbecue Chicken Pizza for one slice of supreme pizza at a restaurant. The typical restaurant slice weighs in with more than 1,000 milligrams of sodium–about half the daily recommended amount.

Mini Pepperoni Pizzas

2 English muffins, *cut in half*

½ cup pizza sauce

1 cup nonfat shredded mozzarella cheese

12 slices reduced-fat pepperoni slices

Preheat oven to 350°. Line baking sheet with foil and spray with cooking spray. Arrange muffin halves on foil; top each with 2 tablespoons pizza sauce, ¼ cup cheese, and 3 pepperoni slices. Bake 6–8 minutes until cheese is melted and lightly browned.

Nutrition per serving: 206 calories, 5.2 g fat, 20 g carbohydrates, 23 protein, 30 mg cholesterol, 1 g dietary fiber, 1,157 mg sodium

Exchanges: 1 starch, 1 vegetable, 2 lean meat

Carb Choices: 1

Snacks for Kids

Shopping List

Dairy
4 oz. nonfat shredded mozzarella cheese

Meat/Fish/Poultry
6-oz. pkg. reduced-fat pepperoni slices

Canned
15-oz. can pizza sauce

Package
English muffins

Snack when you're hungry,
not because you're bored!

Chapter Index

13 Decadent Desserts

Angel Food Cake with Pineapple-Orange Sauce

Everyone loves desserts … some even love to bake them. Tempting all with a wonderful aroma that fills the air, fresh baked treats are simply irresistible.

Now you can have your cake and eat it too. Mouthwatering cookies, silky cream pies, chocolate treats, and more—desserts without guilt. When you make the right substitutions, you can cut the fat without cutting the flavor. The chart below illustrates a few of the simple substitutions that can turn guilt-laden desserts into guilt-free treats. Make small changes and work with your recipes to see what works best.

Instead of ...	Substitute ...	Save ...
Butter or margarine in most cookie, muffin, and cake recipes	Applesauce, crushed pineapple, or prune puree	350 calories and 45 grams of fat per ¼ cup
Whole dairy products	Fat-free dairy products including cheeses, yogurt, sour cream, milk	32–48 calories and 6 grams of fat per 2-tablespoon serving
Sugar- and fat-laden icings and frostings	Marshmallow crème or a sprinkling of powdered sugar	27 calories and 5 grams of fat per ounce
Prepared piecrusts	Nonfat cookie crumbs, graham cracker crumbs, cornflake crumbs, or nonfat crushed granola blended with low-sugar preserves, Butter Buds, or nonfat yogurt	varies
Whole eggs	Egg whites or fat-free egg substitute	30–38 calories and 4 grams of fat per whole egg
Nuts	Dried fruits, fat-free granola, or Grape Nuts	72 calories and 18 grams of fat per ounce
Almonds	Almond extract	165 calories and 6 grams of fat per ounce
Regular dessert toppings	Fat-free dessert syrups and toppings	Up to 278 calories and 25 grams of fat per 2-tablespoon serving
Whipped cream	Nonfat Cool Whip or whipped cream	24 calories and 2 grams of fat per 2-tablespoon serving
Regular ice cream	Nonfat frozen yogurt or ice cream	Up to 200 calories and 20 grams of fat per ½ cup

Decadent Desserts

Angel Food Cake with Pineapple-Orange Sauce

Easy | **Do Ahead** | **Serves: 8**

1   20-oz. can crushed pineapple, do *not drain*

¼   cup orange marmalade

1   tbsp. sugar

2   tsp. cornstarch

12 oz. prepared angel food cake

Combine pineapple, marmalade, sugar, and cornstarch in small saucepan; bring to a boil over medium-high heat. Reduce heat to low; cook, stirring constantly, 2–3 minutes until sauce thickens. Cool slightly; serve over angel food cake slices.

Nutrition per serving: 192 calories, 0.1 g fat, 46 g carbohydrates, 4 g protein, 0 mg cholesterol, 1 g dietary fiber, 116 mg sodium
Exchanges: 3 other carb
Carb Choices: 3

Shopping List

Canned
20-oz. can crushed pineapple

Packaged
12 oz. prepared angel food cake

Baking Goods
sugar
cornstarch

Condiments
orange marmalade

Although it may take a few minutes
longer than buying a premade cake, making a packaged angel food cake mix is still faster than starting from scratch.

Pound Cake with Chocolate Berry Sauce

Easy | Serves: 8

1   13.6-oz. nonfat loaf cake
    (pound cake)

1   16-oz. pkg. frozen mixed
    berries, *thawed and drained*

2   tbsp. fat-free double chocolate
    sundae syrup

8   oz. nonfat Cool Whip, *thawed*

Slice cake into 8 pieces and arrange on dessert dishes. Divide berries and sprinkle over top of cake slices. Carefully fold chocolate syrup into Cool Whip; top each cake slice with ¼ cup chocolate Cool Whip.

Nutrition per serving: 217 calories, 0 g fat, 52 g carbohydrates, 3 g protein, 0 mg cholesterol, 5 g dietary fiber, 282 mg sodium
Exchanges: 3½ other carb
Carb Choices: 3

Decadent Desserts

Shopping List

Frozen
16-oz. pkg. mixed berries
8 oz. nonfat Cool Whip

Packaged
13.6-oz. nonfat loaf cake
   (pound cake)

Dessert Topping
15-oz. bottle fat-free chocolate
   sundae syrup

You can substitute fresh berries for frozen—choose your favorites!

Mandarin Orange Cake

Easy | Do Ahead | Serves: 8

¼ cup egg substitute

1 cup sugar

1 cup flour

¼ tsp. baking soda

1 15-oz. can Mandarin oranges, *drained*

½ cup powdered sugar

2 tsp. skim milk

⅛ tsp. orange-flavored extract

Preheat oven to 350°. Spray 8-inch square baking dish with cooking spray. Combine egg substitute, sugar, flour, and baking soda in medium bowl; mix with electric mixer until creamy and smooth. Fold in Mandarin oranges and mix well. Pour batter into baking dish and bake 25–30 minutes until toothpick inserted in center comes out clean. Cool completely. Combine powdered sugar, skim milk, and orange extract in small bowl; mix until creamy. Cut cake into squares and drizzle with glaze. Let stand 10 minutes before serving.

Nutrition per serving: 210 calories, 0.1 g fat, 51 g carbohydrates, 2 g protein, 0 mg cholesterol, 0 g dietary fiber, 54 mg sodium
Exchanges: 3 other carb
Carb Choices: 3

Shopping List

Dairy
egg substitute
skim milk

Canned
15-oz. can Mandarin oranges

Baking Goods
sugar
flour
baking soda
powdered sugar

Seasonings/Spices
orange-flavored extract

Dust your cake pan with granulated sugar instead of flour before adding batter; your cake will come out easily and taste extra sweet!

Fantasy Fruit and Cake Dessert

Easy | **Do Ahead** | **Serves: 8**

1   10-oz. pkg. frozen strawberries
     in syrup, *thawed*

¼   cup sugar

1   13.6-oz. pkg. nonfat loaf cake
     (pound cake), *cut into
     1-inch cubes*

2   pints whole strawberries,
     *stemmed, hulled, and
     cut in half*

2   16-oz. cans pineapple chunks
     in juice, *well drained*

½   cup double chocolate
     sundae syrup

Combine thawed strawberries and sugar in food processor or blender and process or blend until smooth. Combine cake cubes, whole strawberries, and pineapple chunks in large glass bowl. Drizzle with chocolate syrup and top with strawberry-sugar mixture. Serve immediately. Strawberry-sugar mixture can be prepared ahead, but do not assemble dessert until ready to serve.

Nutrition per serving: 305 calories, 0.4 g fat, 76 g carbohydrates, 4 g protein, 0 mg cholesterol, 6 g dietary fiber, 287 mg sodium
Exchanges: 7 other carb
Carb Choices: 5

Decadent
Desserts

Shopping List

Produce
2 pints strawberries
10-oz. pkg. frozen strawberries
   in syrup

Canned
2 16-oz. cans pineapple chunks
   in juice

Packaged
13.6-oz. nonfat loaf cake

Baking Goods
sugar

Dessert Toppings
15-oz. bottle double chocolate
   sundae syrup

You can substitute angel food cake squares for the loaf cake, if desired.

Apple Spice Cake

Easy | Do Ahead | Serves: 12

1   18.25-oz. pkg. super moist
    French vanilla cake mix
1   21-oz. can Cinnamon 'n Spice
    Apple Pie Filling
½   cup egg substitute
2   egg whites
2   tbsp. sugar
1½ tsp. cinnamon

Preheat oven to 350°. Spray 9×13-inch baking dish with cooking spray. Combine cake mix, apple pie filling, egg substitute, and egg whites; mix until ingredients are blended and smooth. Combine sugar and cinnamon in small cup or zip-top bag; mix well. Pour half the cake batter into baking dish; top with half the cinnamon-sugar mixture. Repeat with remaining batter and sugar mixture. Bake 30–35 minutes until toothpick inserted in center comes out clean. Remove from oven and let cake cool completely.

Nutrition per serving: 246 calories, 3 g fat, 51 g carbohydrates, 4 g protein, 0 mg cholesterol, 0 g dietary fiber, 321 mg sodium
Exchanges: ½ fat, 3 other carb
Carb Choices: 3

Shopping List

Dairy
whole eggs
4 oz. egg substitute

Canned
21-oz. can Cinnamon 'n Spice
   Apple Pie Filling

Baking Goods
18.25-oz. pkg. super moist
   French vanilla cake mix
sugar

Seasonings/Spices
cinnamon

Apple arithmetic:

1 pound apples = 3 medium = 2 cups sliced
3 pounds apples = 8 to 9 medium = enough to make a 9-inch pie

Devil's Food Cheese Cupcakes

Easy | **Do Ahead** | **Freeze** | **Serves: 24**

1 18.25-oz. pkg. super moist
   devil's food cake mix

¾ cup egg substitute, *divided*

2 egg whites

½ cup unsweetened applesauce

1 8-oz. pkg. nonfat cream
   cheese, *softened*

⅓ cup sugar

Preheat oven to 350°. Line muffin tins with paper cupcake liners. Combine cake mix, ½ cup egg substitute, egg whites, and applesauce in large bowl; beat with electric mixer on low speed until smooth and creamy. Combine cream cheese, remaining ¼ cup egg substitute, and sugar in medium bowl; mix until creamy and smooth. Fill cupcake liners ½ full with batter; top each with 1 teaspoon cheese filling and 1 tablespoon batter. Bake 22–25 minutes until toothpick inserted in cupcake (not cheese filling) comes out clean. Cool slightly; remove from pan; cool completely and serve or package for freezer.

Nutrition per serving: 119 calories, 2.5 g fat, 21 g carbohydrates, 3 g protein, 0 mg cholesterol, 0 g dietary fiber, 291 mg sodium
Exchanges: ½ fat, 1 other carb
Carb Choices: 0

Decadent
Desserts

Shopping List

Dairy
6 oz. egg substitute
whole eggs
8-oz. pkg. nonfat cream cheese

Canned
4-oz. unsweetened applesauce

Baking Goods
18.25-oz. pkg. super moist
  devil's food cake mix
sugar

You can cut sugar intake by substituting equivalent amounts of Splenda for granulated sugar.

Chocolate Pudding Cupcakes

Easy | Do Ahead | Serves: 24

1   18.25-oz. pkg. super moist
    vanilla cake mix

1⅓ cups water

½   cup applesauce

¾   cup egg substitute

3   cups prepared fat-free
    chocolate pudding

Preheat oven to 350°. Spray muffin tins with cooking spray. Combine cake mix, water, applesauce, and egg substitute in large bowl; mix well. Fill muffin cups ¾ full with batter. Bake 18–23 minutes until toothpick inserted in center comes out clean. Cool 5–10 minutes; remove from pan and cool completely. When ready to serve: cut off top third of each cupcake, scoop out center, and fill with 2 tablespoons prepared pudding. Replace top and serve.

Nutrition per serving: 114 calories, 1.5 g fat, 22 g carbohydrates, 3 g protein, 1 mg cholesterol, 0 g dietary fiber, 170 mg sodium
Exchanges: 1½ other carb
Carb Choices: 2

Shopping List

Dairy
6 oz. egg substitute

Refrigerated
1 6-pack fat-free chocolate
  pudding cups

Canned
applesauce

Baking Goods
18.25-oz. pkg. super moist
  vanilla cake mix

With a wide variety of cake mixes

available, choose those lowest in fat and calories–be aware of package and serving sizes as they may vary and could affect the amount of finished product.

Caramel Apple Banana Split

Easy | **Serves: 4**

1 cup fat-free caramel dessert topping

4 tsp. marshmallow crème

2 bananas, *peeled and cut in half lengthwise*

2 cups nonfat frozen ice cream or frozen yogurt *(flavor of choice)*

1⅓ cups canned apple pie filling

Combine caramel dessert topping and marshmallow crème in microwave-safe bowl; microwave on High 1–2 minutes until heated. Arrange banana halves in dessert dishes; top each with ½ cup nonfat ice cream. Top with ⅓ cup apple pie filling; drizzle caramel-marshmallow mixture over top and serve.

Nutrition per serving: 496 calories, 0.3 g fat, 116 g carbohydrates, 7 g protein, 0 mg cholesterol, 1 g dietary fiber, 240 mg sodium
Exchanges: 8 other carb
Carb Choices: 8

Decadent Desserts

Shopping List

Produce
2 bananas

Frozen
16 oz. nonfat frozen ice cream or yogurt (flavor of choice)

Canned
21-oz. can apple pie filling

Desserts
8-oz. jar fat-free caramel dessert topping
marshmallow crème

Watch portion sizes–just because it's fat-free does not mean it's calorie-free!

Cinnamon Apple Ice Cream Delight

Easy | Serves: 4

2 cups apple cinnamon whole fruit sorbet

½ cup fat-free caramel dessert topping

½ cup Grape Nuts cereal

Place ½ cup sorbet in each of 4 dessert dishes; top each with 2 tablespoons caramel topping and 2 tablespoons cereal. Serve immediately.

Nutrition per serving: 281 calories, 0 g fat, 71 g carbohydrates, 3 g protein, 0 mg cholesterol, 1 g dietary fiber, 169 mg sodium
Exchanges: 5 other carb
Carb Choices: 5

Shopping List

Frozen
1 pint apple cinnamon whole fruit sorbet

Dessert Topping
12.25-oz. jar fat-free caramel dessert topping

Packaged
Grape Nuts cereal

Substitute any nonfat frozen yogurt, ice cream, or sorbet for the apple cinnamon; pair with a variety of nonfat dessert toppings and sprinkle with chopped nuts or dried fruits.

Pineapple-Mango Ice Cream Treat

Easy | **Serves: 4**

2 cups nonfat, no-sugar-added vanilla ice cream or frozen yogurt

2 cups frozen mango chunks, *thawed and drained*

2 cups frozen raspberries, *thawed and drained*

¼ cup pineapple dessert topping

Place ½ cup ice cream in each of 4 dessert bowls. Top each with ½ cup mango chunks, ½ cup raspberries, and 1 tablespoon pineapple dessert topping.

Nutrition per serving: 300 calories, 0.4 g fat, 72 g carbohydrates, 5 g protein, 0 mg cholesterol, 8 g dietary fiber, 64 mg sodium
Exchanges: 5 other carb
Carb Choices: 5

Decadent Desserts

Shopping List

Frozen

16-oz. nonfat, no-sugar-added vanilla ice cream or frozen yogurt
16-oz. pkg. frozen mango chunks
16-oz. pkg. frozen raspberries

Condiments/Sauces

pineapple dessert topping

Substituting reduced-fat, no-sugar-added ice cream for regular saves 80 unwanted calories. Simply substituting one low-calorie food for the same high-calorie item can cut hundreds of calories each week.

Tropical Fruit Sundae

Easy | **Serves: 4**

1 cup papaya chunks

1 cup fresh pineapple chunks

1 cup mango chunks

2 bananas, *cut in 1-inch pieces*

1/2 cup brown sugar

2 cups nonfat ice cream or frozen yogurt *(flavor of choice)*

Preheat broiler on high heat. Line baking sheet with foil and spray with cooking spray. Arrange fruit pieces on baking sheet; sprinkle with brown sugar and broil just until sugar is melted. Serve hot fruit over ice cream.

Nutrition per serving: 311 calories, 0.6 g fat, 75 g carbohydrates, 5 g protein, 0 mg cholesterol, 3 g dietary fiber, 71 mg sodium
Exchanges: 3 fruit, 2 other carb
Carb Choices: 5

Shopping List

Produce
papaya
pineapple (or packaged fresh
  pineapple chunks)
mango
2 bananas

Frozen
16-oz. nonfat ice cream or
  frozen yogurt (flavor of
  choice)

Baking Goods
brown sugar

You can substitute honey for granulated sugar, but you'll need to make other alterations to the recipe as well. Begin by substituting honey for half the sugar the recipe calls for and reduce the liquid by 1/4 cup for each cup of honey used. Also add 1/2 teaspoon baking soda for each cup of honey and reduce the oven temperature by 25°F to prevent overbrowning. These alterations work best for baked products such as muffins, quick breads, cookies, and cakes.

Melon à la Mode

Easy | **Serves: 4**

1 medium cantaloupe

2 cups nonfat vanilla ice cream

½ cup mango orange dessert topping

Cut cantaloupe in half; scoop out seeds. Cut in half again and place on four dessert dishes. Top each with ½ cup ice cream and drizzle with 2 tablespoons dessert topping.

Nutrition per serving: 256 calories, 0.4 g fat, 59 g carbohydrates, 5 g protein, 0 mg cholesterol, 1 g dietary fiber, 74 mg sodium
Exchanges: 1 fruit, 3 other carb
Carb Choices: 4

Decadent Desserts

Shopping List

Produce
1 cantaloupe

Frozen
16-oz. nonfat vanilla ice cream

Dessert Topping
mango orange dessert topping

Substitute any of your favorite nonfat dessert toppings for mango orange, if desired.

Cinnamon Sugar Bananas with Caramel Topping

Easy | **Serves: 4**

2 bananas, *peeled and cut in half lengthwise*

½ tsp. cinnamon

¼ cup brown sugar

   I Can't Believe It's Not Butter spray

2 cups nonfat ice cream or frozen yogurt *(flavor of choice)*

½ cup fat-free caramel dessert topping

Preheat broiler on High heat. Line broiler pan with foil and spray with cooking spray. Arrange banana halves flat side up on baking sheet; sprinkle each banana half with ⅛ teaspoon cinnamon and 1 tablespoon brown sugar. Spray lightly with "butter" spray. Broil bananas 3–4 minutes until bubbly hot. Arrange bananas in dessert dishes; top with ½ cup ice cream and 2 tablespoons caramel dessert topping.

Nutrition per serving: 325 calories, 0.2 g fat, 75 g carbohydrates, 6 g protein, 0 mg cholesterol, 1 g dietary fiber, 135 mg sodium
Exchanges: 5 other carb
Carb Choices: 5

Shopping List

Produce	Baking Goods
2 bananas	brown sugar

Dairy	Dessert Topping
I Can't Believe It's Not Butter spray	12.25-oz. jar fat-free caramel dessert topping

Frozen	Seasonings/Spices
1 pint nonfat ice cream or frozen yogurt (flavor of choice)	cinnamon

When measuring dessert topping, spray the cup with nonfat cooking spray first to prevent sticking.

Caramel Baked Pears

Easy | **Serves: 6**

2   28-oz. cans pear halves in juice, *well drained and patted dry*

2   tsp. ground cinnamon

½   cup fat-free caramel dessert topping

2   cups nonfat frozen yogurt or ice cream *(flavor of choice)* (optional)

Preheat oven to 350°. Spray 9×13-inch baking dish with cooking spray; arrange pear halves in dish; sprinkle with cinnamon and drizzle with caramel dessert topping. Bake 8–10 minutes until heated through. Serve over nonfat frozen yogurt or ice cream, if desired.

Nutrition per serving: 221 calories, 0.2 g fat, 55 g carbohydrates, 2 g protein, 0 mg cholesterol, 5 g dietary fiber, 57 mg sodium
Exchanges: 3 fruit, ½ other carb
Carb Choices: 4

Decadent
Desserts

Shopping List

Canned
2 28-oz. cans pear halves

Dessert Topping
12.25-oz. jar fat-free caramel dessert topping

Seasonings/Spices
ground cinnamon

Optional
1 pint nonfat frozen yogurt or ice cream (flavor of choice)

If you choose to use fresh pears,

those best for baking include Bartlett, Bosc, and Passe-Crassane.

Raspberry-Peach Cobbler

Easy | **Serves: 6**

2 cups frozen raspberries,
thawed and drained

4 peaches, sliced

1 tbsp. + 1 tsp. sugar

1/4 cup quick-cooking oatmeal

2 tsp. brown sugar

1 tsp. cinnamon

1 tbsp. + 1 tsp. sugar-free
maple-flavored syrup

Preheat oven to 375°. Spray 8-inch square baking dish with cooking spray. Combine raspberries, peaches, and sugar in dish; toss lightly to coat. Combine oatmeal, brown sugar, and cinnamon in small bowl; mix well. Drizzle syrup over oatmeal mixture and toss with fingers until crumbly and moist. Sprinkle over fruit. Bake 15–20 minutes until lightly browned and crisp.

Nutrition per serving: 141 calories, 0.4 g fat, 35 g carbohydrates, 2 g protein, 0 mg cholesterol, 5 g dietary fiber, 2 mg sodium
Exchanges: 2 other carb
Carb Choices: 2

Shopping List

Produce
4 peaches

Frozen
16-oz. pkg. frozen raspberries

Packaged
quick-cooking oatmeal

Baking Goods
sugar
brown sugar

Condiments
sugar-free maple-flavored syrup

Seasonings/Spices
cinnamon

Vary the recipe by substituting nectarines, apricots, or papayas for the peaches.

Baked Rice Pudding
with Berries 'n Cherries

Easy | **Serves: 4**

1/2 cup uncooked rice

2 cups nonfat half and half

2 cups skim milk

1/3 cup sugar

1/2 tsp. cinnamon

1/4 tsp. nutmeg

1/2 cup Dried Berries 'n Cherries

Preheat oven to 325°. Spray 1½-quart baking dish with cooking spray. Combine all ingredients in baking dish; bake 2–2½ hours until rice is tender. Stir several times while baking.

Nutrition per serving: 329 calories, 0.6 g fat, 70 g carbohydrates, 7 g protein, 2 mg cholesterol, 1 g dietary fiber, 64 mg sodium
Exchanges: 5 other carb
Carb Choices: 5

Decadent Desserts

Shopping List

Dairy
16 oz. nonfat half and half
16 oz. skim milk

Packaged
rice
6-oz. pkg. Dried Berries 'n Cherries

Baking Goods
sugar

Seasonings/Spices
cinnamon
nutmeg

You can substitute any of your favorite dried fruits (apricots, dates, raisins, cranberries) for the dried berries 'n cherries.

Black and White Brownies

1   18-oz. pkg. fat-free fudge
    brownie mix

1/2 cup hot water

4   oz. nonfat cream cheese,
    softened

1/4 cup sugar

1/4 cup egg substitute

1   tbsp. flour

Preheat oven to 350°. Spray 8-inch square baking dish with cooking spray. Prepare brownie mix according to package directions. Spread batter in baking dish. Combine remaining ingredients and beat with electric mixer until creamy and smooth. Spoon cheese mixture over brownie batter and swirl with knife (do not completely blend in with batter). Bake 30–35 minutes until toothpick inserted in center comes out clean. Cool brownies at least 15–30 minutes before serving.

Nutrition per serving: 280 calories, 0 g fat, 64 g carbohydrates, 5 g protein, 0 mg cholesterol, 1 g dietary fiber, 470 mg sodium
Exchanges: 4 other carbs
Carb Choices: 4

Shopping List

Dairy
4 oz. nonfat cream cheese
egg substitute

Baking Goods
18-oz. pkg. fat-free fudge
   brownie mix
sugar
flour

For lighter, cakelike brownies, add a little extra egg substitute to the batter; reducing the amount of egg substitute makes the brownies thicker and chewier.

Mocha Fudge Brownies

Easy | **Do Ahead** | **Serves: 8**

1   18-oz. pkg. fat-free fudge
    brownie mix

2   tbsp. instant coffee powder

1/2 cup + 2 tbsp. hot water

2   tbsp. powdered sugar

3/4 tsp. unsweetened cocoa
    powder

Preheat oven to 350°. Spray 8-inch square baking dish with cooking spray. Combine brownie mix, coffee powder, and water in medium bowl; mix until ingredients are blended (batter will be thick). Pour and spread batter into baking dish and bake 30–35 minutes until toothpick inserted in center comes out clean. Remove from oven and cool completely. Combine powdered sugar and cocoa powder; mix well. Sprinkle mixture over brownies, cut, and serve.

Nutrition per serving: 249 calories, 0 g fat, 58 g carbohydrates, 2 g protein, 0 mg cholesterol, <1 g dietary fiber, 360 mg sodium
Exchanges: 4 other carb
Carb Choices: 4

Decadent
Desserts

Shopping List

Baking Goods
18-oz. pkg. fat-free fudge
    brownie mix
powdered sugar
unsweetened cocoa powder

Canned
instant coffee powder

Use a flat metal pastry scraper to cut squares and bars in the pan. It's easier to get a cleaner cut than with a knife, and it cuts through to the bottom.

Cookie Mix #1

4 cups flour
1 tsp. baking soda
1/2 tsp. baking powder
1 1/2 cup brown sugar
1/2 cup sugar

Combine all ingredients in large bowl or zip-top bag and mix well. Cover tightly and store until ready to use with Chocolate Chip or Snickerdoodle cookie recipes.

Shopping List

Baking Goods
flour
brown sugar
sugar
baking soda
baking powder

Use this cookie mix recipe to make a variety of cookies by simply adding low-fat margarine, egg substitute, and flavored extract.

Cookie Mix #2

Easy | **Do Ahead** | **Yields: 6 cups**

4 cups flour

1 tsp. baking powder

½ tsp. baking soda

1 cup powdered sugar

1 cup granulated sugar

Combine all ingredients in large bowl or zip-top bag and mix well. Cover tightly and store until ready to use for sugar cookie recipes.

Decadent Desserts

Shopping List

Baking Goods

flour

powdered sugar

granulated sugar

baking powder

baking soda

This cookie mix recipe works well when preparing rolled or cut-out cookies rather than dropped or bars.

Chocolate Chip Cookies

Easy | Do Ahead | Freeze | Serves: 24

³/₄ cup light margarine, *softened*

¹/₄ cup egg substitute

1 tsp. vanilla extract

2¹/₂ cups Cookie Mix #1
(See recipe on page 340.)

¹/₄ cup miniature chocolate chips

Preheat oven to 350°. Line baking sheet with foil. Combine margarine, egg substitute, and vanilla extract in large bowl; blend until smooth and creamy. Add Cookie Mix; mix well. Fold in chocolate chips. Drop dough by tablespoons onto baking sheet; bake 8–10 minutes until lightly browned. Cool on wire rack.

Nutrition per serving: 98 calories, 1.6 g fat, 15 g carbohydrates, 1 g protein, 0 mg cholesterol, <1 g dietary fiber, 91 mg sodium
Exchanges: ½ fat, 1 other carb
Carb Choices: 1

Shopping List

Dairy
6 oz. light margarine
egg substitute

Baking Goods
Cookie Mix #1 (see recipe)
vanilla extract
miniature chocolate chips

For a change of pace, substitute raisins, chopped nuts, or dried fruit pieces for chocolate chips.

Snickerdoodles

Easy | **Do Ahead** | **Freeze** | **Serves: 24**

³/₄ cup light margarine, *softened*

¹/₄ cup egg substitute

1 tsp. vanilla extract

2¹/₂ cups Cookie Mix #1
(See recipe on page 340.)

2 tbsp. sugar

2 tsp. cinnamon

Preheat oven to 350°. Line baking sheet with foil. Combine softened margarine, egg substitute, and vanilla extract in large bowl; mix until creamy and smooth. Add Cookie Mix #1 and mix well. Combine sugar and cinnamon in small cup or zip-top bag; mix well. Shape dough into 1-inch balls; roll in cinnamon-sugar mixture and place onto baking sheet. Flatten with bottom of a glass cup. Bake 8–10 minutes until lightly browned. Cool on wire rack.

Nutrition per serving: 90 calories, 2.9 g fat, 15 g carbohydrates, 1 g protein, 0 mg cholesterol, <1 g dietary fiber, 91 mg sodium
Exchanges: ½ fat, 1 other carb
Carb Choices: 1

Decadent Desserts

Shopping List

Dairy
6 oz. light margarine
egg substitute

Baking Goods
Cookie Mix #1 (see recipe)
vanilla extract
sugar

Seasonings/Spices
cinnamon

When baking bar cookies, let them completely cool before cutting them or they'll crumble and break apart.

Lemon Sugar Cookies

Easy | **Do Ahead** | **Freeze** | **Serves: 24**

³/₄ cup light margarine, *softened*

¹/₄ cup egg substitute

2 tsp. grated lemon peel

³/₄ tsp. lemon juice

3 cups Cookie Mix #2
(See recipe on page 341.)

sugar

Combine margarine, egg substitute, lemon peel, and lemon juice in large bowl; mix until creamy and smooth. Add Cookie Mix #2 and mix well. Cover and refrigerate 1 hour. Preheat oven to 350°. Line baking sheet with foil. Drop dough by tablespoons onto baking sheet. Dip bottom of glass cup in sugar and press to flatten cookie dough. Bake 6–8 minutes until lightly browned. Cool on wire rack.

Nutrition per serving: 87 calories, 2.9 g fat, 14 g carbohydrates, 1 g protein, 0 mg cholesterol, 0 g dietary fiber, 88 mg sodium
Exchanges: ½ fat, 1 other carb
Carb Choices: 1

Shopping List

Produce
Lemon

Dairy
6 oz. light margarine
egg substitute

Baking Goods
Cookie Mix #2 (see recipe)
sugar

For best results when baking cookies, use a cookie sheet or pan with low sides. Bake in the center or slightly above the center of the oven.

Orange Sugar Cookies

Easy | Do Ahead | Freeze | Serves: 24

- ³/₄ cup light margarine, *softened*
- ¹/₄ cup egg substitute
- 1 tbsp. grated orange peel
- 1¹/₂ tsp. orange juice
- 3 cups Cookie Mix #2
  (See recipe on page 341.)
- sugar

Combine margarine, egg substitute, orange peel, and orange juice in large bowl; mix until creamy and smooth. Add Cookie Mix #2 and mix well. Cover and refrigerate 1 hour. Preheat oven to 350°. Line baking sheet with foil. Drop dough by tablespoons onto baking sheet. Dip bottom of glass cup in sugar and press to flatten cookie dough. Bake 6–8 minutes until lightly browned. Cool on wire rack.

Nutrition per serving: 87 calories, 2.9 g fat, 14 g carbohydrates, 1 g protein, 0 mg cholesterol, <1 g dietary fiber, 88 mg sodium
Exchanges: ¹/₂ fat, 1 other carb
Carb Choices: 1

Decadent Desserts

Shopping List

Produce
orange

Dairy
6 oz. light margarine
egg substitute

Baking Goods
Cookie Mix #2 (see recipe)
sugar

If cookies stick to the foil, return to oven for 30 to 45 seconds. This will soften the bottoms of cookies, making them easier to remove from foil.

Snowball Cookies

Easy | **Do Ahead** | **Freeze** | **Serves: 24**

³/₄ cup light margarine, *softened*

¹/₄ cup egg substitute

³/₄ tsp. almond extract

3 cups Cookie Mix #2
(See recipe on page 341.)

powdered sugar

Preheat oven to 350°. Line baking sheet with foil. Combine margarine, egg substitute, and almond extract in large bowl; add Cookie Mix #2 and blend well. Shape dough into 1-inch balls and bake 10–12 minutes until lightly browned on bottom. Cool completely. Roll cooled cookies in powdered sugar to coat.

Nutrition per serving: 88 calories, 2.9 g fat, 14 g carbohydrates, 1 g protein, 0 mg cholesterol, <1 g dietary fiber, 88 mg sodium
Exchanges: ½ fat, 1 other carb
Carb Choices: 1

Shopping List

Dairy
6 oz. light margarine
egg substitute

Baking Goods
Cookie Mix #2 (see recipe)
almond extract
powdered sugar

These cookies are very similar in flavor and texture to the all-time favorite Mexican Wedding Cakes. You can vary the flavor by using different extracts.

Sugar Cookies

Easy | **Do Ahead** | **Freeze** | **Serves: 24**

3/4 cup light margarine, *softened*

1/4 cup egg substitute

1 tsp. vanilla extract

3 cups Cookie Mix #2
(See recipe on page 341.)

1/4 cup flour

1/4 cup powdered sugar

colored sugar or sprinkles

Combine margarine, egg substitute, and vanilla extract in large bowl; mix until creamy and smooth. Add Cookie Mix #2 and mix well. Cover and refrigerate 1 hour. Preheat oven to 350°. Line baking sheet with foil. Combine flour and powdered sugar in bowl; mix well. Sprinkle mixture on counter top; roll dough in flour-sugar mixture. Using favorite cookie cutters or glass dipped in sugar, cut out dough. Sprinkle lightly with colored sugar. Arrange on baking sheet; bake 8–10 minutes until lightly browned. Cool on wire rack.

Nutrition per serving: 97 calories, 2.9 g fat, 16 g carbohydrates, 2 g protein, 0 mg cholesterol, 0 g dietary fiber, 88 mg sodium
Exchanges: ½ fat, 1 other carb
Carb Choices: 1

Decadent Desserts

Shopping List

Dairy
6 oz. light margarine
egg substitute

Baking Goods
Cookie Mix #2 (see recipe)
vanilla extract
flour
powdered sugar
colored sugar or sprinkles

Sugar sprinkled over tops of cookies

before baking results in a sweeter crust and richer cookies.

Chapter Index

⑭ Holiday Offerings

Pumpkin Pudding Cups

A season for celebrations, family gatherings, taste-tempting treats, glorious gifts, treasured traditions, and a time to give thanks. But who has the time?

If you're like most people, you're busy planning, preparing, and polishing—in an effort to make this year even better than last. But in the whirlwind of acitivty, you're left feeling frazzled. This year, give yourself a break and make some changes. Cope with the chaos and fight the frenzy! If your holiday season means spending hours in the kitchen, get out in record time with these timesaving tips. Plan, prepare, and present the perfect holiday feast with a lot less pressure. Here are just a few ideas to get you started.

- **Clean out your refrigerator** to make room for make-ahead dishes.

- **Peel, slice, and chop vegetables**, bread, or other nonperishable ingredients two to three days prior to cooking day.

- **Defrost foods on time:** Allow one day of defrosting for every 5 pounds of turkey.

- **Read through each recipe,** line up ingredients, prep, and assemble BEFORE you start to cook.

- **Invite friends or family to make a dish.** Even if they just bring rolls or cookies, it saves you time and helps others feel involved in the dinner.

- **Save time with store-bought prepped foods.** Make stuffing with seasoned bread crumbs or croutons; purchase packaged seasoning vegetables to avoid dicing and slicing; make pies with canned fillings and prepared crusts; start sweet potato casseroles with canned potatoes.

- **Save storage space.** Pack cooled stuffing, mashed potatoes, and other nonfragile foods in sturdy zip-top bags. Squeeze out the air, and seal and press food flat so you can stack bags in the refrigerator or freezer. Top baking pans, casseroles, and food dishes with flat baking sheets and place other food on top.

- **Cut cleanup time.** Line cookie sheets and cake pans with parchment paper or aluminum foil. Spray casseroles and baking sheets with nonfat cooking spray to eliminate stuck-on messes. Marinate or store leftover foods in zip-top bags.

Holiday Offerings

Baked Spinach Dip in Bread Bowl

Easy | Do Ahead | Serves: 12

1 lb. round sourdough
   bread loaf

1 cup nonfat mayonnaise

1 cup nonfat Parmesan cheese

1 14-oz. can artichoke hearts,
   drained and chopped

1 10-oz. pkg. frozen chopped
   spinach, *thawed and
   drained*

1 6-oz. can sliced water
   chestnuts, *chopped and
   drained*

¼ cup nonfat shredded
   mozzarella cheese

Cut top off of bread and set aside; remove inside of bread, leaving ½-inch shell. Cut bread into bite-size pieces. Preheat oven to 350°. Line baking sheet with foil and spray with cooking spray. Combine mayonnaise, Parmesan cheese, artichoke hearts, spinach, and water chestnuts in medium bowl; mix well. Spoon mixture into bread bowl; sprinkle with mozzarella cheese. Place filled bread bowl on baking sheet; bake 25–30 minutes until bubbly hot. Serve with reserved bread bites.

Nutrition per serving: 177 calories, 1.3 g fat, 33 g carbohydrates, 9 g protein, 0 mg cholesterol, 2 g dietary fiber, 489 mg sodium
Exchanges: 1 starch, 2 vegetable, ½ other carb
Carb Choices: 2

Shopping List

Dairy
4 oz. nonfat Parmesan
   cheese
nonfat shredded
   mozzarella cheese

Frozen
10-oz. pkg. frozen
   chopped spinach

Canned
14-oz. can artichoke
   hearts
6-oz. can sliced water
   chestnuts

Packaged
1 lb. round sourdough
   bread loaf

Condiments
8 oz. nonfat mayonnaise

Spinach dip can also be prepared and baked in a shallow casserole dish sprayed with cooking spray.

350

Holiday Shrimp Dip

Easy | **Do Ahead** | **Serves: 6**

1   8-oz. pkg. nonfat cream
    cheese, *softened*

1½ tsp. onion powder

2   tbsp. ketchup

1   tbsp. prepared horseradish

2   6-oz. cans small shrimp,
    drained

    assorted crackers (optional)

Combine all the ingredients, except crackers, and mix until completely blended. Cover and refrigerate 6 hours or overnight. Serve with assorted crackers.

Nutrition per serving: 104 calories, 1.1 g fat, 5 g carbohydrates, 18 g protein, 98 mg cholesterol, 0 g dietary fiber, 412 mg sodium
Exchanges: 2 very lean meat, ½ other carb
Carb Choices: 0

Holiday Offerings

Shopping List

Dairy
8-oz. pkg. nonfat cream cheese

Canned
2 6-oz. cans small shrimp

Condiments
ketchup
prepared horseradish

Seasonings/Spices
onion powder

Optional
assorted crackers

Holiday timesaver: Set your table the day before your holiday meal. Set out all food preparation and service utensils.

Caesar Veggie Dip

Easy | **Do Ahead** | **Serves: 6**

½ cup nonfat sour cream

⅓ cup nonfat mayonnaise

¼ cup fat-free creamy Caesar
salad dressing

⅓ cup nonfat Parmesan cheese

2 tbsp. chopped pimientos,
well drained

2 16-oz. pkgs. raw vegetable
pieces (broccoli, cauliflower,
and baby carrots)

Combine sour cream, mayonnaise, salad dressing, and Parmesan cheese in medium bowl; mix well. Sprinkle pimientos over top; cover and refrigerate 30–60 minutes. Arrange raw vegetables on serving platter and place dip in the center.

Nutrition per serving: 93 calories, 0.3 g fat, 17 g carbohydrates, 6 g protein, 0 mg cholesterol, 4 g dietary fiber, 274 mg sodium
Exchanges: 1 vegetable, 1 other carb
Carb Choices: 1

Shopping List

Produce
2 16-oz. pkgs. raw vegetable
pieces (broccoli, cauliflower,
and baby carrots)

Dairy
4 oz. nonfat sour cream
nonfat Parmesan cheese

Condiments
nonfat mayonnaise
fat-free creamy Caesar salad
dressing
chopped pimientos

When selecting fresh cauliflower or cauliflower florets, look for heads that are firm and have compact florets; prepackaged florets save preparation time.

Caramel Yogurt Fruit Dip with Apples

Easy | Do Ahead | Serves: 4

4 tbsp. nonfat cream cheese, softened

½ cup nonfat vanilla yogurt

¼ cup + 2 tsp. fat-free caramel dessert topping

⅛ tsp. ground ginger

3 large apples, *cored and sliced thin*

Combine cream cheese, yogurt, ¼ cup caramel dessert topping, and ginger in medium bowl; beat with electric mixer until creamy and smooth. Cover and refrigerate at least 1 hour before serving with apple slices. Just before serving, drizzle remaining dessert topping on top of dip and swirl to mix lightly.

Nutrition per serving: 190 calories, 0.5 g fat, 44 g carbohydrates, 4 g protein, 1 mg cholesterol, 3 g dietary fiber, 159 mg sodium
Exchanges: 1 fruit, 2 other carb
Carb Choices: 3

Holiday Offerings

Shopping List

Produce
3 large apples

Dairy
4 oz. nonfat cream cheese
4 oz. nonfat vanilla yogurt

Dessert Topping
12.25-oz. jar fat-free caramel dessert topping

Seasonings/Spices
ground ginger

Variation: Try this dip with sliced pears instead of apples.

Creamy Fruit Dip

Easy | **Do Ahead** | **Serves: 8**

1½ cups nonfat vanilla yogurt

1½ tbsp. brown sugar

½ tsp. ground cinnamon

⅛ tsp. ground nutmeg

1 cup seedless grapes

1 pint strawberries,
  washed and hulled

2 kiwifruits, *peeled and sliced*

Combine yogurt, brown sugar, cinnamon, and nutmeg in food processor or blender; process or blend until smooth and creamy. Spoon mixture into bowl, cover with plastic wrap, and refrigerate several hours or overnight. Serve dip with grapes, strawberries, and sliced kiwifruits.

Nutrition per serving: 57 calories, 0.2 g fat, 13 g carbohydrates, 2 g protein, 1 mg cholesterol, 2 g dietary fiber, 29 mg sodium
Exchanges: 1 fruit
Carb Choices: 1

Shopping List

Produce
½ lb. seedless grapes
1 pint strawberries
2 kiwifruits

Dairy
12 oz. nonfat vanilla yogurt

Baking Goods
brown sugar

Seasonings/Spices
ground cinnamon
ground nutmeg

Though filled with festive food feasts, the true meaning of the holidays is about spending time with family and friends.

Mozzarella Sticks with Marinara Sauce

Average | **Do Ahead** | **Serves: 4**

2¼ cups + 2 tbsp. reduced-fat
    baking mix, *divided*

⅔ cup skim milk

2 cups nonfat shredded
    mozzarella cheese

butter-flavored cooking spray

½ tsp. garlic powder

1 cup nonfat pasta or
    pizza sauce

Shopping List

Dairy
8 oz. skim milk
8 oz. nonfat shredded
    mozzarella cheese

Baking Goods
reduced-fat baking mix
    (e.g., Bisquick)

Condiments
8 oz. nonfat pasta or pizza
    sauce

Seasonings/Spices
butter-flavored cooking spray
garlic powder

Preheat oven to 450°. Line baking sheet with foil and spray with cooking spray. Combine 2¼ cups baking mix and the milk in medium bowl; beat until soft dough forms. Sprinkle remaining baking mix on flat surface; knead dough and shape into ball. Divide dough into 8 equal pieces; roll each piece into 2×6-inch rectangle. Sprinkle ¼ cup cheese down center of each dough rectangle; wrap dough around cheese and pinch ends to seal. Arrange cheese sticks in a single layer on baking sheet. Bake 8–10 minutes until crust is golden brown and cheese is melted. Spray cheese sticks with butter-flavored cooking spray and sprinkle with garlic powder. Bake 1–2 minutes. Pour pasta sauce into microwave-safe bowl; microwave on High 2–3 minutes until heated through. Serve mozzarella sticks with pasta sauce.

Holiday Offerings

Nutrition per serving: 483 calories, 1.2 g fat, 101 g carbohydrates, 27 g protein, 1 mg cholesterol, 1 g dietary fiber, 1,811 mg sodium
Exchanges: 1 vegetable, 1 very lean meat, 6 other carb
Carb Choices: 7

Variation: Use 1 cup nonfat cheddar and 1 cup nonfat mozzarella or Swiss cheese instead of 2 cups mozzarella.

Broccoli-Chicken Holiday Bake

Easy | **Do Ahead** | **Serves: 6**

- 1 20-oz. pkg. frozen chopped broccoli, *thawed and drained*
- 3 6-oz. pkgs. grilled chicken breast strips, *cubed*
- 3 cups nonfat shredded cheddar cheese
- 2 10¾-oz. cans condensed 98% fat-free cream of chicken soup
- ½ cup nonfat mayonnaise
- 2 tbsp. bottled lemon juice
- 2 tsp. curry powder
- ¼ cup seasoned breadcrumbs
- ¼ cup nonfat Parmesan cheese

Preheat oven to 350°. Spray 9×13-inch baking dish with cooking spray. Spread half the broccoli in bottom of dish; top with half the chicken and 1½ cups cheddar cheese; repeat layers. Combine soup, mayonnaise, lemon juice, and curry powder. Spread mixture over cheese layer. Combine breadcrumbs and Parmesan cheese in zip-top bag; shake to mix. Sprinkle breadcrumb mixture over top of casserole. Bake 45–50 minutes until bubbly hot and lightly browned on top.

Nutrition per serving: 328 calories, 4.5 g fat, 26 g carbohydrates, 44 g protein, 61 mg cholesterol, 5 g dietary fiber, 1,976 mg sodium
Exchanges: 2 vegetable, 5 very lean meat, 1 other carb
Carb Choices: 2

Shopping List

Meat/Fish/Poultry
3 6-oz. pkgs. grilled chicken breast strips

Frozen
20-oz. pkg. frozen chopped broccoli

Dairy
12-oz. nonfat shredded cheddar cheese
nonfat Parmesan cheese

Canned
2 10¾-oz. cans condensed 98% fat-free cream of chicken soup

Packaged
seasoned breadcrumbs

Condiments
bottled lemon juice
nonfat mayonnaise

Seasonings/Spices
curry powder

Variation: Use a frozen vegetable mix such as broccoli, cauliflower, and carrots or frozen chopped spinach instead of frozen chopped broccoli.

Chicken in Wine Sauce

Easy | **Serves: 6**

¼ cup nonfat chicken broth

1½ lbs. boneless, skinless chicken breasts

½ cup dry white wine

½ tsp. dried dill weed

1 tbsp. lemon juice

3 tbsp. chopped green onions

Spray large nonstick skillet with cooking spray; add broth and heat over medium-high heat. Add chicken and cook 6–8 minutes, turning once while cooking. Combine wine, dill weed, and lemon juice in small bowl; mix well. Pour wine mixture over chicken; bring to a boil over high heat. Reduce heat to low, cover, and simmer 10–15 minutes until chicken is cooked through. Remove chicken from skillet and keep warm. Bring liquid to a boil over high heat; boil 2–3 minutes until liquid is reduced by about half. Pour sauce over chicken and sprinkle with green onions. Serve immediately.

Nutrition per serving: 126 calories, 1 g fat, <1 g carbohydrates, 22 g protein, 55 mg cholesterol, 0 g dietary fiber, 99 mg sodium
Exchanges: 3½ very lean meat
Carb Choices: 0

Holiday Offerings

Shopping List

Produce
green onions
lemon (or bottled lemon juice)

Meat/Fish/Poultry
1½ lbs. boneless, skinless
chicken breasts

Canned
nonfat chicken broth

Other
4 oz. dry white wine

Seasonings/Spices
dried dill weed

Lemon juice serves as a natural tenderizer for chicken, beef, and lamb.

Holiday Honey Mustard Chicken

Easy | **Serves: 4**

1 lb. boneless, skinless chicken breasts

1 tsp. garlic powder

2 tbsp. cornstarch

1¾ cups nonfat chicken broth

1 tbsp. honey

1 tbsp. Dijon mustard

1 16-oz. pkg. frozen pepper stir-fry, *thawed and drained*

Shopping List

Meat/Fish/Poultry
1-lb. pkg. boneless, skinless chicken breasts

Frozen
16-oz. pkg. frozen pepper stir-fry

Canned
14-oz. can nonfat chicken broth

Baking Goods
cornstarch

Condiments
honey
Dijon mustard

Seasonings/Spices
garlic powder

Spray large nonstick skillet with cooking spray and heat over medium-high heat. Season chicken breasts with garlic powder; add to skillet and cook 7–8 minutes per side until chicken is browned. Combine cornstarch, chicken broth, honey, and mustard in medium bowl; mix until blended. Pour mixture over chicken; bring to a boil over high heat and cook, stirring constantly, until mixture thickens. Add pepper stir-fry to skillet, cover and cook over low heat 5–8 minutes until heated through.

Nutrition per serving: 196 calories, 1.4 g fat, 17 g carbohydrates, 25 g protein, 55 mg cholesterol, 1 g dietary fiber, 471 mg sodium
Exchanges: 1 vegetable, 3 very lean meat, ½ other carb
Carb Choices: 1

Unless food will be frozen, it's safest to start preparing most perishable foods no more than a day before a meal.

Garlic-Cheese Chicken

Easy | **Serves: 4**

1 tbsp. + ¼ cup nonfat chicken broth, *divided*

1 tbsp. bottled minced garlic

2 tsp. brown sugar

1¼ lbs. boneless, skinless chicken breasts

¾ tsp. Mrs. Dash seasoning

4 tomato slices

4 oz. nonfat Swiss cheese slices

Shopping List

Produce
1 large tomato

Meat/Fish/Poultry
1¼ lbs. boneless, skinless chicken breasts

Dairy
4 oz. nonfat Swiss cheese slices

Canned
14-oz. can nonfat chicken broth

Baking Goods
brown sugar

Seasonings/Spices
bottled minced garlic
Mrs. Dash seasoning

Spray large nonstick skillet with cooking spray; add 1 tablespoon broth and heat over medium-high heat. Add garlic; cook, stirring frequently, until garlic begins to brown. Stir in brown sugar and mix until sugar is dissolved. Add chicken to skillet; sprinkle with Mrs. Dash seasoning. Cook 2–3 minutes; turn chicken over and cook another 2–3 minutes until chicken is browned. Add remaining chicken broth; cook over medium heat 10–12 minutes until chicken is golden brown and cooked through. Place 1 tomato slice and 1 slice cheese on top of each chicken breast; cover skillet and cook until cheese is melted. Serve immediately.

Nutrition per serving: 103 calories, 1.3 g fat, 4 g carbohydrates, 32 g protein, 69 mg cholesterol, <1 g dietary fiber, 368 mg sodium
Exchanges: 5 very lean meat
Carb Choices: 0

Holiday Offerings

Cut holiday stress by limiting the number of foods you serve to a few favorites. Do you really need all those side dishes and desserts?

Lemon Herb Chicken

Easy | **Do Ahead** | **Serves: 4**

1 lb. boneless, skinless chicken breasts

¼ cup nonfat chicken broth

1 tsp. 1-Step Garlic Herb Chicken Seasoning

½ tsp. lemon-pepper seasoning

sliced lemon (optional)

Spray large nonstick skillet with cooking spray; add chicken breasts to skillet. Pour broth over chicken; bring to a boil over medium-high heat. Reduce heat to low, cover, and simmer 5 minutes. Turn chicken over; sprinkle with 1-Step Seasoning and lemon-pepper seasoning. Cook 10–15 minutes until juices run clear and chicken is cooked through. Garnish with sliced lemon, if desired.

Nutrition per serving: 111 calories, 1 g fat, 0 g carbohydrates, 22 g protein, 0 mg cholesterol, 0 g dietary fiber, 168 mg sodium
Exchanges: 3 very lean meat
Carb Choices: 0

Shopping List

Meat/Fish/Poultry
1 lb. boneless, skinless
  chicken breasts

Canned
nonfat chicken broth

Seasonings/Spices
5.12-oz. 1-Step Garlic Herb
  Chicken Seasoning
lemon-pepper seasoning

Optional
lemon

As a rule, when using fresh raw meat, poultry, or seafood, purchase no more than 1 to 2 days before your holiday meal. Freeze for longer storage. These foods taste freshest if cooked the day of your meal.

Orange Glazed Chicken Tenderloins

Easy | **Do Ahead** | **Serves: 4**

1 tbsp. nonfat chicken broth

1¼ lbs. boneless, skinless, chicken breast tenderloins

⅓ cup orange marmalade

½ tsp. ground ginger

1 tsp. Worcestershire sauce

2 cups cooked brown rice

Spray large nonstick skillet with cooking spray; add broth and heat over medium-high heat. Add chicken tenderloins; cook 5 minutes until browned on one side. Stir in orange marmalade, ginger, and Worcestershire sauce; reduce heat to low, cover, and simmer 15–20 minutes until chicken is cooked through. Spoon sauce over chicken and serve over cooked rice.

Nutrition per serving: 321 calories, 1.3 g fat, 43 g carbohydrates, 34 g protein, 71 mg cholesterol, <1 g dietary fiber, 268 mg sodium
Exchanges: 2 starch, 3 very lean meat, 1 other carb
Carb Choices: 3

Holiday Offerings

Shopping List

Meat/Fish/Poultry
1¼ lbs. boneless, skinless chicken breast tenderloins

Canned
nonfat chicken broth

Packaged
brown rice

Seasonings/Spices
ground ginger

Condiments
orange marmalade
Worcestershire sauce

Variation: You can substitute white or wild rice for brown rice.

Sesame Chicken

Easy | **Do Ahead** | **Serves: 6**

¾ cup seasoned breadcrumbs

⅓ cup nonfat Parmesan cheese

3 tbsp. sesame seeds

⅛ tsp. pepper

1½ lbs. boneless, skinless chicken breasts

½ cup egg substitute

Preheat oven to 375°. Line baking sheet with foil and spray with cooking spray. Combine breadcrumbs, Parmesan cheese, sesame seeds, and pepper in shallow dish; mix well. Dip chicken breasts in egg substitute and roll in breadcrumb mixture to coat. Arrange chicken breasts on baking sheet and spray lightly with cooking spray. Bake 30–35 minutes until crisp and cooked through.

Nutrition per serving: 208 calories, 3.8 g fat, 12 g carbohydrates, 28 g protein, 55 mg cholesterol, 1 g dietary fiber, 258 mg sodium
Exchanges: 1 starch, 3 very lean meat, ½ fat
Carb Choices: 1

Shopping List

Meat/Fish/Poultry
1½ lbs. boneless, skinless chicken breasts

Dairy
nonfat Parmesan cheese
4 oz. egg substitute

Packaged
seasoned breadcrumbs

Seasonings/Spices
sesame seeds
pepper

Variation: Dip chicken breasts in nonfat yogurt, sour cream, or mayonnaise instead of egg whites.

Maple Orange Cranberries

3 cups fresh cranberries

1½ cups maple syrup

2 tsp. grated orange peel

Combine cranberries and syrup in large saucepan; bring to a boil over medium heat. Cook, without stirring, 5–6 minutes. Remove pan from heat, cover, and let stand 5 minutes. Return pan to stove top and cook over medium heat 5–6 minutes; remove from heat, stir in orange peel, cover, and let stand until cool. Spoon mixture into bowl, cover with plastic wrap, and refrigerate until ready to serve.

Nutrition per serving: 246 calories, 0 g fat, 67 g carbohydrates, 0 g protein, 0 mg cholesterol, <1 g dietary fiber, 82 mg sodium
Exchanges: 1 fruit, 4 other carb
Carb Choices: 5

Holiday Offerings

Shopping List

Produce
16-oz. pkg. fresh cranberries
orange

Condiments
12 oz. maple syrup

Save the rinds of lemons, limes, grapefruits, and oranges. After squeezing juice from the fruit, freeze the rinds. You can grate the rinds later when called for in recipes.

Braised Cabbage and Potatoes

Easy | **Serves: 4**

1 lb. green cabbage, *cut in wedges*

1 16-oz. pkg. precooked roasted onion potato cubes

1 cup nonfat chicken or vegetable broth

Preheat oven to 350°. Spray baking dish with cooking spray. Place cabbage and potatoes in dish; pour broth over top and bake 20–25 minutes until tender.

Nutrition per serving: 135 calories, 0.3 g fat, 29 g carbohydrates, 5 g protein, 0 mg cholesterol, 5 g dietary fiber, 437 mg sodium
Exchanges: 1½ starch, 1 vegetable
Carb Choices: 2

Shopping List

Produce

1 lb. green cabbage
16-oz. pkg. precooked roasted onion potato cubes

Canned

14-oz. can nonfat chicken or vegetable broth

Packaged, refrigerated, precooked potatoes are one of the latest timesavers—the peeling and boiling is done for you so you can create fancy dishes in half the time.

Sweet Potato Pancakes

Easy | **Do Ahead** | **Serves: 8**

2 large sweet potatoes,
   peeled, shredded, and
   squeezed dry

½ cup egg substitute

1 tbsp. brown sugar

2 tbsp. flour

1 tsp. allspice

2 tsp. cinnamon

Preheat oven to 300°. Combine all the ingredients in a medium bowl and mix well. Spray large nonstick skillet with cooking spray and heat over medium-high heat. Shape potato mixture into 8 cakes and place in hot skillet; press with spatula to flatten. Cook 2–3 minutes until beginning to crisp; turn pancakes over and cook until brown and crisp on both sides. Wrap pancakes in foil and keep warm in 300° oven while preparing remaining mixture.

Nutrition per serving: 67 calories, 0.1 g fat, 14 g carbohydrates, 2 g protein, 0 mg cholesterol, 1 g dietary fiber, 50 mg sodium
Exchanges: 1 starch
Carb Choices: 1

Holiday Offerings

Shopping List

Produce
2 large sweet potatoes

Dairy
4 oz. egg substitute

Baking Goods
brown sugar
flour

Seasonings/Spices
allspice
cinnamon

Rich in beta-carotene, sweet potato pancakes are an excellent addition to your meal at any time of year.

Special Sweet Potatoes

Easy | Do Ahead | Serves: 6

2 15-oz. cans sweet potatoes packed in brown sugar and spices, *well drained*

½ cup canned crushed pineapple in juice, *drained*

3 tbsp. brown sugar

1 8-oz. pkg. marshmallows

Spray microwave-safe 8-inch baking dish with cooking spray. Place sweet potatoes in dish; mash with fork until smooth. Stir in pineapple and brown sugar; mix well. Microwave on High 4–5 minutes until heated through. Arrange marshmallows in a single layer on top. Preheat broiler on High heat. Broil 45–60 seconds, until marshmallows are lightly browned.

Nutrition per serving: 318 calories, 0.4 g fat, 76 g carbohydrates, 3 g protein, 0 mg cholesterol, <1 g dietary fiber, 70 mg sodium
Exchanges: 2 starch, 3 other carb
Carb Choices: 5

Shopping List

Canned
2 15-oz. cans sweet potatoes packed in brown sugar and spices
8-oz. can crushed pineapple in juice

Packaged
8-oz. pkg. marshmallows

Baking Goods
brown sugar

Canned sweet potatoes are available packed in syrup, solid-packed, or flavor-enhanced with added sugar and spices. If you want to cut calories, select varieties without added sugar or syrup.

Orange Butternut Squash

Easy | **Serves: 4**

1 12-oz. pkg. frozen butternut
  squash

¼ cup orange juice

Microwave butternut squash according to package directions;
drain well; add orange juice and mix until smooth. Microwave
on High 1–2 minutes until heated through. Serve immediately.

Nutrition per serving: 41 calories, 0.1 g fat, 11 g carbohydrates, 1 g protein,
0 mg cholesterol, 2 g dietary fiber, 4 mg sodium
Exchanges: 2 vegetable
Carb Choices: 1

Holiday
Offerings

Shopping List

Frozen
12-oz. pkg. frozen butternut
  squash

Refrigerated
orange juice

Canned and frozen winter squashes

come ready to use in casseroles and other
baked dishes.

Candied Cranberry Sweet Potatoes

Easy | Do Ahead | Serves: 6

4   medium sweet potatoes,
    peeled and sliced

4   Granny Smith apples,
    peeled, cored, and sliced

½   cup dried cranberries

2   tbsp. brown sugar

3   tbsp. apple juice

3   tsp. Butter Buds

3   tbsp. water

Preheat oven to 350°. Spray 2-quart baking dish with cooking spray. Layer sliced sweet potatoes, apple slices, and dried cranberries in baking dish. Combine brown sugar, apple juice, Butter Buds, and water; mix until blended. Pour mixture over potatoes, cover with foil, and bake 40–45 minutes until potatoes are tender.

Nutrition per serving: 311 calories, 1.4 g fat, 50 g carbohydrates, 24 g protein, 39 mg cholesterol, 5 g dietary fiber, 919 mg sodium
Exchanges: 3 starch, 1 vegetable, 2 very lean meat
Carb Choices: 3

Shopping List

Produce
4 medium sweet potatoes
4 Granny Smith apples

Canned
apple juice

Baking Goods
brown sugar

Packaged
dried cranberries

Seasonings/Spices
Butter Buds

Variation: Substitute raisins or other dried fruit for the dried cranberries. You can also save time by using canned apple slices.

Wild Rice Turkey Pilaf

Easy | Serves: 6

4 cups water

¼ cup nonfat chicken broth

2 6.2-oz. pkgs. long grain and
wild rice fast-cook
recipe mix

1 16-oz. pkg. frozen mixed
vegetables (corn, carrots,
green beans, and peas),
thawed and drained

3 cups cooked turkey breast,
cubed

Combine water and chicken broth in large saucepan; add rice and seasoning packets. Bring to a boil over high heat; reduce heat to low, cover, and simmer 5 minutes. Stir in vegetables and turkey; cook over medium-low heat, stirring frequently, until heated through. If mixture is too dry, add additional chicken broth 1 tablespoon at a time until desired consistency and heat through.

Nutrition per serving: 72 calories, 0.2 g fat, 14 g carbohydrates, 4 g protein, 0 mg cholesterol, 2 g dietary fiber, 28 mg sodium
Exchanges: 1 vegetable, ½ other carb
Carb Choices: 1

Holiday
Offerings

Shopping List

Meat/Fish/Poultry
leftover turkey or 1 lb. turkey
breast tenderloins

Frozen
16-oz. pkg. frozen mixed
vegetables (corn, carrots,
green beans, and peas)

Canned
nonfat chicken broth

Packaged
2 6.2-oz. pkgs. long grain and
wild rice fast-cook recipe mix

Try substituting nonfat broth for butter called for in packaged rice mixes—you will save 85 calories and 10 grams of fat per tablespoon.

Rice and Mushroom Stuffing

Easy | Do Ahead | Serves: 8

¼ cup nonfat chicken broth

¼ cup frozen diced onions

1 cup sliced mushrooms

3 cups cooked rice
(white, wild, or brown)

1 tsp. poultry seasoning

⅛ tsp. pepper

Spray large nonstick skillet or Dutch oven with cooking spray. Add chicken broth and heat over medium-high heat. Add onions and mushrooms; cook, stirring frequently, until vegetables are tender-soft. Stir in cooked rice, poultry seasoning, and pepper. Cook over medium-low heat until heated through. If made ahead, place stuffing in microwave-safe 10-inch casserole dish sprayed with cooking spray and reheat in microwave oven on High for 4–5 minutes.

Nutrition per serving: 104 calories, 0.2 g fat, 22 g carbohydrates, 2 g protein, 0 mg cholesterol, 1 g dietary fiber, 27 mg sodium
Exchanges: 1 starch, 1 vegetable
Carb Choices: 1

Shopping List

Produce
8-oz. pkg. sliced mushrooms

Frozen
12-oz. pkg. frozen diced onions

Canned
nonfat chicken broth

Packaged
rice (white, wild, or brown)

Seasonings/Spices
poultry seasoning
pepper

Packaged frozen diced onions are a real timesaver. They also allow you to use a small portion at a time without waste.

Mushroom Barley Skillet Dish

Easy | **Serves: 6**

2½ tbsp. + 2½ cups nonfat chicken or vegetable broth

1 cup diced onions

2 cups sliced mushrooms

¾ cup quick-cooking barley

Spray large nonstick saucepan with cooking spray; add 2½ tablespoons broth and heat over medium-high heat. Add onions and mushrooms; cook, stirring frequently, until vegetables are tender. Add remaining broth; bring to a boil over high heat. Add barley, reduce heat to low, cover, and simmer until liquid is absorbed and barley is tender.

Nutrition per serving: 111 calories, 0.6 g fat, 23 g carbohydrates, 4 g protein, 0 mg cholesterol, 5 g dietary fiber, 350 mg sodium
Exchanges: 1 starch, 1 vegetable
Carb Choices: 2

Holiday Offerings

Shopping List

Produce
8-oz. pkg. sliced mushrooms
diced onions

Canned
nonfat chicken or
    vegetable broth

Packaged
quick-cooking barley

You can substitute frozen diced onions for fresh in almost any recipe.

Green Bean and Carrot Salad

Easy | **Do Ahead** | **Serves: 4**

1 16-oz. pkg. frozen whole green beans, *thawed and drained*

1 8-oz. pkg. shredded carrots

1 red onion, *peeled and sliced thin*

1 red bell pepper, *cored and sliced thin*

½ cup fat-free red wine vinegar salad dressing

Combine green beans, carrots, onion, and bell pepper in large bowl; pour salad dressing over top and toss to mix. Cover and refrigerate until ready to serve.

Nutrition per serving: 104 calories, 0.5 g fat, 23 g carbohydrates, 3 g protein, 0 mg cholesterol, 5 g dietary fiber, 145 mg sodium
Exchanges: 4 vegetable
Carb Choices: 2

Shopping List

Produce
8-oz. pkg. shredded carrots
1 red onion
1 red bell pepper

Frozen
16-oz. pkg. frozen whole green beans

Condiments
fat-free red wine vinegar salad dressing

Fresh, frozen, and canned green beans are either whole, "French-style," or "cut." How do you know what to choose? Whole green beans have not been cut or sliced; French-style refers to green beans sliced lengthwise; and "cuts" or "short cuts" are sliced crosswise.

Apple Cinnamon Cake with Vanilla Glaze

Easy | **Do Ahead** | **Serves: 8**

1 19-oz. pkg. fat-free apple-cinnamon muffin mix

1¼ cups water

¼ cup canned apple pie filling

1½ tsp. cinnamon

½ cup powdered sugar

2 tsp. nonfat half and half

½ tsp. vanilla

Preheat oven to 350°. Spray 8-inch square baking dish with cooking spray. Combine muffin mix and water in medium bowl; mix well. Spread half the batter into baking dish. Combine canned apple pie filling with pouch from muffin mix; spread over batter and sprinkle with cinnamon. Top with remaining batter. Bake 25-35 minutes until toothpick inserted in center comes out clean. Remove from oven and let cake cool completely. Combine powdered sugar, half and half, and vanilla in small bowl; mix until creamy and smooth. Drizzle glaze over cooled cake. Let stand 5-10 minutes before serving.

Nutrition per serving: 301 calories, 0 g fat, 72 g carbohydrates, 4 g protein, 0 mg cholesterol, 4 g dietary fiber, 657 mg sodium
Exchanges: 5 other carb
Carb Choices: 5

Holiday Offerings

Shopping List

Dairy
nonfat half and half

Baking Goods
19-oz. pkg. fat-free apple cinnamon muffin mix
21-oz. can apple pie filling
powdered sugar

Seasonings/Spices
cinnamon
vanilla

When preparing muffins or cakes that call for oil, substitute crushed pineapple or applesauce. You'll keep all the moistness without the calories and fat.

Pumpkin Pudding Cups

Easy | **Do Ahead** | **Serves: 4**

½ cup nonfat half and half

1 cup canned pumpkin puree
  (not pumpkin pie mix)

¼ cup egg substitute

1 tbsp. water

1 tsp. vanilla extract

½ tsp. pumpkin pie spice

¼ cup nonfat Cool Whip,
  thawed

cinnamon

Pour half and half in microwave-safe dish; microwave on High 2–3 minutes just until boiling. Add pumpkin, egg substitute, water, vanilla, and pumpkin pie spice; mix until blended. Spray four 6-ounce custard cups with cooking spray. Pour pumpkin mixture into cups; arrange cups in a circle on a microwave-safe dish. Microwave on Medium 15–20 minutes, turning several times while cooking. Cook until knife inserted 1 inch from edge comes out clean and center is thickened. Cover custard cups with plastic wrap and refrigerate at least 1 hour until completely set. When ready to serve, top each pudding with 1 tablespoon Cool Whip and sprinkle with cinnamon to taste.

Nutrition per serving: 51 calories, 0 g fat, 9 g carbohydrates, 2 g protein, 0 mg cholesterol, 0 g dietary fiber, 47 mg sodium
Exchanges: ½ other carb
Carb Choices: 1

Shopping List

Dairy
4 oz. nonfat half and half
egg substitute

Frozen
8 oz. nonfat Cool Whip

Canned
16-oz. can pumpkin puree
  (not pumpkin pie mix)

Seasonings/Spices
vanilla
pumpkin pie spice
cinnamon

Make sure you select the proper can. There is a big difference between pumpkin puree and pumpkin pie mix! The wrong can will surely mess up a great dessert!

Mini Banana Loaves

Easy | **Do Ahead** | **Freeze** | **Serves: 20**

2 cups mashed bananas

¾ cup egg substitute

2 large egg whites

¾ cup sugar

¾ cup brown sugar

4 cups flour

2 tsp. baking soda

2 tsp. ground cinnamon

Preheat oven to 350°. Spray four 4-inch mini loaf pans with cooking spray. Combine bananas, egg substitute, egg whites, sugar, and brown sugar in medium bowl; beat until creamy and smooth. Add flour, baking soda, and cinnamon and mix until ingredients are moistened. Divide batter among loaf pans; bake 35–40 minutes until toothpick inserted in center comes out clean. Cool slightly, remove from pans, and let cool before slicing.

Nutrition per serving: 187 calories, 0.4 g fat, 43 g carbohydrates, 4 g protein, 0 mg cholesterol, 1 g dietary fiber, 118 mg sodium
Exchanges: 3 other carb
Carb Choices: 3

Holiday Offerings

Shopping List

Produce
6 ripe bananas

Dairy
6 oz. egg substitute
whole eggs

Baking Goods
sugar
brown sugar
flour
baking soda

Seasonings/Spices
ground cinnamon

Don't throw away those overripe bananas–they work great in breads, cakes, and muffins.

Index

Index

Index

Index

Index

Metric Information

The charts on this page provide a guide for converting measurements from the U.S. customary system, which is used throughout this book, to the metric system.

Product Differences

Most of the ingredients called for in the recipes in this book are available in most countries. However, some are known by different names. Here are some common American ingredients and their possible counterparts:

- Sugar (white) is granulated, fine granulated, or castor sugar.
- Powdered sugar is icing sugar.
- All-purpose flour is enriched, bleached or unbleached white household flour. When self-rising flour is used in place of all-purpose flour in a recipe that calls for leavening, omit the leavening agent (baking soda or baking powder) and salt.
- Light-colored corn syrup is golden syrup.
- Cornstarch is cornflour.
- Baking soda is bicarbonate of soda.
- Vanilla or vanilla extract is vanilla essence.
- Bell peppers are capsicums.
- Golden raisins are sultanas.

Volume and Weight

The United States traditionally uses cup measures for liquid and solid ingredients. The chart below shows the approximate imperial and metric equivalents. If you are accustomed to weighing solid ingredients, the following approximate equivalents will be helpful.

- 1 cup butter, castor sugar, or rice = 8 ounces = ½ pound = 250 grams
- 1 cup flour = 4 ounces = ¼ pound = 125 grams
- 1 cup icing sugar = 5 ounces = 150 grams

Canadian and U.S. volume for a cup measure is 8 fluid ounces (237 ml), but the standard metric equivalent is 250 ml.

1 British imperial cup is 10 fluid ounces.

In Australia, 1 tablespoon equals 20 ml, and there are 4 teaspoons in the Australian tablespoon.

Spoon measures are used for smaller amounts of ingredients. Although the size of the tablespoon varies slightly in different countries, for practical purposes and for recipes in this book, a straight substitution is all that's necessary. Measurements made using cups or spoons always should be level unless stated otherwise.

Common Weight Range Replacements

Imperial / U.S.	Metric
½ ounce	15 g
1 ounce	25 g or 30 g
4 ounces (¼ pound)	115 g or 125 g
8 ounces (½ pound)	225 g or 250 g
16 ounces (1 pound)	450 g or 500 g
1¼ pounds	625 g
1½ pounds	750 g
2 pounds or 2¼ pounds	1,000 g or 1 Kg

Oven Temperature Equivalents

Fahrenheit Setting	Celsius Setting*	Gas Setting
300°F	150°C	Gas Mark 2 (very low)
325°F	160°C	Gas Mark 3 (low)
350°F	180°C	Gas Mark 4 (moderate)
375°F	190°C	Gas Mark 5 (moderate)
400°F	200°C	Gas Mark 6 (hot)
425°F	220°C	Gas Mark 7 (hot)
450°F	230°C	Gas Mark 8 (very hot)
475°F	240°C	Gas Mark 9 (very hot)
500°F	260°C	Gas Mark 10 (extremely hot)
Broil	Broil	Grill

*Electric and gas ovens may be calibrated using celsius. However, for an electric oven, increase celsius setting 10 to 20 degrees when cooking above 160°C. For convection or forced air ovens (gas or electric) lower the temperature setting 25°F/10°C when cooking at all heat levels.

Baking Pan Sizes

Imperial / U.S.	Metric
9×1½-inch round cake pan	22- or 23×4-cm (1.5 L)
9×1½-inch pie plate	22- or 23×4-cm (1 L)
8×8×2-inch square cake pan	20×5-cm (2 L)
9×9×2-inch square cake pan	22- or 23×4.5-cm (2.5 L)
11×7×1½-inch baking pan	28×17×4-cm (2 L)
2-quart rectangular baking pan	30×19×4.5-cm (3 L)
13×9×2-inch baking pan	34×22×4.5-cm (3.5 L)
15×10×1-inch jelly roll pan	40×25×2-cm
9×5×3-inch loaf pan	23×13×8-cm (2 L)
2-quart casserole	2 L

U.S. / Standard Metric Equivalents

⅛ teaspoon = 0.5 ml
¼ teaspoon = 1 ml
½ teaspoon = 2 ml
1 teaspoon = 5 ml
1 tablespoon = 15 ml
2 tablespoons = 25 ml
¼ cup = 2 fluid ounces = 50 ml
⅓ cup = 3 fluid ounces = 75 ml
½ cup = 4 fluid ounces = 125 ml
⅔ cup = 5 fluid ounces = 150 ml
¾ cup = 6 fluid ounces = 175 ml
1 cup = 8 fluid ounces = 250 ml
2 cups = 1 pint = 500 ml
1 quart = 1 litre

Metrics

I would like to thank the following family and friends for helping me make this cookbook possible. Thank you all for your love and generous support. I am extremely grateful to you all.

Gary, Happy Anniversary! 24 years! Your solid strength, creative mind, and loving ways keep me strong, inventive, and loving. We've come a long way, baby, and I love ya, Gar! We are a great team! Thank you for your unconditional love, hugs, and kisses. I do need them every day.

Jamie, I just simply love you with all of my heart and soul! You are dynamic and genuinely a sweetheart. May all of your dreams be yours! You have taught me so much in my life, and I am grateful and blessed that you are my daughter. Thank you, Jams.

Acknowledgements

Scott. Hey, Sunshine—you rock! NBA basketball here you come! I believe in you! You will be whatever you want and whatever you dream. You know our motto: work hard, stay focused, breathe, and bring those angels everywhere you go and just be the best that you can be. I love you, Mr. Scott!

Mom and Dad, thanks for always believing in me! I love you both!

Grandma, I love you!

Jacie, you are always there for me—your love overflows, and I am so lucky you are my sister.

Jeff, Diane, Alex, and Casey, your nonstop energy and drive is contagious! I love you all!

Journey Home is a wonderful nonprofit charitable organization that Diane has created. Please check out their website: journeyhome.org.

Snooky and Harlan, thanks for always being there. I love you.

Mikki Eveloff, you are spectacular and an incredible inspiration. Thank you for all of your amazing hard work and commitment. I appreciate every second of your time and high energy and for always being "on call" and exceeding all expectations. Thank you, Mikki!

Debbie Kohl, you never cease to amaze me. Your middle name is "crunch." You always come through and astonish me every time. I respect you and your time. Thank you! Debbie Kohl, M.S., R.D., my exceptional nutritionist, can be reached at 602-266-0324.

Linda Raglan Cunningham, Jennifer Darling, Stephanie Karpinske, and Amy Nichols, the extraordinary people at Meredith that have made this cookbook possible. Thank you for always being there to help and for your marvelous support and fabulous energy. I am grateful to you all. Thank you!

Marilyn Allen and Coleen O'Shea, my creative and powerful literary agents. Thank you for your hard work, persistence, and loving ways about you both. You are phenomenal and I appreciate you both very much. Thank you!